Dragon and Eagle

DRAGON

and

EAGLE

United States-China Relations: Past and Future

EDITED BY

MICHEL OKSENBERG

ROBERT B. OXNAM

Basic Books, Inc., Publishers   *New York*

The endpaper map is from *East Asia: Tradition and Transformation* by John K. Fairbank, Edwin O. Reischauer, and Albert M. Craig. Copyright © 1973 by Houghton Mifflin Company. Reprinted by permission.

Library of Congress Cataloging in Publication Data

Main entry under title:

Dragon and eagle.

   Bibliography: p. 361
   Includes index.
     1. United States—Foreign relations—China—Addresses, essays, lectures. 2. China—Foreign relations—United States—Addresses, essays, lectures. I. Oksenberg, Michel, 1938–   II. Oxnam, Robert B.
E183.8.C5D7   327.73′051   77–76472
ISBN: 0–465–01686–3

CONTENTS

Part III
BILATERAL INTERACTIONS

Part IV
MULTILATERAL INTERACTIONS

Contents

Part V
INTERACTIONS AROUND CHINA'S RIM

Part VI
THE LEGAL CONTEXT

CONTRIBUTORS

JEROME A. COHEN is director of the East Asian Legal Studies Program of the Harvard University School of Law. He is author of a number of books and articles on China's legal institutions and diplomatic practice.

WARREN I. COHEN is Associate Professor of History at Michigan State University. He specializes in American-East Asian relations, and is the author of *The American Response to China*.

WALDO H. HEINRICHS, JR. is Professor of History at Temple University, specializing in U.S. military history. His major work is *American Ambassador: Joseph C. Grew and the Development of the U.S. Diplomatic Tradition*.

MICHAEL H. HUNT received his doctorate from Yale University in American diplomatic history and Chinese history, and is now Assistant Professor of History at Yale. He is the author of *Frontier Defense and the Open Door: Manchuria in Chinese American Relations, 1895–1911*.

STEVEN I. LEVINE is a specialist on Sino-Soviet relations. He is a staff member of the Social Science Department of the

Rand Corporation and has taught in the Columbia University political science department. He is now preparing a book on international relations in Manchuria in the late 1940s.

STANLEY B. LUBMAN received the law degrees of LL.B and JSD from Columbia University, where he was also trained as a China specialist. After teaching Chinese law at the School of Law at the University of California (Berkeley) he returned to private practice and now travels often to China on behalf of American clients. He is special counsel to the law firm of Heller, Ehrman, White & McAuliffe in San Francisco.

MICHEL OKSENBERG is Professor of Political Science and Associate of the Center for Chinese Studies at the University of Michigan. Currently on leave, he is serving as an analyst on the staff of the National Security Council. He is the author of many articles on China, and was editor of *China's Developmental Experience*.

ROBERT B. OXNAM is Associate Professor of History at Trinity College. He is currently serving as Program Director of The Asia Society's China Council. His publications include several articles on Chinese history and the book *Ruling from Horseback: Manchu Politics in the Oboi Regency, 1661–1669*.

TU WEI-MING is Professor of History at the University of California at Berkeley. He is the author of the recently published *Neo-Confucian Thought in Action: Wang Yang-ming's Youth*.

PETER VAN NESS teaches in the Graduate School of International Studies of the University of Denver, specializing in

Chinese foreign policy. He is the author of *Revolution and Chinese Foreign Policy.*

LYMAN P. VAN SLYKE is Associate Professor of History at Stanford University, specializing in modern Chinese history. He is the author of *Enemies and Friends: The United Front in Chinese Communist History,* and visited China in 1975 as a member of a delegation studying rural small-scale industry.

ALLEN S. WHITING is Professor of Political Science and Associate of the Center for Chinese Studies at the University of Michigan. Among his many publications are *China Crosses the Yalu* and *The Chinese Calculus of Deterrence.* Professor Whiting served as director of the Office of Research and Analysis for the Far East in the U.S. Department of State from 1962 to 1966, and as deputy U.S. Consul General in Hong Kong from 1966 to 1968.

ALEXANDER WOODSIDE is Professor of History at the University of British Columbia in Vancouver. His latest work is *Community and Revolution in Modern Vietnam.*

ACKNOWLEDGMENTS

This volume emerges as part of a 1975–78 project of the China Council of The Asia Society entitled "Sino-American Relations in Historical Perspective." The Asia Society is a nonprofit, nonpolitical educational organization dedicated to deepening American understanding of Asia and to promoting thoughtful trans-Pacific discourse. Its China Council undertakes national programs for public education on Chinese affairs, providing outreach through regional councils and collaborative projects, a variety of media-related activities, and a series of studies on modern Chinese history and China's role in the contemporary world. The editors and the authors express their gratitude to The Asia Society as a whole and to its China Council for assistance in developing this volume. The membership of the China Council, many of whom provided extensive review of this project in draft form, is listed on the following page.

Special thanks go to two individuals who served as key consultants in this project. Dorothy Borg of Columbia University urged us to consider carefully the general diplomatic context in which Sino-American relations have unfolded and to examine both the American and Chinese sides of the relationship—advice we have endeavored to follow throughout. Alexander Eckstein, the eminent American expert on the Chinese economy, counseled us to take a broad viewpoint, encompassing Asian affairs in general and incorporating a long sweep of history in U.S.-China relations. Professor Eckstein's death in December 1976 was a great loss to Chinese studies in the United States. We shall miss his wisdom and insights, and we dedicate this volume to his memory.

In the course of preparing this volume, the China Council collaborated in organizing several regional conferences and seminars in which many of the authors participated, exchanging their ideas with a wide spectrum of local representatives. We want to express our gratitude in particular to the following organizations which assisted us in this endeavor: The Johnson Foundation (which held a major conference on Sino-American relations at its magnificent center at Wingspread, in Racine, Wisconsin), the Boston World Affairs Council, the Chicago Council on Foreign Relations, the University of Washington's East Asian Resource Center, the University of Wisconsin–Milwaukee's Institute of World Affairs, the Pittsburgh World Affairs Council, the Middle Atlantic Association for Asian Studies, the University of Pittsburgh's East Asian Studies Program, the Great Neck Adult Education Program, and the Yale-China Association. And our thanks are extended to the organizations which have supported this project and the general activities of the China Council: the National Endowment for the Humanities, the General Service Foundation, the Rockefeller Foundation, the Luce Foundation, The Johnson Foundation, and the National Committee on U.S.-China Relations.

Finally, our deep appreciation is expressed to the staff of the China Council—Peggy Blumenthal, Richard Bush, Terrill Lautz (program associates), Barbara Suomi (administrative assistant), and Renee Tugman (secretary)—for their help in preparing the manuscript.

While acknowledging with gratitude this assistance from individuals and organizations, we wish to emphasize that the views expressed in this volume are those of the editors and authors alone.

M.O.

R.B.O.

March 1977

MEMBERS AND ASSOCIATES OF THE CHINA COUNCIL

Charles W. Bailey
Jackson Bailey
A. Doak Barnett
Robert W. Barnett
Richard Baum
Carol E. Baumann
James M. Becker
Gordon A. Bennett
Peter Bennett
Richard Bernstein
David Biltchik
Tom Brokaw
Franklin R. Buchanan
Mark E. Buchman
Mary B. Bullock
Parris H. Chang
George Chaplin
Samuel Chu
Harlan Cleveland
Ralph N. Clough
Jerome A. Cohen
Ralph C. Croizier
Irv Drasnin

John King Fairbank
Richard A. Freytag
Edward Friedman
Joel Glassman
James P. Grant
Harry Harding
Bill Hosokawa
James C. Hsiung
Akira Iriye
F. Tomasson Jannuzi
Joyce K. Kallgren
Stanley Karnow
Geoffrey Kean
Donald W. Klein
D. W. Y. Kwok
Lionel Landry
Nicholas Lardy
Lee Lescaze
Victor Li
Kenneth Lieberthal
Timothy Light
Winston Lord
Stanley B. Lubman

Donald E. MacInnis
Patrick G. Maddox
Richard A. Melville
Harriet Mills
Martha T. Mills
Ronald N. Montaperto
Donald J. Munro
Reg Murphy
Douglas P. Murray
Andrew J. Nathan
Michael J. O'Neill
Allan W. Ostar
Eugene C. Patterson
Christopher H. Phillips
Lucian W. Pye
Edward Rhoads
John E. Rielly
Carl Riskin
Arthur H. Rosen
Norman Ross
Robert A. Scalapino
B. Preston Schoyer
Peter J. Seybolt
Clifford A. Shillinglaw
Gaston I. Sigur
Crocker Snow, Jr.
Richard H. Solomon

Jonathan D. Spence
Shirley Sun
Phillips Talbot
Jerald F. terHorst
Ross Terrill
Eugene A. Theroux
James C. Thomson
Audrey R. Topping
James R. Townsend
Daniel Tretiak
Tang Tsou
Lyman P. Van Slyke
Ezra F. Vogel
Frederic Wakeman
William Watts
Tu Wei-ming
James M. Wesley
Peter White
Theodore H. White
Allen S. Whiting
Gerry Wielenga
Fay Willey
Edwin A. Winckler
Roxane Witke
Michael Witunski
Franklin J. Woo
Frederick T. C. Yu

Part I

INTRODUCTION: THE FUTURE AND THE PAST

1

MICHEL OKSENBERG

Sino-American Relations in a New Asian Context

AMERICANS have become inured to a litany about the severe foreign policy challenges to which we must respond: halting the arms race, advancing the dignity of all human beings, establishing a more stable, equitable economic order, setting in motion processes which will achieve peaceful reconciliation between contending regional forces, and solving the world's energy, food, and population problems. Of course, these problems *are* more than cliché, and failure to grapple forthrightly with them will affect us all.

Parts of this chapter appeared in Michel Oksenberg, "The United States and China" in Volume XII of a major project of the Commission on Critical Choices for Americans. The fourteen volumes of this project have been published by Lexington Books, D.C. Heath & Company. Volume XII is entitled *China and Japan: A New Balance of Power*. Reprinted by permission of the publisher. All rights reserved © 1976 by Third Century Corporation.

China specialists might plead, however, that the list ignores one of the most significant global challenges of our era: the inclusion of China as an equal into an international political framework. Until the mid-1800s, China dominated the terms of exchange; then later the West dictated to Peking how it would interact with the rest of mankind. But in the last quarter century, the Chinese people have rapidly built a new social, economic, and political system. What are the implications of this regenerated and quickly developing China for the search for world order? What adjustments will be necessary in current international law and customs—which grow out of Western tradition—in order to accommodate the views of a fourth of mankind? Efforts to address the litany of global problems will not succeed unless the Chinese dimension and Chinese views of these problems are considered from the outset. When listing our global problems, therefore, Americans had best recall that China is still there too.

Americans daily read of the regional flashpoints that could erupt in war: the Mideast, Southern Africa, and Korea. We also know of the problems over Panama, Ireland, Cyprus, Pakistan, the Philippines, and Thailand. A few years ago, of course, Indochina would have headed these regional tensions and conflicts.

The list is intriguing, for with the exception of Korea, none of the trouble spots involve East and Southeast Asia; that region of the world temporarily seems stable. As Robert Oxnam makes clear, a generation of confrontation in the region may have come to an end with the termination of the Vietnam War and President Richard M. Nixon's trip to China. Americans have a remarkably short memory, and what once was thought unlikely—a Pacific that deserved its name—now seems quite possible. In some respects, we have emerged from the Vietnam War in better shape than we had anticipated. A balance of power favorable to the United States has emerged in the Western Pacific. It is one of the few regions in the world where we have some firm allies and where our presence is welcomed.

The foreign policy challenge in this region is to explore opportunities rather than solve problems: to help consolidate the favorable situation and to use the relationships with China and Japan for our mutual global advantage.

Two key factors explain the new era in East Asia. One is the region's unprecedented economic prosperity. Japan has emerged as the world's third largest economic power, while South Korea, Taiwan, Hong Kong, and Malaysia have grown at an average 8–10 percent per year for over a decade. East Asia has surpassed Western Europe as the United States' largest foreign trade area, reflecting the extent to which the region's prosperity is due to the expansion of international trade and the vitality of the foreign trade sector in many of the region's economies. Global economic recession or growing protectionism would obviously have a destabilizing impact upon the area.

A second and equally important reason for the recent stability is the new Sino-American relationship. That new relationship has been a key factor in Peking's reevaluation of its interests in Asia. As the United States appeared less threatening than the Soviet Union in Peking's eyes, the Chinese endorsed the Japanese-American defense treaty. Allen Whiting stresses this point in his essay: the years of Peking-encouraged attacks on the treaty came to an end in Tokyo as Mao Tse-tung and Chou En-lai told visiting Japanese and Americans alike that their mutual relations were important to security in Northeast Asia. Michael Hunt notes that although the Chinese back the volatile Kim Il-sung in North Korea, they nonetheless have come to recognize the benefits of stability on the Korean peninsula and have not pressed for the immediate withdrawal of U.S. forces from South Korea. Alexander Woodside observes the Chinese encouragement of a strong ASEAN (the Association of Southeast Asian Nations) alliance. The Chinese now see benefits from a continued U.S. military presence at Subic Bay and Clark Air Force Base in the Philippines, for America's forward bases are no longer displayed against China but serve as a counter to the Soviet Union's expanding naval presence in the Pacific.

Farther afield, the United States and China have discovered parallel strategic interests in the South Asian subcontinent and the Indian Ocean (to prevent the Soviet Union or India from establishing a position of dominance), in the Mideast and Southern Africa (to counter the Soviet thrust in the regions), and in Western Europe (to maintain a strong NATO). Only a decade before, the United States had identified China as the major obstacle to world peace and had directed its "counterinsurgency warfare" against what Washington at that time perceived as the greatest threat to global stability: guerrilla war and the export of revolution. In the mid-1960s too, Mao derided the military strength of the United States, which he still proclaimed the "number one enemy." Ten years later, the global Soviet forward thrust had driven Peking and Washington on a more nearly parallel course. During the 1971–76 era, Richard Nixon, Henry Kissinger, and Gerald Ford also indirectly sought to involve the People's Republic of China in a number of transitory issues: the negotiations to end the Vietnam War; an effort to establish a coalition government in Cambodia including Lon Nol, the Khmer Rouge, and the then-deposed Prince Sihanouk; the U.S. support of Pakistan in the Indo-Pakistani War of 1971 and the response to the creation of Bangladesh; the 1972–73 effort to establish a North-South dialogue in Korea; and the U.S. opposition to the Soviet- and Cuban-backed forces in Angola. In each of these instances, Washington managed the issue in part with an eye to including China. As long as Peking perceived Washington to have firm resolve against the Soviets, the U.S. approach elicited a basically positive response from the People's Republic.

Several factors seem to have guided Chinese policies toward the United States in the 1970s. Steven Levine develops this notion that the U.S.-China détente has been largely a partnership of convenience born of mutual concern about the Soviet

Union. The Chinese see U.S. military power in the Western Pacific and in South and Southeast Asia as a major obstacle to Soviet encirclement of the People's Republic. Thus the Chinese have also urged a strong NATO which pressures the Soviet Union's western flank and prevents increased Soviet emphasis on its border with China. In addition, as Stanley Lubman suggests, the Chinese seek access to U.S. technology. Computers, offshore oil-drilling technology, and possibly defense-related technology would accelerate China's economic development and enhance its national security. Finally, China is interested in improving relations with the United States as a way of resolving the vexing Taiwan issue. Peter Van Ness notes that the Nixon-Kissinger gambit encouraged the Chinese to believe that the United States would soon withdraw its troops from Taiwan, end its formal military commitment to the island, and thus pave the way for diplomatic relations between Peking and Washington. Thus, although the Sino-Soviet dispute is a key factor in Sino-American détente, the main factor that made détente politically acceptable in Peking was American flexibility on the Taiwan issue.

While China has approached the United States with a clear sense of its interests, the same cannot be said for all Americans. To be sure, in 1971, Nixon and Kissinger saw the advantage to be derived vis-à-vis the Indochina War and the SALT talks. But beyond that, Americans seem to have had difficulty identifying the American interest in consolidating the Sino-American relationship. The significance of the relationship beyond its strategic and economic dimensions is less obvious, and specific methods for developing a better relationship with China are yet to be developed.

As Oxnam indicates, however, three aspects of Sino-American relations are more certain. First, a relationship built on sentiment rather than on the common interests of both sides will not endure. Second, a well-meaning effort to improve relations that is uninformed by history is likely to repeat the errors of the past. Third, neither side has much leverage over the other; no single major development is likely to make the relationship a more substantial one. The establishment of full diplomatic relations will be but one step in a much longer process, and will not eliminate the strains in Sino-American affairs. The relationship can be cemented only through the aggregation of smaller actions. It must be laboriously pieced together as we look ahead to future decades.

The American Interest in China

To begin with interests only minimally involved, commercial rewards are not likely to be major. This is the key finding of Stanley Lubman's analysis of Sino-American trade. Chinese reluctance to accept direct foreign investment is likely to persist. To be sure, select sectors of the American economy may develop a profitable exporting relationship, particularly those which enjoy a competitive edge in international trade: the agricultural sector, the computer industry, the aerospace industry, and purveyors of petroleum exploration technology. On the import side, China could become a modest supplier of petroleum and petroleum products over a ten or fifteen year period; in addition, China has substantial deposits of such nonferrous metals as tungsten, tin, manganese, and molybdenum. Further, China could be an attractive source of labor-intensive commodities. But the overall capacity and willingness of China to engage in trade in the years ahead is likely to remain limited.

Further, as Waldo Heinrichs concludes, the United States will not face a massive, direct military threat from China for the foreseeable future. True, Peking will gradually acquire intercontinental missiles that will affect our national security calculations. The Chinese also seem to be developing a blue-water navy, but that probably will not materialize until the

1990s. Militarily, then, barring a massive infusion of capital and technology, China will remain a regional power for some time to come. Thus, it is not China's direct threat to the United States but rather America's credible military presence in the Western Pacific and possibly the Indian Ocean that will link the interests of the two and provide a basis for conflict, cooperation, or accommodation.

The overriding American interest should be the independence and internal effectiveness of the People's Republic, in its capacity to maintain the unity of the people and provide them with sufficient food, clothing, shelter, and employment. This interest is valid solely on the humanitarian ground that we wish a quarter of mankind well. But it is also in the world's interest that China not become a major claimant on external food supplies and that it remain self-sufficient or even become a net contributor to world energy supplies. As Premier Chou En-lai often jokingly reminded American guests, the Chinese government did the world a favor simply by feeding its population. His words had insight, for failure of the Chinese government to meet the minimum welfare demands of its populace or to retain its unity would have significant, adverse international consequences. A major new burden would be placed upon already overtaxed aid-dispensing agencies. To put this issue in proper perspective, from 1960 to 1972 the People's Republic stood alone among the developing countries as a net *contributor* rather than a recipient of foreign aid and credit, and maintained a slight balance in its favor in its foreign trade accounts. From 1956 through 1972, it extended more than $2.5 billion in credits and grants, although not all commitments were fulfilled. And while Peking has been a major world importer of grain—for the last decade, an average of 3 percent of world grain shipments have gone to the People's Republic—it has received none as relief but has purchased it all.

At a time when much of mankind lacks effective structures

of political authority, the People's Republic commands attention and respect simply for its organizational achievement. As a result of this organization, however, the aspirations of the entire Chinese populace have been awakened. China's quest for greatness—for wealth and power—has involved a maximum national effort. The mass media penetrate nearly every rural village, and the government now provides nearly universal opportunity for five years of schooling to rural young people and nine years to urban young people.

Chinese under forty years of age—the bulk of the population—have matured under communism. The vast majority possess little knowledge about and have had little contact with the outside world; their education has been more than tinged by virulent nationalistic appeals. This younger generation of Chinese will eventually guide the nation, controlling its expanding military capacity. Possibly, if this generation were to become frustrated in its effort to continue China's progress, it could direct its frustration outward. While China has not exhibited expansionist tendencies thus far, her leaders recognize that the possibility cannot be excluded in the future. And the current generation of China's leaders have bequeathed to their successors unrealized or internationally unrecognized territorial claims that point in all directions: along the Amur, over Taiwan, far into the South China Sea, along the Northeast Frontier Agency and in Ladakh, and in Sinkiang. Such irredentist claims conceivably could be used by a frustrated Chinese leadership in the future to divert domestic discontent. There is a real time pressure, then, to establish as firm contacts as possible with Chinese of all generations *now*, to minimize the chances of future hostility.

But more is at stake than reducing the chances of future hostility. The world seems to be entering an era of profound pessimism over man's capacity to surmount the crises of poverty and overpopulation in the developing countries. In this sense, China has become one source of inspiration—not a totally attractive, pleasant beacon, to be sure, but nonetheless one hope that an impoverished nation, if sufficiently endowed with resources, can galvanize itself and eliminate starvation and disease. China is now poised to advance significantly. If China were to fall behind again, if problems of malnutrition, extensive underemployment, and political disorder again occur in China, then pessimism about man's future is appropriate. With all the discipline and sacrifice of the past twenty-five years, if the Chinese do not achieve a breakthrough, then who can? On the other hand, Chinese success may have a particularly timely effect upon the world's deprived—important because the impoverished must at this juncture retain a confidence in themselves and a vision of the possible.

While the Chinese economy has performed well during the past twenty years, continued expansion at growth rates satisfactory to the Chinese probably requires importation of some select technology and capital equipment. It follows that the U.S. interest is to help facilitate the flow of knowledge and the export of whole plants to China. For recognition—and with it settlement of the claims issue, the extension of most-favored-nation status, and the availability of Export-Import Bank financing to assist Chinese purchases—would marginally yet perhaps significantly increase China's trade potential and slightly hasten her economic growth. Perhaps more important, moves in this direction would enhance China's stake in a stable international economic community.

In short, the American interest is an increasingly prosperous and informed China, able and willing to contribute to the creation of a stable world order. Another way of defending this view is briefly to portray future Chinas that obviously would be inimical to American interests: (1) a highly nationalistic, expansionist, militant China, seeking hegemony over countries on its periphery; (2) a weakened China, feeling vulnerable and seeking its security and technology through an exclusionary alliance with an American adversary —maybe the Soviet Union again or perhaps at some point a Japan that is less tied to the United States; (3) a distintegrating

China that becomes a major claimant on the world's food supplies and a focal point of competition for influence; (4) a frustrated China, militarily unable to project its own power beyond its borders and politically unable to play a responsible role in building a new international order and as a result acting as a somewhat irrational, disruptive force, preventing the efforts of others to structure a durable peace.

At the present time, none of these alternatives seems likely. The record of the past twenty-five years shows generally that when the Chinese have had the opportunity, they have acted responsibly and cautiously. Of course, exceptions exist and the public rhetoric does not always coincide with more private statements and with actual deeds. But on balance, as the Levine and Whiting articles demonstrate, Chinese foreign policy can be largely explained as a realistic response to the global power balance. The American interest is to maintain that balance in such a way that China will help maintain an order in East Asia that will be beneficial to both powers.

Yet, as Robert Oxnam has argued, Americans must avoid a critical problem from our past outlooks on China—the mistaken belief that U.S. policies will have a decisive effect on China's future. To be sure, in our military and strategic positions, as in our commercial policies, we should be cooperative and supportive, not hostile and threatening. But ultimately, China's future must and should be in Chinese hands and in Peking's response to domestic needs and to Asian and global developments.

The Relationship of Values

Four revolutions have shaped the modern world. The American and French revolutions fostered governments dedicated to the pursuit of liberty. During the twentieth century, the United

States has been significantly responsible for the attractiveness of these ideas throughout the world: that man should participate in his own governance, that the state should protect the dignity of the individual, and that political freedom is essential as means to these ends. Although the American experience as a global power has often been tarnished by the shortsightedness of many of its policies, these ideals remain an important source of inspiration for human rights and freedoms.

The Russian Revolution impressed another message upon mankind. Coming at the end of World War I, which demonstrated the potential of the modern state, the Russian Revolution gave birth to a state that used its power to accelerate economic growth. If the key institutional legacy of the American Revolution is elections, the key legacy of the Soviet experience is planning. The state controls and plans the economy for the common good. Interestingly enough, in the 1930s both the United States and Germany deliberately sought to revive their economies in non-Bolshevist ways, but both the New Deal and Nazi Germany accepted the premise that the way out of the depression was through increased government management of the economy. The Soviet experience, both directly and indirectly, legitimated the encroachment of public bureaucracies upon the marketplace.

The Chinese Communist revolution has given institutional force to other powerful ideas: economic equality and the capacity of the dispossessed to improve their lot through will and organization. Here is a nation that now has nearly 900 million people. Thirty years ago, it experienced enormous discrepancies in wealth and income. Amidst the great opulence of Shanghai, where some of the world's richest families then resided, carts made daily rounds to pick up the bodies of beggars who had died in the street the night before. The Chinese revolution led by Mao Tse-tung and his associates ended many of these gross economic inequities, although at a high cost in terms of individual freedom and political justice.

China remains a poor country in per capita income—less than $300 a year. Nonetheless, the Chinese government has brought many of the benefits of industrialization to its populace at an earlier stage than elsewhere. Heretofore, it was axiomatic that modernization occurred at the cost of the peasantry. That certainly was the Soviet experience, and in the American case, the farmers of the South and Midwest remained totally vulnerable to economic uncertainties until the New Deal. The Chinese developmental pattern since 1949 challenges the dogma. Economic security and redistribution can occur as industrialization spreads; income disparities can be narrowed. The pursuit of economic growth and a more equitable distribution of income are compatible goals. But the resulting Chinese political order is devoid of meaningful political freedom; it is a utilitarian society, without frills and with little concern for beauty and aesthetics.

Through the ideas of the revolutions that established them, three continental states have become the repositories of principles which coexist in tension—liberty, growth, and equality. Yet each value speaks to an important aspect of the human condition. It would not be in the interest of mankind to see any of these principles eliminated or fundamentally compromised. So, the underlying challenge in developing a viable international order involves the search for ways which allow the United States, the U.S.S.R., and China to remain true to their respective revolutionary traditions.

To an important extent, the evolution of Sino-American relations will be a litmus test of the balance of ideas in the world. Can the ideas of Jefferson and Mao Tse-tung, of political freedom and economic equality, coexist as we seek areas of cooperation? That, in part, is the significance of the Sino-American relationship. For if the terms of exchange between these two societies can become genuinely reciprocal, then we may discover that there is less tension between the values of our two revolutions than is currently believed.

Chinese Nationalism

Americans, however, must hold no illusions on this score. There is no escaping the challenge of the Chinese revolution and the reassertion of the Chinese. After a century of political decay, internal disorder, and foreign encroachment, the nation has galvanized its energies. From 1950 through 1970, the United States hoped it could isolate China: ignore the problem and it would go away. That simpleminded strategy did not work. Rather, it yielded hostility and tension in East Asia, leading to American involvement in two major land wars in Asia and a series of dangerous confrontations.

To his credit, President Nixon understood that the People's Republic of China was a major force on the world scene and that a more forthcoming response would redound to our strategic benefit. This was a major conceptual breakthrough. Until Nixon's initiative, many Americans tended to fear various forms of Asian nationalism—Japanese, Korean, Chinese, or Vietnamese. The Nixon initiative was a dramatic effort to work with the energies of Chinese nationalism for the American interest. Herein lies a second significant aspect of our relations with China. For 400 years, Westerners were drawn to China and mainland East Asia: first the Spanish and Portuguese, then the British, the French, the Russians, and finally the Americans. Commercial, religious, military, and diplomatic involvements formed the complex fabric of Western colonialism. But with the Guam Doctrine and the American withdrawal from Vietnam, for the first time since the early 1800s, no Western troops are on the mainland of East and Southeast Asia (with the noticeable exception of Korea). To be sure, as Waldo Heinrichs notes, the United States retains the Seventh Fleet in Pacific waters, forces in the Philippines, a residual presence in Taiwan, and a major defense commitment to Japan. Those involvements are strategic rather than colonial in nature, and are not intended to defend positions of American dominance. Rather, their purpose is to maintain stability and prevent others from establishing positions of dominance.

The age of imperialism in East Asia seems to have drawn to a close. Instead, those forces of nationalism which swept Japan in the late nineteenth century—the quest for independence and the creation of new sources of national power and wealth—have come to characterize the whole area. The specific nature of nationalism in each Asian country reflects its distinct culture and its particular experience with Western (or Japanese) colonialism.

Finally after tragic misjudgments of Asian nationalism over the past half century, in Japan and Vietnam as well as China, Americans seem to be developing a greater sensitivity to the complex, multiple nationalisms of the region. What has been the nature and origins of Chinese nationalism? Mao Tse-tung, Chou En-lai, and the other founders of the People's Republic came of political age during the May Fourth movement of 1919. Spearheaded by students, that movement protested the injustice of the Versailles Peace Conference. In violation of President Wilson's proclaimed ideals and in disregard of the Chinese contribution to the allied effort in World War I, the powers assembled in France ceded the treaty privileges of Germany in China to the Japanese. The Chinese students were shocked and angered. The May Fourth generation sought to create a China that would never again be humiliated and disregarded in similar fashion. They were determined to win a respected, dignified voice for China in the councils of nations. From this vantage, the entry of the People's Republic into the United Nations in 1971 was the ultimate vindication of a life of sacrifice and devotion to their country by Mao, Chou, and their associates. China had entered the world state as an independent, equal force. Mao and Chou had succeeded beyond their wildest dreams. They had forged a nation-state admirably equipped to deal with the world of 1919.

Now the May Fourth generation has passed, and a new generation is coming to the fore whose initiation into politics came with the war against Japan. While Mao's quest for national greatness was circumscribed by China's military weakness, his successors may gradually acquire the capability to act on other visions. For this reason, one cannot assume continuity in China's nationalistic quest, although the current rhetoric remains within the May Fourth intellectual framework: the desire to create a wealthy, powerful country with a modern culture and a large industrial base.

Yet, Chinese nationalism will not be easy to accommodate. The articles by Tu Wei-ming, Warren Cohen, and Lyman Van Slyke are pivotal to the analysis, with each author illuminating a dimension of the problem. Cohen portrays the difficulty Americans have had historically in feeling any empathy with the Chinese self-image. Tu reveals the ambivalence and tensions inherent in China's will for greatness. And Van Slyke illuminates the point that Americans and Chinese focus upon different attributes as key to their national essence: the Chinese, their culture; the Americans, their technology. Neither side accurately interprets the nationalistic expressions of the other. We sometimes conclude that assertions of Chinese cultural greatness imply a desire to force that culture upon those beyond the realm; after all, this is what we intend when we assert our cultural greatness. On the other hand, the Chinese are suspicious that American efforts to export technology are intended to erode foreign cultures; after all, the Chinese are skeptical of a civilization that treats technology as having intrinsic merit. The Cohen, Tu, and Van Slyke essays, then, enhance our understanding of Chinese nationalism. The implication of their essays is that the United States has responded ineffectively to Chinese nationalism because we have assumed that Chinese nationalism is similar to ours. To bridge Chinese and American nationalisms requires understanding different concepts of nationhood, national purpose, and national essence.

Dealing with China

The challenge of dealing with China, in other words, must be traced to deeper considerations. The People's Republic is but twenty-five years removed from a great rural-based revolution during which peasant armies overwhelmed the urban areas. The cities of China not only were the centers of bureaucratic and commercial power, but with the emergence of the treaty port system, they became the focal point of the Western presence in China as well. During the late Ch'ing (1842–1911) and Republic (1911–49) eras, many Chinese in the treaty ports—particularly among the intellectuals and large entrepreneurs—shifted their gaze from the interior of China to the world beyond. Frequently foreign educated, many of the urban elite took world standards and ideas as their point of reference. Certainly the weakened cultural links between the large urban centers and the rural hinterland were a major factor in the distintegration of China under the impact of the West.

The rural tide which swept over the cities had several consequences. For one thing, many members of the Western-oriented elite fled China, and most who remained behind were subjected to harsh control. The links between the cities and the Western world were severed, and the activities in the urban areas—particularly after the Chinese abandonment of the Stalinist model of development—were more tightly integrated with the countryside. In addition, the cities themselves acquired a rusticated air, while the benefits of modernization spread rapidly to the countryside. Renewal of foreign contacts could jeopardize this pattern of development. At least, many Chinese leaders apparently now fear that the urban areas, where external influences would be particularly felt, could again drift from their rural moorings.

The foreign policy consequences of this characteristic of the Chinese revolution are reinforced by Chinese concepts of the purpose of the state and of the basic nature of man. As Donald Munro has argued with eloquence and insight, traditional concepts survive in Chinese Marxism. Man is considered perfectible, not born in sin. The task of the state is to nurture the moral potential of the populace. We see the absence of Hobbes or Locke—of the state conceived to protect the individual from the avarice of his fellowman. Further, in both traditional and Marxist China, man's obligations are owed to the network of social relations in which he is embedded, and not to the development of his individual identity. The task of the state is to cultivate, through education, this sense of obligation. The rulers of both traditional and contemporary China, in short, have considered one of their principal tasks to be the creation of a moral order. This aspect of China is not likely to change, simply because Chinese are not reevaluating the basic philosophical assumptions about man and the state which give rise to their social and political forms of organization. The reluctance to risk Chinese virtues in a corrupt world and the inclination to create barriers between the enlightened and the heathen therefore will also remain.

Nor is this concept of morality likely to encompass an aggressive or expansive missionary effort. For virtue is not disseminated primarily through the dispatch of zealous native missionaries who seek to create new moral communities as in the Western Christian tradition. To be sure, the Chinese send intelligence agents and underground workers abroad. But as to proselytizing an ideology, potential converts are more likely to be brought to the virtuous center and then encour-

aged to return home to spread the word. Thus, the missionary
work is accomplished by staying at home and encouraging
others to imbibe the virtues of the realm.

Implicit in this view is a conception of hierarchy and
mutual obligation. We do not wish to imply that the Middle
Kingdom syndrome persists or that individual Chinese are
unable to establish good personal relations on an equal foot-
ing. Nor do we wish to assert that Chinese diplomats are unable
to maneuver successfully in the current, rather unstructured
international system. Clearly the opposite is the case. Yet,
indications exist that as a nation, the Chinese do not feel entirely comfortable with bilateral relations among equals. Although Peking proclaims that its policies are based on mutual
benefit, the way it structures those relationships creates a
strong sense of hierarchy—particularly the way visits by world
leaders are made to appear to the Chinese populace as exer-
cises of deference which in turn elicit Chinese magnanimity.
Visiting heads of state tend to be accorded the same ritual, obtain the same pictures with Chinese leaders, and receive
roughly the same coverage in the *People's Daily*. The emphasis
upon equality in ritual underscores the Chinese reluctance to
deal more equitably in matters of substance.

Even more revealing in this regard was the Chinese perception of the Sino-Soviet alliance. According to their own descriptions, the Soviets were the "elder brother" and the Chinese the
"younger." To be sure, Chinese conceptualization of the
alliance was a good deal more complicated than that homey
formulation, but Mao's disaffection with the U.S.S.R. was related to Moscow's failure to act as a proper "elder brother"
should: to allow his strength to be used by other members of
the clan, to share his wealth, and to be a model worthy of
emulation. Interestingly, the more recent Chinese complaints
about the United States may grow out of a somewhat similar
perspective. Namely, Washington is not acting as an enlightened leading capitalist power ought to act: unyielding in its

opposition to its Soviet opponent. In short, the Chinese perceptions of hierarchy and preferences for ritual may lead to unspoken expectations different from those of their partners.

The establishing of links with China is complicated by yet another consideration. Networks of personal relations based on old ties are terribly important in expediting affairs in the large Chinese bureaucracy. Even today, Chinese governmental bureaucracies hardly consist of impersonal, corporate settings where behavior is regulated through contract. Mutual trust and confidence—human relationships—rather than extensive formal rules and codes order the social system. China is, after all, a society in which the skills of managing interpersonal relations are sufficiently widespread that it survives without any lawyers or psychologists. Relations among officials tend to be diffuse and not just limited to professional concerns. People who work together in the same bureaucracy tend to live together in ministry apartment blocks. Marriage among co-workers is widespread, children of office mates typically attend the same schools, and office workers belong to the same political study groups. Contrast this with the highly mobile, litigation-minded, contract-oriented American who is trained for the corporate world of functionally specific relations, and one senses the problems of knitting the two societies closer together. The problem is then compounded by the official state policy which, out of fear of ideological corruption, deters Chinese foreign-affairs specialists from establishing the kinds of diffuse personal relations with foreigners that prevail in their own society. Paradoxically, then, the Chinese government demands its foreign affairs specialists to develop the skills of operating in the impersonal corporate-legal-contractual world of international transactions. They master these skills marvelously but thereby become aliens in their own society.

One senses out of all of this—the rural base of the Chinese revolution, the commitment to creating a moral order, the penchant for hierarchial relations entailing mutual obligations, a system based on personal ties—that a distinctly *Chinese* state has been regenerated in East Asia, not a recreation of previous empires to be sure, but nonetheless a state drawing heavily for its principles of statecraft from the rich Chinese experience in governance. Therein lies the enormity of the challenge to American foreign policy in the years ahead—the task of creating a framework of interaction for two societies based on such different assumptions about man and his potential. Historically, civilizations have flourished when they responded with flexibility and awareness to such challenges; they have perished when they resist or avoid the task.

2

ROBERT B. OXNAM

Sino-American Relations in Historical Perspective

THE 1972 visit of President Richard Nixon to the People's Republic of China was one of the most spectacular moments in diplomatic history. On February 21, Americans watched on television screens as Nixon stepped off Air Force One at Peking Airport and greeted Premier Chou En-lai while a Chinese band struck up "The Star-Spangled Banner." The scene seemed so improbable that it made the occasion appear all the more momentous. Twenty years earlier, American GI's and Chinese troops fought each other to a bloody stalemate in Korea. Less than ten years earlier Vice-President Hubert Humphrey and Secretary of State Dean

In this introduction the author has drawn on some of the themes expressed in Michel Oksenberg and Robert B. Oxnam, *China and America: Past and Future* (New York: Foreign Policy Association, 1977).

Rusk had explained that a major reason for American troops fighting in Vietnam was the containment of Chinese Communist expansionism.

Against this background President Nixon's meeting with Chairman Mao on February 21 was a remarkable event —the outspoken American anti-Communist and the leader of the Chinese Communist revolution greeted each other with warm double handshakes and spent more than an hour in cordial conversation. The news media in both countries conveyed these images to the American and Chinese peoples: Walter Cronkite, Barbara Walters, and others offered extended live commentary, while the Chinese official newspaper, *People's Daily,* covered several pages with pictures and articles about the Nixon trip. When the visit ended on February 28, there seemed to be widespread agreement about Nixon's statement that "this was a week that changed the world."

The 1970s: From Euphoria to Uncertainty

During the early 1970s, U.S.-China détente seemed to fulfill Nixon's euphoric prophecy on several levels. The Shanghai Communiqué, issued on February 28, 1972, provided the diplomatic framework for the new era of détente. In the Communiqué both countries recognized the vast difference in ideology and social structure, but both sides committed themselves to trade, cultural exchanges, diplomatic discussions, and progress toward "normalization of relations." On the difficult issue of Taiwan, the two sides stated separate positions, which seemed to leave room for future negotiations.

Events from 1972 to 1974 seemed to fulfill the spirit of the Shanghai Communiqué admirably, and leaders in both countries (and in Taiwan as well) seemed to feel that "normalization" would occur in the relatively near future. In 1973 liaison offices were established in Peking and Washington and were headed by senior diplomats (Huang Chen from China and David Bruce, replaced by George Bush and then Thomas Gates, from the United States). The liaison offices performed many of the functions of full-scale embassies. Trade, a trickle at first, reached almost $1 billion in 1974; Chinese exports were primarily consumers' goods and textiles, while American exports included not only wheat and corn but also high-technology items such as Boeing 707 aircraft, Pratt and Whitney jet engines, RCA satellite systems, and chemical fertilizer plants from the M. W. Kellogg Company. Americans clamored for visas to the People's Republic. By 1975 some 10,000 Americans had visited China, and several hundred Chinese had journeyed to the United States. Many of the visits had a spectacular quality. All told, large numbers of Chinese listened to the Philadelphia Orchestra and watched American track and field, swimming, and gymnastic teams. Smaller numbers of highly influential Chinese entertained American congressmen, newspaper editors, university presidents, international affairs experts, scientists, and businessmen. Millions of Americans were enraptured by the performances of Chinese acrobats and the exhibition of Chinese archeological discoveries which drew record crowds to museums in Washington, Kansas City, and San Francisco. The China enthusiasm which spread across America—fed by television documentaries, newspaper and magazine articles, a flood of new paperback visitors' reports, and slide shows galore—was accompanied by a more restrained Chinese hospitality and seeming admiration for Nixon (even after his public career disintegrated under the impact of the Watergate episode).

This high tide of Sino-American détente had powerful repercussions in international and Asian affairs with benefits for both countries. Shortly after the advent of "Ping-Pong diplomacy" in mid-1971, the United States ceased its effort to prevent China's entry into the United Nations, and the People's Republic gained its long-awaited goal of occupying

China's seat in the United Nations (a seat previously held by the Republic of China). In 1972 the Japanese established diplomatic relations with the People's Republic, an event treated with great fanfare in both Tokyo and Peking as it seemed to terminate the bitter Sino-Japanese hostility of the previous century. The new Sino-American relationship sent reverberations into other parts of the globe as well. Moscow viewed the relationship with caution and concern because the complex new Moscow-Peking-Washington triangle left the Soviet Union in a more disadvantageous position. Peking leaders used the situation to escalate ideological attacks on the Soviet "revisionists" and "superpower hegemony," while the Sino-Soviet border tensions of the late 1960s appeared to ease somewhat. Washington leaders found new leverage in pushing the Soviets toward détente and nuclear arms limitation talks. At the same time the United States was able to extricate itself from its disastrous involvement in Vietnam while the Chinese applauded the continued American presence in the Pacific as a counterweight to Soviet expansionism.

By the mid-1970s, however, several factors tended to slow down the earlier momentum, and U.S.-China relations appeared stalemated. Most importantly, the mutual strategic interests which had initiated the era of détente—a desire for greater leverage against the Soviet Union, for a rapid U.S. withdrawal from Vietnam, for a post-Vietnam U.S. military presence in the Pacific—had been partially achieved by mid-decade. But these short-term solutions created a new set of problems for leaders on both sides who began asking themselves, "Where do we go from here in U.S.-China relations?" Furthermore, leadership shifts in Peking and Washington exacerbated the sense of uncertainty. The Nixon-Mao and Kissinger-Chou duos had faded into history through death and domestic political turbulence. The late 1975 trip of President Ford to the People's Republic was a pale reflection of the 1972 voyage, and Ford seemed too preoccupied with the challenge from conservative Ronald Reagan to risk any moves toward Peking. The rapid American withdrawal from Vietnam, furthermore, left Ford unwilling to make any other Asian initiatives that might be seen as evidence of a further weakening of U.S. resolve. Former President Nixon's second voyage to China early in 1976, at the special invitation of Chairman Mao, left many Americans confused about Chinese intentions, while it underscored Mao's irritation at Ford's slow progress on relations with China. Although both American candidates reiterated their commitment to "normalization" in the 1976 campaign, neither placed much emphasis on China policy in their debates and campaign statements. In China as well, the political upheavals of 1976—the death of Chou En-lai, the April riots in Peking, the death of Mao Tse-tung, the purge of the "gang of four," and the emergence of Chairman Hua Kuo-feng—tended to focus Chinese attention on domestic events. By early 1977, the two new administrations in Washington and Peking were making cautious overtures, but the sense of rapid movement and personalized diplomacy had been drained away.

Although more than 2,000 Americans continued to visit the People's Republic each year, trips to China were losing their quality of specialness. And there were problems in cultural exchanges as well. In 1975 the American side cancelled a visit of Chinese performing artists because of a last-minute inclusion of a song about "liberating Taiwan," and later that year the Chinese refused a delegation of American mayors because they felt the inclusion of the mayor of San Juan compromised the Chinese advocacy of Puerto Rican independence. In 1976, Sino-American trade had dropped back from a 1974 high of $933 million to a more modest $336 million (much of this decline is explained by Chinese cancellation of grain orders in 1975 and by a Chinese desire to have a favorable balance of trade which they achieved in 1976).

In short, by the late 1970s we seemed to be moving from a period of mutual expectations in Sino-American relations to a period of greater uncertainty on both sides. Each country had achieved some short-term goals, but both countries seemed unsure about where to go from there. The Taiwan dilemma remained the immediate stumbling block to normalization. Taiwan has been the island home of the Chinese Nationalists (formerly led by Chiang Kai-shek) since their defeat by the Chinese Communists in the late 1940s. The United States had sent its Seventh Fleet to patrol the Taiwan Straits in 1950, and in 1954 signed a Mutual Defense Treaty with the Republic of China (the Nationalist government on Taiwan). Washington saw these acts as part of its "containment" strategy, but Peking perceived them as intervention in the Chinese Civil War. Since then, the United States has poured billions of dollars of aid into Taiwan, and has established strong commercial relationships (two-way trade amounted to $4.8 billion in 1976). The United States has supplied a considerable proportion of Taiwan's heavy weaponry and military aircraft, while gradually removing American military forces from the island (down to 1,400 troops by March 1977).

The nub of the Taiwan issue is that the People's Republic sees the island as part of its rightful territory. It has set three conditions for normalized relations with the United States: the severance of U.S. formal diplomatic relations with Taipei, the termination of the Mutual Defense Treaty, and the withdrawal of all American military personnel from Taiwan. The U.S. government, on the other hand, considers that it has a historical and moral interest in the peaceful resolution of the Taiwan issue, and the American people clearly wish to retain commercial and cultural contacts with the island. Uncertain of Peking's peaceful intent, the United States wants to ensure that Taiwan has the capacity to deter the People's Republic should it attempt a military solution. The dilemma is how to achieve a flexible solution which establishes full diplomatic relations. This solution cannot be seen as a Taiwan "sellout" in Peking (which would embarrass the new leadership), in Washington (where pro-Nationalist sentiments of the

1950s might be revived and jeopardize necessary congressional approval), in Taipei (which might, under duress, declare independence, suffer economic panic, or develop nuclear weapons), or in other capitals (particularly in Tokyo because the Japanese have substantial commercial interests in Taiwan).

Taiwan, therefore, is a thorny issue for all parties concerned. At stake are principles, diplomatic and military calculations, and definitions of national interest in Asian affairs. In principle, U.S. recognition of the Peking government is long overdue, for it has authority over almost 900 million people and now occupies China's seat in the United Nations. But the United States also has an ongoing interest in Taiwan, for under the American aegis the 17 million people on that island have developed their own prosperous economy and life style. In terms of diplomatic and military reality, the Taiwanese government and economy probably have sufficient independence and resilience to absorb the shock of American derecognition, provided that guarantees of Taiwan's security are sufficient and credible. Taiwan has a strong defensive military capacity of its own, including a standing army of 500,000 men and an array of potent weapons (F-5E jet fighters, tanks, artillery, destroyers, and Nike-Hercules and Hawk missiles). It seems highly unlikely that Peking would risk the loss of life and equipment, the loss of international prestige, and the resistance from the United States and Japan that would be involved in an attempt to conquer Taiwan by force.

This leads us to look at the Taiwan question in terms of U.S. and People's Republic national interests in Asian and global affairs. A short-term settlement is certainly possible that enables both sides to remain true to their respective principles. But why should either side be willing to be flexible? Indeed, what is beyond the goal of normalized diplomatic relations? What are the realistic potential benefits for both countries? Is it reasonable to expect that diplomatic relations will lead to greater trade and cultural-educational exchanges? Does normalization promise greater long-term stability in Asian affairs? Will it lead to greater Sino-American cooperation in multi-lateral negotiations on such issues as Korea and offshore economic resources? Will it lead to greater Sino-American cooperation in international bodies dealing with energy resources, food and population issues, arms control, international economic concerns, and so forth? On the other hand, what are the likely consequences of a relationship that is not normalized? Can we preserve a subdiplomatic status quo or are Sino-American relations likely to deteriorate unless there is normalization?

Historical Patterns in Sino-American Relations

The authors of this volume have reached no consensus on the important issues, but they all believe that such issues should be addressed with a knowledge of more than the immediate past. Looking over the past two centuries, one can identify several persistent patterns that have characterized the Sino-American relationship. These patterns are worth noting because they establish the context for the current era of détente, and because they point out some past problems that may still persist.

Poles Apart. First of all, history and geography seem to have conspired to create a fundamental and inescapable fact. The physical and cultural gaps between our societies have been and remain enormous. We are poles apart both physically and perceptually. As China experienced its turbulent transition from ancient empire to a unique developing country under Communist control, the United States has grown from a small newly independent republic to the world's most affluent and powerful nation. The vastly different histories and recent experiences of China and the United States have produced divergent traditions and current outlooks. Visitors from each country still experience a strong cultural shock when traveling to the other—just as the Chinese immigrants and American missionaries did a century ago.

Both countries are continental in size, and throughout much of their history each has been geographically and culturally isolated from events elsewhere in the world. America, bracketed by two oceans, has devoted much of its energies to developing its own resources and resolving its own domestic problems. Similarly, China, insulated by mountains, deserts, and a long ocean boundary, has developed an introspective outlook, seeking to defend its borders while concentrating on problems at home. Both countries have relatively self-sufficient economic systems with a small percentage of overall resources drawn from foreign trade. Thus, it has been natural for Americans and Chinese to see themselves as the center of the world.

In terms of public perceptions, China has seldom figured importantly in American eyes, nor America in Chinese eyes. Schoolchildren learn little about the other country in their textbooks (except that one gets there by "digging straight down"), while adults generally develop only a superficial knowledge consisting largely of stereotypes (reinforced by the limited coverage in our respective mass media). Only a relatively few individuals and groups have come to understand the other society in any depth, but their influence at home has been short-lived and their images of China or America have often been developed in idealized terms. Indeed some of the outsiders—the missionaries in China and the Chinese immigrants in America—have been seen as disruptive and subversive influences.

All of these factors have influenced policy-makers in both Peking and Washington to see U.S.-China relations as a low priority issue in the broad context of their domestic and foreign policy options. From the vantage point of the White

House as from the Forbidden City in Peking, it is difficult to
see a society halfway round the world as central to one's interests. Few American presidents or secretaries of state have
taken a strong interest in Chinese or Asian affairs, and few
Chinese leaders have developed a close awareness of American society. When we have looked abroad, American policy
has grown from an essentially Europe-centered outlook and
Chinese policy from an essentially Asia-centered viewpoint.
When Chinese and American interests have intersected, the
relationship has generally been motivated by broader geopolitical considerations, such as a mutual concern about
Japan or Russia, rather than from direct bilateral interests.
And after a brief flurry of concern in Peking and Washington,
the relationship has usually lapsed back to its low-priority
status.

Conflicting Self-images. Given this remoteness, it is not surprising that each society has evolved quite different conceptions of itself and its appropriate role in world affairs. Indeed
in order to understand the spotty history of Sino-American
relations, it is important to note that each country has its own
competing sets of self-images that deeply influence American
outlooks on China and Chinese outlooks on America. In this
sense, the Sino-American relationship has often served as a
double-sided mirror, each country developing policies that
fulfill one or another of its self-images, while seldom clearly
understanding developments in the other society.

In very broad terms, we can see a historic tension in American foreign policy between those approaches that fulfill American moral yearnings and those that arise from the American
sense of practicality and toughness. Although policy makers
have endeavored to capture both sides of this dichotomy, the
tension has persisted, and nowhere has it been more evident
than in American policies toward China. The roots of this tension can be traced to the nineteenth century when the United
States, with no distinct China policy, was content to enjoy

the privileges won by British firepower and aggressive diplomacy. In those years, American missionaries sought the moralistic goal of bringing spiritual enlightenment to the Chinese people ("400 million souls"), while American traders sought the more pragmatic goal of opening China to unrestrictive commerce with the West ("400 million customers"). The Open Door policy, developed by Secretary of State John Hay in 1899–1900 during an era of great power rivalry to extract concessions from a weakened China, incorporated both sides of the American outlook. It called for the "equality of commercial opportunity in China" (the tough approach), while also promising to protect the "administrative and territorial integrity of China" (moralism par excellence). Although the United States failed to realize either side of the statement, the Open Door was the official framework for American policy up to 1949, offering a broad umbrella for a variety of strategies.

This tension has persisted down to the contemporary era and has permeated American deliberations over an appropriate China policy. Should America maintain its role as "defender of the free world" and thus preserve its alliance with Taiwan at all costs? Or should it follow a more realpolitik strategy and recognize the People's Republic in the interest of future cooperation in Asian affairs? Indeed as we look more closely at the debate, moral and pragmatic arguments can be summoned on both sides. Americans still face the dilemma of trying to define themselves as they search for an appropriate policy toward China.

Although the Chinese historical experience has been radically different from the American, a similar tension in self-imagery has characterized Chinese outlooks as well. Two hundred years ago, at the height of China's last dynasty, the imperial court retained its traditional vision that China was the "Middle Kingdom," the sophisticated center of all civilization to which all "barbarians," including those from the West, should pay homage. But in the course of the nineteenth and early twentieth centuries this monistic self-definition crumbled before the onslaught of Western imperialism and domestic revolution. Long before the last Chinese dynasty collapsed in 1912, many intellectuals recognized that China could no longer be defined as an expansive Confucian culture; instead it had become a beleaguered nation-state. How was China to become a modern country, achieving the "wealth and power" of the West and Japan, while still retaining its integrity and special sense of identity? This question prompted the great intellectual debates of the first two decades of the twentieth century and the great revolutionary conflicts of the next three decades, and it continued as a source of tension in the almost three decades of the People's Republic. The basic issue is whether China should be viewed as a spiritual and ideological entity or as a material entity evaluated in terms of economic progress and popular well-being. Of course, the ideal answer for all Chinese intellectuals and politicians has been to say that they seek *both* spiritual values and material achievements. In the nineteenth century the slogan was "Chinese values as the essence, Western technology for practical purposes," and in contemporary China the goal for both the state and the individual has been to combine "red and expert."

But, in fact, this tension over Chinese self-definitions has persisted unresolved and is at the heart of the division between the so-called "radicals" and "moderates." As with American self-images, the conflicting Chinese outlooks have colored attitudes towards Sino-American relations. Should China preserve its commitments to a radical version of Maoist ideology and thus continue its policy of "self-reliance" and minimal contact with the United States and other Western countries? Or should China place greater emphasis on economic modernization and thus seek closer political and economic ties with the United States and the West?

These internal tensions over self-definitions help explain the historical volatility in Sino-American relations which has

led to frequent and sudden changes in policies. Shifting definitions of priorities on both sides, often because of a new leadership or because of dramatic changes in the world situation,
can lead to a powerful redirection of policies. Thus, in the
ebb and flow of self-images, American realpolitik and Chinese
pragmatism have sometimes combined for limited mutual
advantages (such as the détente of the 1970s), while American moralism and Chinese ideological emphasis have often
formed an explosive combination (such as the mutual hostility of the 1950s).

Changing Definitions of the Other Society. Closely related
to these fluctuations in self-image are the changing definitions
of the other which both societies have evolved over the long
course of Sino-American relations. In this respect, the relationship has been more than a mirror, for it has constituted a
void into which both societies have projected their best hopes
and their worst fears about mankind. "China" and "America" thus become abstractions for the other country, arche-
types of the ultimate good or the ultimate evil. The net effect
of these shifting self-images and changing definitions of the
other society has been to produce a cyclical character to the
overall relationship. Harold Isaacs, focusing on the American
side of the relationship, called this phenomenon the "love-
hate" cycle; the observation is just as accurate for the Chinese
side.

As one probes more deeply into these "love-hate" cycles,
certain features of U.S.-China relations become clearer. First
of all, before 1950 the American and Chinese cycles of policies and perceptions were seldom synchronized. Hateful notions on one side were often matched by rather positive images
on the other side. This lack of synchronization stemmed from
the fact that from the outset it was a grossly asymmetrical
relationship. The American march onto the stage as an Asian
power in the early twentieth century coincided with the height
of imperialist aggression, disunity, warlordism, and revolution
in China. In Warren Cohen's terminology, the period from

1900 to 1949 was an era of "paternalism" in American outlooks on China—a paternalism born of an Americanized
dream for China's future. China was viewed as a pitiful giant
whose strength and stamina could be restored only through
large doses of American aid and American idealism. In cari-
catured form, the vision was summed up by Senator Kenneth Wherry: "With God's help, we'll lift Shanghai up and
up, ever up, until it's just like Kansas City."

Yet this early twentieth century American vision for China
was never realized. To be sure, the reformist dimensions of
the vision yielded some fragmentary results (schools, universities, hospitals, engineering projects, and welfare programs) and
a modest China trade developed. But in overall policy terms
the vision remained illusive—partly because American goals
overstated its realistic capacities and interests, and partly because the United States seldom acted on the basis of realistic
appraisals of what was happening in China. Throughout
most of the period from 1900 to 1949, in spite of the powerful
rhetoric of the Open Door, China remained a low-priority
issue in American policy making. Thus, Theodore Roosevelt's
realpolitik approach, based on a contempt for a weakened
China and a respect for close Japanese-American relations,
did not foresee the long-term consequences of Japanese expansionism nor the potentials of a future nationalistic China.
In contrast, the idealism of Woodrow Wilson's League of Nations and his principle of "self-determination" failed because
of a lack of understanding of the intensity of great power
rivalries in Asia and a lack of support at home. And the
Franklin Roosevelt administration of the 1930s, caught up in
an era of economic depression and isolationism, followed suit
offering high-sounding rhetoric but no willingness to use American force to deter Japanese aggression in China. By the 1930s,
China had become a great moral concern for many Americans who donated millions of dollars to missionary enterprises
and relief programs, but the defense of China was not deemed
worthy of American military intervention.

On one level, the American entry into World War II after Pearl Harbor seemed to mark a break with previous policies and attitudes—now America and China were allies in a common cause against Japan and the American presence in China increased markedly. But upon closer examination, the American involvement in China during the 1940s also displays a mix of moralist and realpolitik approaches, some new and some reminiscent of earlier approaches. China still remained a low-priority consideration during the war, when the main emphasis was on the European theater and on island-hopping in the Pacific, and after the war, when Americans had little interest in committing troops to the Nationalist cause against the Chinese Communists in the Civil War (1946–49). The mix of realpolitik and moral strains in American policy centered on the desire for a unified and democratic postwar China and led many Americans to pin their hopes on Chiang Kai-shek's Nationalist movement. Chiang's democratic and Christian rhetoric were more evident to most Americans than the disunity of his Nationalist forces, the increasing loss of popular support and demoralization of the late 1940s, and the growing strength of the Communist movement.

The Communist victory in 1949 brought an abrupt end to the American involvement on the Chinese mainland and to the era of American "paternalism." Then the Korean War led to a new phase of American moral concern and military intervention, this time focused on the island of Taiwan where Chiang Kai-shek established his new Nationalist headquarters. This dramatic change of events left many Americans confused and bitter. What had gone wrong? Was it a Soviet conspiracy? Was it a Communist conspiracy in the American State Department? Who lost China? Few in the United States recognized that the real problem with the American vision for China was that it was an *American* vision. It was based on an inflated estimate of our capacities to influence events in China and on inaccurate definitions of Chinese politics and society.

Turning to the Chinese side of the story in the early twentieth century, we see not one but two broad attitudes toward Americans. Tu Wei-ming appropriately calls these attitudes "admiration" and "ambivalence." For two decades after the turn of the century, Chinese intellectuals looked across the globe for foreign models that would answer China's quest for a new ideology and for a modernized society and economy. During that period many intellectuals focused on the United States as a nation with powerful industry and technology and a potent set of liberal ideals. But such views were inevitably filtered through Chinese eyes, often overlooking problems in American society and the possibility that American solutions might not be applicable to Chinese difficulties. Indeed that seemed to be one of the lessons of the Revolution of 1911. Sun Yat-sen, the key leader of the revolutionary movement, had incorporated various American ideals into his ideology, and the Republic of China, established in 1912, included several American principles in its constitution. But the Republic was short-lived and quickly collapsed before the forces of Chinese monarchism and warlordism. In spite of that experience, the high tide of Chinese interest in America came near the end of World War I as Woodrow Wilson's rhetoric captured the attention of many young Chinese. In 1919 that idealized version of America came to an end with the Versailles Treaty when Wilson agreed to turn over the former German concession areas in China to the Japanese. The principle of "self-determination" now seemed empty and Wilson was no longer a hero but a betrayer of the Chinese quest for sovereignty.

The era of "admiration" passed and a new era of "ambivalence" emerged. Some Chinese hung on to their respect for American values and tried in vain to create a liberal democratic alternative to the Communist and Nationalist revolutionary movements. But most Chinese political leaders began to look elsewhere for inspiration, most frequently to the Russians, whose 1917 Bolshevik Revolution seemed to provide a more promising model for Chinese circumstances. By the

1930s, Mao Tse-tung was developing his unique form of Communism based on agrarian support and guerrilla warfare, while Chiang Kai-shek was building a Nationalist movement based on urban and military support and an ideology that seemed to mix Confucianism, Christianity, and authoritarianism. During the 1940s, both Mao and Chiang looked to the United States not as a source of values, but rather with the hope of finding military and economic support for their respective movements. In terms of Chinese self-image, although America had lost much of its spiritual and ideological appeal, it remained a strong source of potential support and inspiration on the practical and technological side.

In the 1950s, the grossly asymmetrical nature of the Sino-American relationship passed into history and was suddenly replaced by a fearful symmetry. The Korean War of 1950–53 initiated a twenty-year period of hostility and confrontation. It was a moral and ideological crusade on both sides, and each defined the other as the most villainous society on earth. Casting aside the *Good Earth* imagery, Americans defined China in images derived from the Fu Manchu and "blue ants" stereotypes. The Chinese, meanwhile, came to see the United States as the "Number One Enemy" and used Uncle Sam dummies for bayonet practice.

And yet, tragically and paradoxically, the downswing of hate may have been necessary for the upswing of détente that emerged in the 1970s. As Waldo Heinrichs observes, the bloody stalemate of the Korean conflict did not lessen hostility on either side, but at least it tended to undercut Mao's view that Americans were "paper tigers" and that People's Liberation Army soldiers fought like the proverbial "Chinese fire drill." A grudging but genuine respect was growing for the military potentials on both sides, a respect that tended to keep both from escalating the offshore islands crises and the Vietnam conflict into a full-scale war between the United States and China. It was mutual recognition of equality on the field of battle that helped pave the way for new diplomatic, economic, and cultural interactions based on the same principle of equality. The détente of the 1970s thus permitted both sides to preserve their moral and ideological self-images, while it pushed both to stress their more pragmatic strains and to define each other in more rational terms. The Shanghai Communiqué of 1972 captured the situation well when it announced:

There are essential differences between China and the United States in their social systems and foreign policies. However, the two sides agreed that countries, regardless of their social systems, should conduct their relations on the principles of respect for the sovereignty and territorial integrity of all states . . . .

Domestic Polemics. A fourth broad pattern is that the Sino-American relationship has occasionally become a heated domestic issue in both societies in spite of the fact that both countries usually tend to treat U.S.-China relations as a low-priority issue in foreign affairs. The explanation for this seeming paradox takes us back to an earlier point. The competing self-images in each society are sometimes championed by competing political groups and factions. In this sense, the China issue or the American issue can become an important test case for various political interests within our respective societies. Small but vocal minorities can thus capture the political and media spotlights and create an intense controversy over U.S.-China relations.

Close ties between certain groups of Americans and Chinese have sometimes intensified their controversies. In the past, Christians, businessmen, and military personnel on both sides often developed enduring friendships and intense interests in each other's lives and countries. These personal bonds led many to take a strong interest in the politics of U.S.-China relations, seeking policies in their own country that would protect the interests of friends in the other country. Politics and passions then became mixed as the two societies became linked at subdiplomatic levels.

A classic instance in the United States was the "China Lobby" whose strongly pro-Nationalist and sharply anti-Communist activities can be traced to certain American congressmen and journalists with an enduring affection for Chiang Kai-shek's Nationalists. In the election of 1948, the China Lobby supported losing Republican Thomas Dewey, who had endorsed substantially increased economic and military support for Chiang's failing Nationalist cause. Then in the several years after the Communist victory and the outbreak of the Korean War, the China Lobby became a major force in American politics, asking the haunting but ill-posed question, "Who lost China?" Fingers pointed to diplomats, scholars, and other Americans who had argued for a more realistic, balanced appraisal of Chinese Communist Party strengths and Kuomintang weaknesses in the 1940s. In the resulting furor, many fine China experts in the State Department were forced to leave their posts and American China policy became frozen for two decades.

Similar instances of domestic divisions over policies toward the United States have occurred in Chinese politics as well. The most recent example occurred in the early 1970s when the Mao-Chou overture to the United States aroused some domestic opposition. Defense Minister Lin Piao appears to have been a major opponent of the détente strategy, arguing at the very least for a balanced Chinese posture toward Moscow and Washington, and possibly for a new effort to rekindle closer Sino-Soviet relations. Some observers have also speculated that the so-called radicals may have opposed the policy of Washington-Peking détente on the grounds that it compromised ideological purity and threatened the principle of "self-reliance." Such differences over Chinese policies toward the United States are likely to continue in the future, reflecting not only the vicissitudes of American postures but more importantly the continuing tensions within Chinese domestic politics.

The slowing of progress toward normalization in the mid-1970s is partially due to domestic factors in both societies. The period of Mao's and Chou's deteriorating health intensified succession politics in Peking and sapped their ability to push the U.S. relationship farther. On the American side, Nixon's Watergate problems and the Reagan challenge to President Ford weakened their capacities to make a move toward Peking that might have aroused criticism from the conservative wing of the Republican Party. And then both Ford and Carter, recognizing the potential volatility of the China issue and drawn to other foreign policy concerns, made few remarks about U.S.-China relations in the course of the 1976 campaign.

Because the Sino-American relationship is a loaded issue in both countries, the easiest alternative for political leaders is to duck the issue and dodge the possible criticisms. Mao Tse-tung and Richard Nixon constituted notable exceptions to this general rule—Mao because of his acknowledged role as supreme leader of the People's Republic and Nixon because of his long-established credentials as a conservative anti-Communist. But other leaders, including those in the post-Mao and post-Nixon eras, may be more reluctant to grasp the thorny problem.

Here we arrive at a critical point. Major changes in Sino-American relations depend heavily on presidential leadership in the United States and the Politburo leadership in the People's Republic of China. As we saw in the early 1970s, moves at the top can have a decisive impact on attitudes in both countries and are a determining factor in the overall relationship. And without that leadership, the Sino-American relationship is likely to become a more divisive issue in both countries, thus further inhibiting moves from either side.

Short-range Calculations. Finally, because of all the patterns cited above, when policy makers on both sides have dealt with U.S.-China relations, they have tended to operate on the basis of immediate, short-range calculations. They need to feel a great sense of urgency or momentous opportunity before making major moves. Such was the case in 1899–1900 when the United States developed its Open Door policy and it appeared that China was about to become colonized by other foreign powers. Similarly in 1941 the Japanese attack on Pearl Harbor suddenly pushed the United States into a military alliance with China. And once again in 1950 the Korean War created a crisis for both sides, eventually pulling the Chinese into the conflict, while prompting the United States to develop a "containment" policy toward China. Between these crisis points of mutual concern, the interest in Washington and Peking seems to have lapsed, and no carefully conceived long-range strategy has emerged to deepen and sustain the relationship.

In the present decade, Washington and Peking saw a major opportunity in a rapprochement strategy because of several short-term interests of mutual concern. A primary interest was to prevent the Soviet Union from encroaching on China's sovereignty and from establishing positions of primacy on China's periphery as well as in the Middle East, Africa, and Western Europe. Such common interests also extended to other related issues: the rapid withdrawal of American troops from Vietnam while maintaining a strong U.S. presence in the Pacific; the maintenance of stability on the Korean peninsula so that neither the United States nor China would be drawn into another land war in Asia; and the effort to prevent Taiwan from declaring independence, acquiring nuclear weapons, or turning to the U.S.S.R. for its security.

While all of these goals seem worthy, all are based on short-term calculations and particularly on the parallel strategic interests of the United States and China vis-à-vis the Soviet Union. The détente between Peking and Washington thus becomes heavily dependent on the U.S.-China-U.S.S.R. triangle. Any shifts in that triangular pattern can have strong effects on the Sino-American relationship. Since 1972, the Chinese have increasingly expressed concern about the willingness of the United States to contain possible Soviet expansionism in Asia. At the same time, Chinese perceptions of the Soviet threat have diminished considerably since their border conflicts in 1969. The Soviets are still perceived as serious opponents in Peking, and as vile representatives of the principles of "revisionism" and "hegemonism," but a limited thaw may appeal to the post-Mao leadership since it would ease border tensions while opening another source of technology.

In short, the "mutually perceived enemy" approach is not likely to provide the basis for longer-term relationships between the United States and China. In an earlier era, we saw that the triangle involving the United States and China against Japan that formed in the wake of Pearl Harbor began to collapse after the holocaust of Hiroshima. Triangles in politics, as in orchestras, can sometimes sound important notes but they are unlikely to sustain attention for very long. While the Soviet factor will remain a significant element in Sino-American relations, we need to look beyond to other powerful potentials of the Peking-Washington connection—greater economic and diplomatic cooperation among the great powers in Asia (China, Japan, the Soviet Union, and the United States); resolution of the dangerous situation in Korea; negotiations over competing maritime claims in the eastern Pacific; joint U.S.-China involvement in multilateral negotiations on arms control, energy resources, food supply, and the international economic system; and bilateral trade and cultural and scientific exchanges.

The Past and Future of Sino-American Relations

Readers who scour these pages in search of an ideal prescription for the future of U.S.-China relations will surely be disappointed. Both history and the present situation indicate that there are no panaceas for the relationship. Certainly the problems of the past cannot be overcome by "weeks that changed the world" nor even by months or a few years. Instead of searching in vain for some tidy set of policy recommendations, the authors of this volume are convinced that the greatest need is for a new way of thinking about the relations between the world's most populous society and the world's most affluent society. In this respect, the approaches suggested in this volume are designed to have relevance not only to opinion makers and policy makers, but also to the broader public concerned about international affairs and American relations with Asia. Indeed, historical problems in Sino-American relations can be traced in part to policy makers, whose interests in the issue are often fleeting, and in part to the general public, whose concerns seldom focus on Asian affairs.

To encourage new ways of thinking about U.S.-China relations, let us underscore some general observations from these introductory essays. First of all, *the relationship must be understood in historical context.* That history did not begin with the Nixon-Mao meeting in 1972, nor with the eras of World War II, the Chinese Civil War, or the Korean War, but instead takes us back to the nineteenth century when Chinese and Americans first began to interact. To be sure, that history is filled with instances of new policies and new perceptions, feelings of breakthrough and of setbacks, new actors and new approaches on both sides. But in a general sense, the history of Sino-American relations provides the broad continuum in which policies are conceived and perceptions are developed. As we have seen, that history suggests some general patterns which have continued relevance to the present and future of the relationship. In short, while none of the authors is arguing the ominous and dubious proposition that history will repeat itself in specific terms, all are agreed that the potentials and problems in the relationship cannot be fully understood without broad historical reference points.

Second, *we need to examine both sides of the Sino-American relationship not only in terms of our direct interactions, but also in terms of the domestic considerations and constraints in the United States and China.* As we pointed out earlier, each side has tended to see the relationship as a mirror for its self-images and as a void into which it can project abstracted versions of the other society. Both societies have often seen "the Chinese" or "the Americans" in monolithic terms. Americans have generally missed the complexities of Chinese society and have frequently generalized about a "Chinese mind" or "Chinese characteristics." Only limited numbers of Chinese have ever met an American and thus it becomes easy to see Americans in generalized terms as "evil imperialists" or "friendly people" depending on time and circumstance. Therefore, at the same time that we consider the bilateral interactions that constitute much of the content in U.S.-China relations, we must also observe the separate and distinct domestic contexts in which policies and perceptions arise. On the one hand, such an outlook helps us understand why the Sino-American relationship has been such a low-priority issue on both sides; and on the other hand, it helps us recognize why the relationship occasionally has become an explosive domestic issue in both countries.

Third, *we need to envision a future relationship in a broad and long-term perspective.* Historically, the policy makers and the general public on both sides have seen Sino-American relations in terms of immediate needs and an immediate future. This crisis mentality has tended to focus attention on short-term factors—most frequently on the military and strategic considerations of the moment—and then attention turns elsewhere as the crisis passes. Thus, the relationship has hopped through history in topsy-turvy fashion, leaping from crisis to opportunity to crisis again, and both sides have proved incapable of sustained interest over an extended period of time.

Thus, this volume is written not to advocate a particular

policy, but rather to encourage all parties to see a long-term future in U.S.-China relations, a future that extends beyond the next three to five years, and instead looks ahead at least to the end of the present century. This long-term approach requires that both sides avoid operating in one-dimensional perspectives and instead see the potentials of U.S.-China relations in terms of four interrelated factors: (1) mutual perceptions, (2) bilateral interactions, (3) interactions in Asian affairs, and (4) global and strategic considerations. It is hoped that these four factors, which provide the organizational structure for this volume, will offer a conceptual framework for a more optimistic future while recognizing that the past provides ample grounds for pessimism.

Part II

MUTUAL PERCEPTIONS

ROBERT B. OXNAM

Introduction

IT is appropriate to begin our investigation of Sino-American relations by focusing on the images and perceptions that Americans have of Chinese and Chinese of Americans. Frequently, international relations are treated only as a set of "objective factors"—the interactions among nations, armies, economies, and statesmen—and thus the more subjective opinions and attitudes within each society are missed. In the case of U.S.-China relations, those subjective factors have played important roles. Opinion and policy have been interwoven in both countries, and the changing opinion-policy outlook in one country has often led to shifts in the attitudes and policies of the other.

In the two essays that follow, Warren Cohen and Tu Weiming examine the changing historical outlooks from the American and Chinese perspectives respectively. Their insights greatly amplify some of the introductory observations —the limited knowledge of the other society, the importance of self-image, the changing definition of the other country, the "love-hate" cycles, and the potential for domestic polemics. Both authors have endeavored to capture the shifting perceptions as they relate to ideologies, politics, and emotions in the United States and China. And in seeking to explain the formation and reformation of perceptions, the authors look broadly into popular literature, mass media coverage, leadership opinion, policy pronouncements, military and economic developments, and direct contacts between Chinese and Americans.

Looking at these essays together, we can draw two further conclusions. First, although we can trace a chronology of changing perceptions for each society, one should not assume that earlier attitudes pass away in strict sequence. Instead, the divisions between such eras are often blurred and earlier outlooks frequently persist as subordinate themes in a new era. The net result is to create a wide range of possible responses to the other society. Second, in the 1970s both sides seem to have evolved "split-level perceptions" of the other. The Chinese are very precise in this matter: they make a sharp distinction between "the American people" for whom they profess an abiding friendship and "the American government" which is still perceived as an "imperialist superpower." American perceptions are somewhat more difficult to define because they seem to encompass a broader spectrum and because the U.S. official position does not draw a clear-cut line between the government and people of China. Nevertheless, we find some parallels among visitors who return from China observing the "remarkable accomplishments in economic terms" but also "the enormous costs in political freedom." Both societies thus appear to hedge their bets, extending a new sense of friendliness and admiration on one level while preserving an older set of suspicions on the other.

On balance, the present era does seem to have brought some changes in the perceptual basis for Sino-American relations—some bridging of the culture and knowledge gaps (particularly on the American side), increased attention to the importance of the relationship on both sides, and a quieting of domestic squabbles (again particularly on the American side). But while the 1970s offer the promise of a more productive era in terms of perception and understanding, we have just begun the process. The history of shortsighted perceptions and stereotypes is just behind us, and thus both authors close their essays on an appropriately uncertain note.

3

WARREN I. COHEN

American Perceptions
of China

EN ROUTE to their independence, a band of American colonials in Boston staged history's most famous tea party. Tea from Amoy, China, made that operation possible. China produced tea. China produced porcelain. The first publication of Ben Franklin's American Philosophical Society expressed admiration for the industriousness of the Chinese people. George Washington knew the Chinese were "droll" in shape and appearance—and years later was astonished to learn that they were not white. Tea and porcelain; industrious, droll, and yellow: little suggests that colonial Americans knew or cared much more than that about China or the Chinese.

For most of the 200 years after independence, the prevailing American attitude toward China was indifference and disinterest—with a veneer that varied from contempt to sympathy, and more recently, to fear. Until World War II, those few Americans interested in world affairs focused largely on Europe. Culturally, most Americans were a part of Western civilization. Their roots, the origins of their ideas, were European. Economically and strategically, Europe was the center of power. China was a distant world where everything was upside down, where people ate dogs and wore white to funerals, where women wore pants and men wore gowns. Asian history and geography have received scant attention in the education of Americans. Even in the midst of the Pacific war in 1942, a poll indicated that *60 percent* of the American people could not locate China on a map.[1]

But indifference and ignorance do not prevent a people from having images of other people. Without ignoring constant undercurrents of indifference and contempt, a rough periodization of American attitudes, reflecting changing perceptions, can be constructed:

1784–1841	Era of Deference
1841–1900	Era of Contempt
1900–1950	Era of Paternalism
1950–1971	Era of Fear
1971–	Era of Respect

This periodization is meant to be suggestive. Attitudes selected to define one era will also be found in others. Eras overlap and indeed recent history indicates that Americans have inherited a wide array of attitudes toward China and are capable of rapid shifts in outlook.

But this periodization is useful to show how American public perceptions relate to U.S.-China relations—setting the broad context for policy making while often being influenced by

[1] Unless otherwise specified, cited public opinion data *prior to* 1947 is drawn from Hadley Cantril, ed., *Public Opinion* (Princeton, N.J.: Princeton University Press, 1951); and *after* 1947 from George H. Gallup, ed., *The Gallup Poll: Public Opinion, 1935–1971*, 3 vols. (New York: Random House, 1972). Both volumes are organized chronologically.

shifts in policies in Washington or Peking. Similarly, "American" attitudes, perceptions, and images must be considered at different levels: general public, special interest groups such as the missionaries, businessmen, and scholars involved with China, and policy makers. For policy makers and special interest groups, the written record is rich and can be analyzed. Government actions can be traced. But methods of gauging mass opinion are of relatively recent origin. The results of increasingly sophisticated polling techniques are available beginning in the 1930s. For the first 150 years of Sino-American contacts, however, we can generalize only about the information available to the public.

Era of Deference: 1784–1841

In 1784, when the first American merchant vessel reached Canton, the United States was a weak, underdeveloped country. Its leaders sought security—from external threats and for internal development. Remote China was peripheral to the fears and aspirations of the founding fathers. But trade was important—and a few American merchants now excluded from the British colonies looked to China, as to other parts of the world, for new opportunities. Quickly they established themselves in Canton. They had the blessings of the United States government and favorable tariff arrangements, but little more. They made their own way to Asia, took their risks, and operated only within the severe limits imposed upon them by Chinese authorities. There were no contacts between the American and Chinese governments: no treaties, no diplomatic missions, no diplomatic contacts. The Chinese regarded foreigners as barbarians, to be regulated by the traditional tribute system —and the Americans were no different. Americans, like all foreigners, had to submit, however resentfully, to whatever regulations and penalties the Chinese saw fit to impose.

The notorious Terranova case of 1821 strikingly illustrates the situation. Terranova was a seaman on an American ship whom Chinese authorities seized and executed in retribution for the death of a woman allegedly killed by debris falling from the vessel. Warned that refusal to turn Terranova over to Chinese authorities would mean exclusion of Americans from the Canton trade, local American merchants and the American government acquiesced, whereupon the local viceroy commended the Americans in Canton for their submissive behavior. Similarly, when Edmund Roberts at President Andrew Jackson's direction searched in the Orient for trade opportunities and treaties, he was unable to establish communications with Chinese authorities—except to receive orders to leave immediately. And he did, to the relief of American businessmen who feared his presence would antagonize the Chinese, ultimately hurting rather than expanding trade. Under the tribute system, the Chinese dictated the terms of contact, and that passionate nationalist Jackson was forced to be restrained. Until 1841, successive American administrators were aware that they simply lacked power in China to obtain more favorable terms of contact. While Americans had to tread carefully in Canton, they did not have to like the Chinese or their experiences in China. Few Americans who passed through Canton found kind words for the Chinese. Traders were appalled by the despotic government they found there and by the apparent dishonesty of Chinese officials and businessmen. They were angered and frustrated by the restrictions imposed on them and by the contempt with which Chinese officials treated them. No less ethnocentric than the Chinese, they found local costumes, customs, and cuisine ludicrous. Respect for Chinese culture—widespread in Europe in the eighteenth century— was rare among Americans. A relatively egalitarian, frontier society had less appreciation, less use for the finer arts of Chinese civilization.

The missionaries who began to arrive in the 1830s found the Chinese government hostile and the propagation of Chris-

tianity banned under pain of death by strangulation. This
resistance to salvation, and the intensity of wicked Chinese
heathenism troubled them deeply. They soon came to share
the merchants' longing for the use of Western secular power
to make the Chinese more receptive to Western influence,
trade, and Christianity.

While Americans at home, still caught up in the Anglophobia of the times, generally opposed the British involvement
in the Opium War, Americans in China unhesitatingly supported the British cause. Merchant and missionary cheered as
the British humbled the Chinese. Victims of Chinese arrogance, they welcomed the destruction of the tribute system, of
Chinese controls on their operations. Witnessing the slaughter
of Chinese troops, one American missionary wrote that he regarded British troops as instruments of God clearing away the
rubbish that impeded the advancement of Divine Truth.

Cultural differences between Chinese and Americans while
China appeared strong had elicited fear and caution from
Americans who had contact with the Chinese. But defeat in
the Opium War and further humiliations at the hands of Euro-
peans changed American perceptions of Chinese power.
Stripped of superior power, the cultural peculiarities of the
Chinese elicited only contempt. The "foreign devils," the
"big noses," no longer had to accept Chinese arbitrariness.
Now the Western barbarian dictated the terms of contact and
scorned the Chinese.

Era of Contempt: 1841–1900

In the latter half of the nineteenth century, American policy
generally followed guidelines set down by the British, and the
numbers of Americans in China increased only modestly to a

few hundred merchants, missionaries, diplomats, and adventurers. But it was a crucial era in defining American attitudes toward the Chinese—indeed echoes of this era of contempt have been heard throughout much of the twentieth century as well. The British victory in the Opium War enabled them to redress many of the grievances which had previously vexed Westerners. China was forced to open five new ports in 1842 and eleven more in 1858 after another conflict. Chinese tariffs were no longer imposed arbitrarily but embodied in a treaty that could be modified only with British consent. Westerners accused of crimes were tried by their own consular officials through the process of extraterritoriality. Merchants enjoyed expanded opportunities for trade, regularized and predictable procedures, and the protection of Western law backed by British troops stationed in Hong Kong. Missionaries enjoyed the same protection as merchants and after 1858 were free to roam much of the interior of China to proselytize wherever they pleased. These battalions of the Lord against the heathen were, in the words of one American missionary, "closing the fight, and Confucius, Buddha and Lao-tsz [*sic*] shall surely go down before the Lord of Hosts."

The Chinese extended the privileges wrested from them by the British to Americans and other foreigners rather than have the British extend such favors unilaterally and reap any consequent gratitude. But by 1844 the American government was ready to insist on having its own treaty. Gone was the deference to which the Chinese seemed entitled in the early years of the Republic. President John Tyler, in a letter carried by his agent, Caleb Cushing, addressed the Chinese Emperor much as he might have addressed the chief of an Indian tribe whose land the American government had decided to confiscate.

Through the Opium War (1839–42), the Arrow War (1856), and even as late as the Sino-Japanese War (1894–95), the U.S. government never indicated much concern over China's fate. American interests were restricted to trade and missionary work. American leaders never seriously entertained territorial ambitions. But they did not hesitate to insist on the same privileges for Americans in China that the British, French, and others had fought the Chinese to obtain. China was viewed as a weak, backward country, from which the United States could extort concessions by diplomacy, by use of the most-favored-nation clause in Sino-American treaties, but most of all, by following in the wake of British gunboats.

Writings on China, now available to a larger public with the advent of the "penny press" just before the Opium War, provided Americans with unfavorable images of the Chinese people, their culture, and their government. The violent episodes of the Taiping Rebellion (1850–64) were reported regularly. And intellectual leaders like Horace Greeley of the *New York Tribune* and E. L. Godkin of *The Nation* joined a host of less respected writers in maligning the Chinese. Greeley in 1854 described them as "uncivilized, unclean, and filthy beyond all conception . . . lustful and sensual in their disposition; every female is a prostitute of the basest order." And for Godkin, writing in 1869, the Chinese were barbarians whose chief virtues were "their fitness for servile duties and their want of social ambition." [2] To be sure, as long as domestic labor was scarce and the Chinese were willing to wash clothes, cook, clean house, and build railways, they were commended for being thrifty, industrious, and law-abiding. But these images of the Chinese survived only among businessmen eager for sources of cheap labor. With the end of the gold rush, labor was in oversupply and Californians perceived no further need for the Chinese. California led the rest of the country in purveying unfavorable images.

By 1868, there were more than 100,000 Chinese in the

[2] As quoted in Stuart Creighton Miller, *The Unwelcome Immigrant* (Berkeley and Los Angeles: University of California Press, 1969), pp. 169, 168.

United States. In that year, the United States signed a treaty with China providing Chinese immigrants with most-favored-nation treatment, thereby giving them the right to the same treatment accorded immigrants from England, Ireland, or Germany. But growing numbers of Americans appeared to want fewer Chinese, not more. Although Americans welcomed hundreds of thousands of immigrants who came each year from *Europe,* and most states took official steps to encourage immigration, the American vision had no room for the Chinese. The American's preference was for immigrants most like himself—and the Chinese were the most exotic. Chinese immigration was in fact considered so distinct from European immigration that it was possible for Irish immigrants to lead anti-Chinese movements without fear of stirring a general nativist reaction.

Perceptions of the Chinese as peculiarly depraved, perhaps even nonhuman, led to frequent violence against them. Individual Chinese were beaten, humiliated, and occasionally murdered. Bret Harte expressed his horror in the famous obituary to Wan Lee: "Dead, my reverend friends, dead. Stoned to death in the streets of San Francisco, in the year of grace 1869 by a mob of half-grown boys and Christian school children."[3] And in the 1870s and 1880s, anti-Chinese agitation grew increasingly violent, with lynchings, boycotts, and mass expulsions. Powerful pressure to exclude Chinese immigrants grew too great for Congress to ignore. The promise of most-favored-nation treatment, to which the United States was bound by treaty, was ignored, and Congress passed laws severely restricting and ultimately suspending Chinese immigration. In 1880 both major political parties opposed further Chinese immigration in their platforms. And still the hostility mounted. In 1885, 28 Chinese miners were brutally murdered in Wyoming and smaller-scale atrocities continued to occur.

[3] Cited in Harold R. Isaacs, *Images of Asia* (Cambridge, Mass.: M.I.T. Press, 1958), p. 113.

China had no gunboats to send to America, no way to protect its people in the United States, no way to force the United States to honor its treaty obligations. Chinese were considered disgusting. Their country was weak. They need not be tolerated. They could be mistreated. Americans were not yet ready to take up the white man's burden. And when some were, it was usually on behalf of the Chinese who stayed home.

Era of Paternalism: 1900–1950

After the turn of the twentieth century, as immigration remained a serious issue and aroused antagonism among young Chinese revolutionaries, the United States was gradually becoming a world power and beginning to evolve foreign policies toward various regions of the globe. In this policy perspective, China remained a minor concern of the U.S. government throughout most of the early twentieth century. The "Open Door" policy remained little more than high-sounding rhetoric during the five decades that it supposedly guided policy toward China (1899–1949). Yet for many Americans this was an era of great concern over issues that related to China. For those in U.S. government circles, China was a geopolitical concern, a focal point for British, French, Japanese, Russian, and American interests. For American merchants in the early 1900s, China was inaccurately portrayed as a great market for U.S. goods. For missionaries and foundations, China was a world concern, a beleaguered country that could benefit from American spiritual, technological, educational, or medical aid. Out of this era there emerged a new set of attitudes toward China and the Chinese.

Nothing that happened within China in the late nineteenth

century caused Americans to elevate their regard for the Chinese. Routed by the Japanese, carved into spheres by the Europeans, the country and its people continued to appear contemptible. The striving to be free of foreigners in the so-called Boxer Rebellion in 1900 was viewed in the West as reactionary resistance to modernization, and the murders of missionaries and Chinese Christians were taken as evidence of extraordinary viciousness.

But at the turn of the century, Americans were conceiving a new imperial role for themselves in world affairs, and this new self-image affected American perceptions of China. Brooks Adams and Alfred Thayer Mahan, the ideologues of American imperialism, placed great stress on the importance of the power struggle in East Asia, and their views were often echoed in the writings and speeches of Henry Cabot Lodge and Theodore Roosevelt. The world balance of power seemed at stake in European and Japanese rivalries over China. The weight of the United States in that balance might be critical.

These outlooks provided the basis for the Open Door policy, and its chief architect was the American official William W. Rockhill. Rockhill was convinced that an independent China able to keep order within its own boundaries was essential to the balance of power in Asia. He contended that the United States should use its new position in Asia and its growing influence in the world to preserve China from domination by European and Japanese imperialism.

In the late 1890s, as imperialist pressures in China mounted and as American exporters urged the U.S. government to protect their interests, President William McKinley and Secretary of State John Hay accepted Rockhill's draft of the Open Door notes—a message directed to each of the powers in China asking that they promise, within their spheres of influence, not to discriminate against the trade of other countries or to interfere with Customs Service collection of duties. The goods of all nations were to receive equal treatment throughout China, and markets would be available to those who sought them, including the Americans. And if the Customs Service was permitted to function as before, the Chinese government would have revenue necessary for *it* to function.

The notes seemed an ideal solution to the administration's quest for a new policy toward East Asia. They satisfied pressures from those who, like Rockhill, were concerned with power politics, from those who sought the expansion of American economic interests, from romantic nationalists eager to see the United States playing a larger role in world affairs—all without risking an overseas involvement that would disturb a people notoriously skittish about foreign entanglements.

Hay's notes were not intended as an act of benevolence toward the Chinese, who were not consulted about them. Indeed, Sino-American relations were greatly strained at the very time Rockhill and Hay were formulating their "Open Door" policy. American acquisition of Hawaii and the Philippines had led to the extension of American discriminatory policies against Chinese to those Pacific islands. In September 1899, the month in which the notes were sent, the Chinese minister to the United States protested against the "utter disregard of the American government for the friendly relations which should exist between the two governments." In other words, the first set of Open Door notes did not indicate an end of contempt for China at the governmental level. They did indicate a greater degree of interest in China among businessmen, intellectuals, and government officials.

But the locus of power in the world remained Europe, and it was to Europe that most Americans concerned with markets or the security of the United States looked. Only the greatly revitalized American missionary movement found Asia and particularly China more suitable for its efforts. But the missionaries functioned in China only as part of the treaty system, forced upon an unwilling Chinese government, and operating under the protection of gunboats. Measured in terms of converts, missionary successes were few, but the Christian attack on Chinese customs antagonized many Chinese, especially the gentry—the backbone of traditional Chinese society. Having worked toward the transformation of traditional society through the introduction of Western ideas, many missionaries concluded that the collapse of the old order was prerequisite to the fulfillment of the Christian mission and then welcomed the Japanese victory over China in 1895. The aftermath of the war brought not Christianity triumphant, however, but rather more widespread antimissionary activity and ultimately the Boxer War—with atrocities against hundreds of missionaries and thousands of Chinese Christians.

Weak country, depraved and cruel people—worthy only of contempt. In the midst of the Boxer War in 1900, when a possible Russian seizure of Manchuria might have precipitated the dismemberment of China, Secretary Hay sent off another round of notes in which he expressed concern for the territorial integrity and independence of China. These notes, together with those of the previous year, expressed what came to be known as America's traditional Open Door policy toward China and served as the basis for the myth of the United States as China's protector. Neither set of notes committed the United States to aid China: they were merely expressions of how the American government considered its interests would be served best. Indeed, many Americans with experience in China, including missionaries, took a very hard line on the Boxer settlement, warning that the Chinese would mistake generosity for weakness. They cherished not China, but the opportunities to reform that "benighted" country, to fulfill their Christian missions, or to make profits.

Nonetheless, an element of compassion for the Chinese began to emerge in the public media: Chinese were victims of European and Japanese imperialists. And with it grew a sense that John Hay with his Open Door notes had saved the Chinese from dismemberment. Hay was not eager to dispel the illusion, which reflected so well on him and cost so little.

Some Americans pitied the Chinese; others despised them.

All saw them as weak, backward, in need of guidance to find their way safely into the modern world. Theodore Roosevelt epitomized this view. His personal contempt for the Chinese was so great that "Chinese" became a derisive adjective in his vocabulary. When he thought the Russians were behaving stupidly in 1905, he accused them of "Chinese folly." When he wanted to condemn his fellow Americans for military laxity, he compared them to the Chinese. Most picturesquely, when President Woodrow Wilson spoke of being "too proud to fight," Roosevelt wrote: "If I thought the mood was permanent, I would feel that Uncle Sam would do well to wear a pigtail at once." He was contemptuous of what he saw as a Chinese lack of patriotism, Chinese cowardliness, Chinese backwardness.

But the new currents surging through American society in the early years of the twentieth century strengthened the shift from contempt to condescension and paternalism. Adherents of "progressivism" and its religious manifestation, the social gospel movement, saw the "heathen Chinee" not as objects to be despised but rather as a people to be uplifted, to be remade in the American image. And signs of progress, once sought, were soon found.

Reforms in China in the last years of the Ch'ing dynasty caught the fancy of American writers, and even Roosevelt in the last year of his presidency wrote of China's awakening—by which he meant greater receptivity to Western thought. The revolution of 1911 elicited a warm response in the United States. The creation of the Chinese Republic was portrayed as emulation of the United States, an image reinforced by Sun Yat-sen's close association with Americans and his interest in American constitutional principles. American journalists and missionaries expressed the belief that the Chinese had at long last opted for the American model, had become a sister republic, led by westernized Chinese who would soon guide their people toward Christianity and democracy.

During the administration of William Howard Taft a group of younger diplomats emerged who were eager to use American power and influence to check imperialism in China. The key to their plans was not the protection of China per se, but rather the containment of European and Japanese imperialism to preserve China as a region for American economic expansion. "Dollar diplomacy" was their catch phrase. When the Chinese revolution broke out in 1911, the Taft administration did not share the euphoric vision of certain American publicists, but stood by the European and Japanese governments in withholding recognition until the new regime promised to honor economic concessions forced upon the old.

The Wilson administration seemed more protective of China, more eager to help the world's newest republic, less willing to extort economic advantages. But Wilson's idealism collapsed, both for Wilson himself and for many Chinese who had cherished his vision of self-determination in the aftermath of World War I. At the Versailles Treaty negotiations, Wilson acceded to Japanese demands to take over former German concessions in China. Few in America realized that a whole generation of Chinese saw Wilson's act as a great betrayal— and they participated in a new upsurge of nationalism strongly directed against both Americans and Japanese. Wilson had sought to create an international organization which could do for China and the world what the United States could not do itself. In this respect Japanese participation seemed essential, and Wilson hoped that the League of Nations would rectify any inequities committed against China.

Paradoxically, many Americans remained under the impression, often fostered by missionaries, that the Chinese saw the United States as their protector against European and Japanese imperialism. This image was reinforced by the Nine Power Treaty of the Washington Conference, an international agreement sponsored by the United States to respect China's sovereignty and territorial integrity. The conference proceedings also provided a striking example of American paternalism. The U.S. delegation worked vigorously to modify the "unequal treaties," but acted *for* rather than *with* the Chinese delegation. Chinese efforts to assert themselves evoked irritation rather than admiration.

Probably most of all, American missionaries—in their writings, their speeches, their appeals for financial assistance— gave the American people a sense that they were doing something for the Chinese people—and that their sacrifices and their efforts were appreciated. Americans saw themselves, their role in China, as being strikingly different from the role played by Europe and Japan.

And because Americans assumed that they were assured of China's friendship, they alone of the powers involved in China could sincerely hope for a strong, independent China. They could be sympathetic to modern nationalism in China because they assumed that when the nationalists became strong —as strong as Chinese could become—they would throw out the imperialists—and open the doors to the United States. In short, America's self-image was critical—how Americans assumed that the Chinese saw them.

But in the nationalist ferment of the 1920s, and particularly during the Northern Expedition of 1927 when Nationalist (KMT) troops sallied north from Canton to unify China, Chinese acted hostilely and violently toward Americans in China. Where was Chinese gratitude for American protection and assistance? Even as sophisticated an observer as J. V. A. MacMurray, who became American minister to China in 1925, was confused by the aggressive nationalism he encountered. He had served in China before the World War and loved the China he remembered. Now he found a people no longer willing to defer to foreigners who enjoyed the privileges of the treaty system—and he blamed this behavior on the Russians, who were supporting the nationalist movement.

Many missionaries accepted this explanation of Russian-fostered Chinese aggressiveness as well. And there is also evidence that the principal mission boards suppressed news of antiforeign, anti-Christian behavior to protect fund-raising efforts. But unlike MacMurray, a number of missionaries came to see Chiang Kai-shek's Kuomintang as a party they could trust and Christian Chiang became the Protector of the Faith. Missionary hopes increased as Chiang staffed his new government with countless products of mission schools and as American-educated, Christian Chinese like T. V. Soong and H. H. K'ung appeared in positions of prominence in the Nationalist regime.

Aided by peace organizations eager to forestall the use of force in world affairs, friends of China like Roger Greene of the Rockefeller Foundation and A. L. Warnshuis of the American Board of Foreign Missions wrote, spoke, and lobbied for the peaceful surrender of the "unequal treaties," of the imperialistic privileges Americans enjoyed in China. A *Literary Digest* poll showed newspaper editors to be overwhelmingly favorable to the peaceful revision of the treaty system.[4] The administration of Calvin Coolidge did not try to buck an aroused public. MacMurray and the American business community in China were ignored as Coolidge and his advisors chose to cast the United States in the role of friend of the Chinese revolution headed by a young Christian couple named Chiang.

As Japanese troops overran Manchuria in 1931 and Japanese planes bombed Shanghai in 1932, the Great Depression and not events in China held the attention of Americans, government officials, and general public alike. But China's plight aroused considerable compassion within the American peace movement, and the American government, especially Secretary of State Henry Stimson, was critical of Japan's

[4] *The Literary Digest,* 5 February 1927, pp. 7–9.

resort to force. China as a victim of Japanese aggression received sympathetic coverage in the press and periodical literature. A *Literary Digest* analysis of newspaper editorials and
a State Department analysis of public opinion concluded that
Americans were sufficiently disturbed by Japanese actions to
favor calling Japan to account. However, Americans were not
interested in China, but in the postwar peace system that
Japan seemed in the process of destroying.[5]

The mid-1930s in the United States were the years of the national commitment to alleviate misery at home. President
Roosevelt could express his sympathy for China in most elo-
quent terms, but he disregarded China's interests when they
conflicted with his programs for recovery or demanded American military action. State Department officials responsible for
East Asian policy were concerned primarily with the avoidance
of conflict with Japan. In Washington a consensus emerged
with a perception of a weak China led by men interested
only in personal power, a China unworthy of American
assistance.

Simultaneously, however, some Americans in China were
becoming more optimistic about China's future. Nelson Johnson reported that Chiang and his wife, "unlike most Chinese," behaved decently, "like Protestant Anglo-Saxons."
Roger Greene of the Rockefeller Foundation became convinced that Chiang had developed a genuine concern for his
country and his people. Greene was favorably impressed by
developments in Chinese law, by government flood control,
and by rural reconstruction projects. Protestant missionaries
found Chiang's regime soliciting their support in a New Life
Movement based at least in part on the YMCA and as Christian cadres in Chiang's anti-Communist campaigns. Struggling to save China without adequate financial support from

[5] *Literary Digest,* 10 October 1931; 24 October 1931; 31 October
1931; 23 January 1932; United States Department of State Archives,
Hornbeck Memorandum to Stimson, 6 December 1931, 793.94/4314.

America, accustomed to the obstruction of local officials, the missionary movement found the overtures from the Chinese government irresistible—and thought they saw a new China that was progressive, very much on the right track.

But apart from moments of great international crisis, the general public was unaware of events in China, its perceptions of China more likely to be formed by images found in novels, movies, and comic strips. These images were not consistent. There was Fu Manchu, the arch villain of the Sax Rohmer novels—master of deceit, capable of a million exquisite tortures—cruel, vicious, a throwback to Genghis Khan, a personification of the yellow peril. In dozens of variants this image could be found in American popular culture. But there was also Charlie Chan—honest, shrewd, self-effacing, filled with more sayings of Confucius than a barrel of fortune cookies. And for Americans coming of age in the 1930s and 1940s there was the image presented by Pearl Buck of the peace-loving, industrious, stoic peasant. Her *Good Earth* sold more than 2 million copies, and approximately 23 million Americans saw the movie.

Interviews conducted by Harold Isaacs in the mid-1950s suggested that conflicting images of the Chinese might be held simultaneously. Very likely individual Americans conceived of several stereotypical Chinese to whom they could refer as suitable for a given occasion—much as the Chinese later conceived of Americans as divided into a peace-loving democratic faction and a warmongering reactionary faction.

For the 1930s, a number of polls give us something better than impressionistic estimates of public attitudes toward the Chinese. In October 1935, January 1937, and February 1939, Americans were asked to indicate the countries or people in the world they liked best. In *none* of the three polls did as many as 1 percent list China or the Chinese as their favorite. (Despite traditional Anglophobia, 54 percent of the sample selected England as the country they liked best in 1937.) After the Sino-Japanese war was under way and Americans were asked to choose between the Chinese and the Japanese, their sympathies were overwhelmingly with the Chinese. But as late as February 1940 a majority opposed loans to the Chinese— even though these loans could be used only to purchase farm products and other nonmilitary goods in the United States. In the same month, Americans were asked what foreign country was most likely to threaten the peace of the United States. China was not on the list. In July 1940, by a margin of 46 percent to 12 percent, respondents preferred to allow Japan to control China rather than risk war with Japan. By October 1941, however, approximately 60 percent of those polled were willing to send spare military supplies to China.

The results of the various polls reinforce the idea that China was remote from public concerns, neither a highly favored nation nor a feared nation. Victims of Japanese aggression, the Chinese had the sympathies of the American people, but little more. Not until after the Tripartite Pact, not until the Roosevelt administration had granted credits and extended lend-lease aid despite indications of public opposition, did the polls indicate support for aid to China. Presumably the public would not have troubled to help China on its own but was quite ready to follow presidential leadership when offered.

And Roosevelt was reluctant to lead his country into any program of assistance to China that might lead to war with Japan. He felt that events in East Asia were not nearly so important as those in Europe. Japan did not constitute a threat to the security of the United States of a magnitude comparable to that posed by Hitler's Germany. When the war in Europe began, Roosevelt brushed aside the demands of pro-Chinese lobbyists and concentrated his attention on the war in Europe; he was determined to avoid any diversion in East Asia, an area seen as peripheral to vital American interests. Although the Chinese government and its American friends grew increasingly hostile to the Roosevelt administration, they had no recourse. Not until the summer of 1940, when the Japanese had threatened British and French positions in Southeast Asia and begun flirting anew with Nazi Germany, did the United States take significant action to retard the Japanese war effort. Even then Roosevelt was persuaded not to prevent the sale of all scrap iron and oil. Ultimately, it was Japan's decision to ally with Germany—the Tripartite Pact of September 1940—that convinced Roosevelt and American opinion leaders that the security of the United States might be affected by the outcome of the Sino-Japanese War—that China was worth more than sympathy. American aid to China increased, and in May 1941, China became eligible for lend-lease assistance.

With the attack on Pearl Harbor, war came to America and China became an honored ally—but a second-class one. Roosevelt and his advisers continued to focus their attention on Europe. China was allotted the task of keeping Japan busy until the major job was completed in Europe. Roosevelt, no less than Churchill or Stalin, denied Chiang Kai-shek an equal role in the making of strategic or logistical decisions. The Chinese could have what was not needed elsewhere, provided a way could be found to transport these items.

Thus, America entered its alliance with China in World War II with the era of paternalism still intact. But as American ties with China became more intimate, American images of China became more complex and seemed to reflect all the views inherited from the experiences since the 1840s.

As the war raged, a July 1942 poll showed that Americans at home had chosen the *Good Earth* stereotype for their image of the Chinese. They were viewed now as industrious, honest, and brave, and considered preferable to Jews and blacks as neighbors, roommates, or working colleagues. But some Americans in China were turning against the Chinese. Soldiers detested the "slopeys." Many government officials and journalists concluded that the Chinese did not want to fight the Japanese, but were husbanding their resources while the United

States won the war for them. Some Americans thought Chiang's regime, with its secret police stifling dissent, was little better than Hitler's. They were disgusted by corruption and the suffering of the Chinese people—while officers and high government officials lived in relative luxury. By 1943 such images were seeping into newspapers and popular magazines as they began publishing unflattering portraits of Chiang's government. Even old friends of the Chinese people, like Pearl Buck, expressed concern publicly. Such criticism intensified after mutual dissatisfaction led Chiang to demand the recall of General Joseph W. Stilwell, who was a sharp opponent of Chiang's political and military policies.

The liberation of China was a sideshow in the war against the Axis. China received all of the praise and some of the loyalty due an ally but little of the substance. The United States renounced its privileges under the "unequal treaties" and talked much of China as a great power after the war. Roosevelt's conception of China as a great power was ultimately incorporated into the United Nations Organization—in part to keep China fighting, compensation for material neglect. But Roosevelt and his advisers also acted on the assumption of a China grateful to the United States, dependent on the United States—as Churchill suspected, a loyal vote on the side of the United States.

A series of polls taken in America in the 1940s indicate a substantial interest in the military alliance during the war, but a sharp drop in American willingness to provide support to Chiang's Nationalists as civil war was waged in China from 1946 to 1949. Polls taken throughout 1942 indicated that by an average margin of 85 percent to 5 percent Americans thought China could be depended on to cooperate with the United States after the war.

In June 1945, a *Fortune* poll reported 43 percent of those polled chose China to be one of America's principal partners in keeping the peace in the Pacific—but almost 50 percent selected Great Britain. Interest in a military alliance with China, favored by a margin of 56 to 23 percent in 1943, had fallen off to 42 to 38 percent by April 1944—before the recall of Stilwell. By August 1946, a majority (57 percent) had heard about the civil strife in China. But when asked what the United States should do about it, only 6 percent were willing to help Chiang—and another 1 percent wanted the Russians kept out. As the Cold War developed and anti-Soviet attitudes in the United States intensified, public attitudes on aid to Chiang followed not the curve of anti-Communism but rather the trajectory of his declining fortunes. In April 1948 the polls indicated approval of aid to Chiang by a 55 to 32 percent margin, but by the end of the year another poll indicated that a proposed $5 billion aid package to keep China from "going Communist" was opposed by a ratio of 35 to 32 percent. By May 1949 the public had apparently written off the Nationalist regime; only 22 percent wanted to keep up the effort to help it, while 47 percent preferred inaction or considered it too late for any action. In August 1949, after the government released the famous "White Paper" on China, polls indicated negative attitudes toward Chiang, especially among those who had some knowledge of the White Paper. The informed group opposed aiding Chiang by 60 to 23 percent and were unfavorably disposed to him by a margin of 56 to 24 percent. But even those who had never heard of the White Paper responded unfavorably to Chiang, 35 to 21 percent, and opposed aid to his forces, 44 to 25 percent.

These opinion surveys reinforce the observation that in the late 1940s most Americans continued to see China as remote, not central to American interests, and caught up in a civil war in which Chiang's Nationalists were fighting a losing cause and American military aid should not be extended. The Truman administration seemed to express the same opinion. The George Marshall mission of 1946 endeavored in vain to recon-

cile Communist-Kuomintang differences. But failing to prevent the war, and concluding that the Soviets did not intend
to occupy Manchuria and North China, Marshall withdrew from his frustrating task. By 1946–47, some State Department officials, most notably George Kennan, argued that a
Communist China would not be likely to pose a serious threat
to the United States or to other areas of the Asian mainland for
some time. By the late 1940s, both President Harry S. Truman
and Secretary of State Dean Acheson had come to the reluctant conclusion that a Communist victory was inevitable and
that American military aid to Chiang was folly.

But the China issue captured the attention of a small but
vocal minority of American congressmen, businessmen, journalists, returned missionaries—an amorphous group that came
to be known as the "China Lobby." Their pressures kept the
Truman administration from cutting its losses and completely
extricating itself from the Chinese Civil War. And their influence set the stage for one emotional aspect of the 1950s Mc-
Carthy era—the congressional hearings and media attention
given to the perplexing but illogical question, "Who lost
China?" As fingers pointed to certain government officials and
scholars, American policy toward China became a volatile
domestic issue in the United States and a vehicle for political
opportunism.

On the eve of the Korean War, however, most in the U.S.
government had written off China—with regret, but not
dismay. In the view of policy makers, China was too weak to
make much difference. Population mattered less in the balance of power than technology and resources. China was weak
and disorganized, poor in resources, struggling with a prein-
dustrial economy and a hungry, unskilled, and passive people.
It was regrettable that the Chinese people should have to endure Communist oppression, but there was nothing much that
could be done about it. China continued to be viewed with
contempt for its weakness and pity for the misery of its people,

but this condescending view persisted only until the Red hordes came pouring across the Yalu.

Era of Fear: 1950–71

The era from 1950 to 1971 was a destructive and frightening period in U.S.-China relations as a confluence of factors brought the United States to military confrontation with the People's Republic and led to a new set of American attitudes based on fear. Fu Manchu, opium dens, dark streets in China-town, Nanking in 1927, the Boxer Rebellion way back in 1900. There *had* been times when Chinese were feared, when perceptions of Chinese included the possibility of hostile, cruel yellow men capable of gross barbarities. But fear of China as a nation had never existed. A few writers at the turn of the century had been able to conceive of a powerful China, overwhelming the world by the sheer weight of its population—the yellow peril. But a constant humbling by other imperialists, an inability to unite and defend itself against the Japanese had all but erased such imagery. In a July 1942 poll, Americans were asked to select words from a card that would describe the Chinese. Although they were allowed to select as many characteristics as they pleased, the respondents could hardly conceive of a dangerous China. Four percent thought the Chinese war-like, 4 percent thought them treacherous, and 2 percent found them cruel. Twenty-four years later, in March 1966, 23 percent thought them warlike, 19 percent treacherous, and 13 percent cruel. Polls in April 1964 showed that close to 60 percent of the American people thought the Chinese were a greater danger to world peace than the Russians—and among college-educated Americans that percentage soared to 74 percent.

The turning point came in 1950 when the United States Army and the People's Liberation Army met head-on in Korea. General Douglas MacArthur had been contemptuous of the Chinese and did not think the People's Republic would dare to intervene in Korea and risk confrontation with American forces. And if they did, he was confident that they would be no match for the American fighting man, supported by overwhelming firepower. He was wrong on both counts, of course. Contact with Chiang Kai-shek's poorly fed conscript armies during World War II had misled American military men. They could not conceive of a well-trained highly motivated Chinese army—of a peasant army so convinced of the righteousness of its cause as to be willing to fight and die for it, to be willing to confront the vastly superior military technology of the United States.

Throughout the 1950s, China was perceived as a Soviet puppet, and the 1950 Sino-Soviet Treaty tended to reinforce that impression. The Chinese people presumably had no reason to hate or to fight Americans. Left to their own devices, they would be friendly, grateful for America's historic contribution to China. The United States had lost China—and it had fallen into Soviet hands.

When Americans were asked in December 1950 if the Chinese had intervened on their own or under orders from the Russians, 81 percent of the respondents blamed Russia. Only 5 percent thought the Chinese had acted at their own initiative. Dean Rusk, then assistant secretary of state, contended that the Chinese were being "driven by foreign masters." He referred to Mao's government as a possible "colonial Russian government—a Slavic Manchukuo on a larger scale. It is not the Government of China. It will not pass the first test. It is not Chinese." [6]

A poll taken the first week of December 1950 indicated that

[6] *U.S. News and World Report,* 1 June 1951, pp. 24–25.

the public was very responsive to the idea of seating the People's Republic in the UN Security Council if the Chinese would stop fighting in Korea. In February 1951, the Gallup organization asked Americans if they would be willing to risk their lives or have one of their family risk his life to keep the Russians from taking over Western Europe. Forty-nine percent were willing, while 42 percent were not. When asked if they were willing to take the same risks to stop the Chinese Communists from taking over Korea and other countries in Asia, only 36 percent gave an affirmative answer—and a resounding 56 percent refused.

But as the war progressed and Chinese Communists killed American boys, as reports reached America of human waves overrunning U.S. lines and of the brainwashing of prisoners of war, images of the Chinese changed. Government officials and Americans with experience in China focused on Chinese germ-warfare charges and tended to blame all on the Communists, on a Moscow-directed international conspiracy. For the public, however, the sinister and evil Chinese, killers and torturers of our loved ones, conjured up old images of Fu Manchu and Genghis Khan. All of the old imagery reappeared in China Lobby propaganda, in newspapers, magazines, and movies, and, perhaps most important, on television.

Official rhetoric all through the 1950s was strongly hostile to the Chinese. McCarthyism fed on the controversy over policy toward China. Recognition and seating in the United Nations were deemed out of the question by President Dwight D. Eisenhower and Secretary of State John Foster Dulles. The newly organized China Lobby, known as the Committee of One Million, gained widespread public support to keep "Red China" out of the United Nations. Both Eisenhower and Dulles adhered to the same position. Indeed, Eisenhower later threatened John F. Kennedy, warning that he would reenter public life if there was a danger of the People's Republic being admitted to the United Nations.

So deeply rooted was the image of the Sino-Soviet menace that the split in the Communist bloc initially was interpreted as a quarrel over tactics. Again and again, Dean Rusk warned Americans not to take comfort from the split, that the Communists were merely arguing about the means with which to destroy us. And Rusk and nongovernmental opinion leaders noted that of the two great Communist powers, it was the Chinese who were taking the tougher pose, demanding confrontation with the West. In 1961, asked whether China or the Soviet Union would be a greater threat to world peace by 1970, 49 percent thought Russia and only 32 percent were more worried about China. By 1964, China had soared ahead with 56 percent in April, 59 percent in November. By 1967, amid the apparent irrationality of the Cultural Revolution, 71 percent of the respondents saw China as a greater threat to world peace with only 20 percent more worried about the Soviet Union.[7]

American perceptions of an aggressive China increased with the Sino-Indian war in 1962. In the early 1960s some experts on China had argued that Chinese rhetoric had to be discounted, that China's actions were defensive rather than aggressive—and this opinion was being voiced within the State Department and by advisors to President Kennedy. But the war with India undermined the credibility of those who argued Chinese concerns were primarily defensive. The liberal intellectual community, where these views were strongest, was also highly sympathetic to India. Kennedy and Rusk were unhesitating thereafter. Particularly in the last year of his life, Kennedy worked toward détente with the Soviet Union and softened his rhetoric toward the Russians but consistently described China as a menace.

The Chinese role in Africa, Indonesia, and Vietnam was also seen as aggressive and threatening. Roger Hilsman, a later critic of Vietnam policy, argued that Vietnam had to be held

[7] *Gallup Opinion Index,* Report No. 76 (October 1971).

to contain Chinese expansion directed toward India. Even John K. Fairbank, working arduously for an improvement of Sino-American relations, argued in 1966 that while we offered sweeteners to attract the Chinese to the world community, "Military containment on the Korean border, in the Formosa Straits, and somehow in Vietnam cannot soon be abandoned." [8] One defense of America's war in Vietnam, repeated ad nauseum in the mid-1960s, was that it was essential for the taming of Chinese revolutionaries. They had to be contained as the United States had contained the Russians in Europe. Only then would they be willing to live in peace with their neighbors.

But in certain sectors of American government there were new indications of a desire to improve relations with the People's Republic in the 1960s. In 1961, by a 53 percent to 32 percent margin, Americans wanted the United States to take steps to improve relations with China. Even a majority of Republicans, who had been most hostile to the PRC in the 1950s, favored such steps. Forty-seven percent favored the establishment of trade relations with the Chinese and only 35 percent were opposed. In December 1963, Assistant Secretary of State Hilsman indicated that the United States was prepared to coexist with Mao's China—and few Americans seemed disturbed. In October 1966, as fears of China were reaching a maximum in the United States, the Gallup organization asked two samples about admitting the People's Republic to the United Nations. The ordinary sample showed continued strong opposition, 56 percent to 25 percent. But when a sample taken of people appearing in *Who's Who* was asked, an enormous difference appeared. Among the elite group 64 percent favored admitting China to the United Nations and only 32 percent opposed it.

Similarly, A. T. Steele's study of public attitudes conducted

[8] John K. Fairbank, *China: People's Middle Kingdom and the United States* (Cambridge, Mass.: Harvard University Press, Belknap Press, 1967), p. 101.

in the mid-1960s found indications that the American public would respond readily to signs of Chinese interest in improving relations. Steele also found that the inhibitions of the Mc-Carthy era were fading among academics and that younger Americans were less rigid in their opposition toward the People's Republic. He concluded that with time, hostilities born of the Korean War and the McCarthy era would fade.[9]

His prognosis was correct. As relative calm returned in the late 1960s after the Cultural Revolution, the Chinese seemed less bellicose, and opinion leaders and government officials in the United States sensed public receptivity to rapprochement. Slowly and cautiously, the Nixon administration signaled its willingness to improve relations with China. First travel and then trade restrictions were eased. The Seventh Fleet was withdrawn from the Formosa Straits and ambassadorial talks with the People's Republic in Warsaw, broken off during the Johnson years, were resumed.

Because these steps were taken by a Republican president who long personified the cold warrior, and because the public response indicated that these steps had the support of the American people, the era of hostility was coming to an end. At the policy level, it became apparent in the late 1960s that the Sino-Soviet split involved more than an argument about the proper tactic for burying the West. Specialists on Chinese affairs had argued throughout the last years of the Johnson administration that Peking was far more worried about the Soviet Union than about American activities in Vietnam. They saw signs that the Chinese, focusing their hostility on the Russians, were interested in improving their relationship with the United States and were aware that the United States had moved to a policy of "containment without isolation." Whereas the Johnson administration was bemired in the affairs of Southeast Asia, still apprehensive about attacks from the China Lobby, the Nixon administration—and particularly

[9] A. T. Steele, *The American People and China* (New York: McGraw-Hill, 1966), chap. 6.

Henry Kissinger—seemed capable of fresh vision, a fresh approach, in 1969. The fresh approach came—and proved to be an enormous success.

Era of Respect: 1971–

By May 1971, for the first time, more Americans were in favor of admitting the People's Republic to the United Nations than were opposed. Similarly, after it became known that Kissinger had conferred with the Chinese and arranged a trip for Nixon, public fears of China dropped sharply. A new era had arrived, in which the Chinese would be treated—for the first time—with respect, as equals.

In February 1972 the American public was treated to the unlikely sight of Richard Nixon, president of the United States, a staunch leader of anti-Communist forces, hobnobbing, swapping toasts with Red Chinese leaders in Peking, smiling appreciatively through a performance of the Red Detachment of Women and applauding with enthusiasm at its conclusion. In the months that preceded and followed Nixon's trip to China, American interest in things Chinese soared. As the American and Chinese governments moved to relax the tensions between them, American fears of the Chinese and hostility toward them seemed to drop away.

Chinoiserie filled the stores in the early 1970s. Szechuan and Peking style restaurants proliferated. Stories of Chinese successes in the distribution of food and medical care, as well as of the use of acupuncture as an anesthesia, filled the papers. The Chinese were industrious, progressive, honest, civil. Senator J. William Fulbright in particular marveled at the civility of Chinese society. And the polls showed that Americans *liked* the Chinese. A 1973 poll found only 44 percent of Americans ages 30–49 with favorable attitudes toward the

Chinese—but 56 percent of those 21–29 and 61 percent of the 18–20 group.[10]

At the policy level China received the deference due a powerful nation. Latter-day tribute missions flowed westward across the Pacific. Recognition, formal diplomatic relations, were almost certainly delayed only by the extraordinary circumstances of the Watergate scandal—by Nixon's inability to risk alienating conservative Republicans who might be able to preserve his presidency. Similarly, Gerald Ford, faced with a conservative challenge in 1975–76, hesitated, but fear of Chinese aggressiveness had vanished and there was no longer any doubt that most Americans were prepared to accept the normalization of relations with China.

By the mid-1970s, however, while the era of respect still characterized American public outlooks on China, there was a greater uncertainty about the future of U.S.-China relations. A 1975 Gallup Poll commissioned by the Republic of China indicated that 61 percent of the American people wanted a normalized relationship with "Mainland China" and 70 percent wanted to maintain relations with the Republic of China —though some have noted that the term "Mainland China" may have prejudiced the poll.[11] But it does seem that Americans remain in a quandary and that decisive presidential leadership is needed to point to future directions over the terms of normalization.

Conclusion

Perhaps the historic attitude of Americans toward China is clearest when contrasted with American admiration for Japan's rapid westernization. The Japanese had abandoned

[10] *Gallup Opinion Index,* Report No. 96 (June 1973).
[11] *New York Times,* 7 November 1975, p. 6.

the past and built a powerful modern nation, but the Chinese seemed to wallow in ancient glories. Americans, a people whose dominant ideology incorporated the idea of progress, who worshiped the new and saw ever-increasing greatness ahead, could not respect a people whose finest moments were behind them. The "people of plenty," living in a land containing all things in abundance, believing that anything could be done given the will, could not understand the psychology of a people whose land had been depleted over a period of 2,000 years.

But the contrast between American attitudes toward China and Japan reveals something else, of greater relevance for understanding American policy. Because of Japan's strength and China's weakness, it was China that elicited American sympathy in the first half of the twentieth century, China that needed the protection of the United States. It was China that could be saved, China where Americans might take up the white man's burden, where America's mission might be fulfilled in a world otherwise divided among European imperialists.

A second point worth noting is that a people's image of another people can be affected by its perception of itself and by how it assumes it is perceived by the other people. During the 1930s and 1940s, when Americans saw themselves as China's champions *and* thought the Chinese shared that image and were grateful to Americans, they liked the Chinese. Americans responded favorably to the Chinese Communists during World War II in part because they seemed to like Americans more than Chiang and his cohorts did. When Mao's line became intensely anti-American, American attitudes toward the Chinese shifted. After an initial effort to blame the Russians, to distinguish between what the beloved Chinese *really* thought and what Moscow ordered them to express, Chinese belligerence was taken seriously and reciprocated. Similarly, when Mao's line changed in the 1960s, when Americans perceived that his hostility was redirected toward the Russians, American hostility quickly melted. By 1973 only 20 percent of the American people indicated strongly negative feelings about the Chinese.

For the future, the superficiality of American attitudes toward the Chinese remains an important consideration. Because Chinese culture is radically different from Western culture, because Chinese are not like Americans or Europeans, the American public is never likely to understand China. Respect for China's new strength and determination, however, should endure. Self-reliance, whether called for by Emerson or by Mao, is a trait Americans can readily admire. The "Chinese homer" or "Chinese degree," terms of derision from bygone years, are disappearing from the language. But whether American images of China will be positive or negative depends on events, on whether the two nations move closer together or are to confront each other hostilely again. Public opinion is unlikely to drive the United States into an antagonistic relationship with China, but if the exigencies of international politics or China's internal politics lead to renewed antagonism, public opinion will surely become negative again. Chinese criticism of the United States and of the American role in China will sour American attitudes. Praise for the United States, for the peace-loving and democratic American people, will win friends. Chinese actions, as interpreted by American opinion leaders, especially government opinion leaders, and Chinese rhetoric, as made available to the public, are surely the keys to future American images of China.

4

TU WEI-MING

Chinese Perceptions
of America

AN inquiry into the Chinese intellectual perceptions of America has a twofold significance. Given the fragmentation of the modern world, the study of mutual perceptions is a vitally important step toward the formulation of a more comprehensive and coherent value orientation that dissimilar cultures can share. Although the development of new political and administrative structures that can accommodate diverse interests is difficult to achieve, the willingness of the parties concerned to understand and appreciate radically different world views is a prerequisite. Furthermore, while historically the Chinese intellectual perceptions of America have had very little relevance to American self-examination, it may not be totally academic to investigate what these perceptions mean in a new light. It is not inconceivable that observations made from a "wholly other" perspective may turn out to be exceedingly suggestive for intellectual self-identification at home.

This exploratory essay probes the underlying Chinese images of America, and, in a preliminary way, analyzes the mind of modern China through whose eyes America is perceived. It takes into account the confluence of historical and cultural forces that have shaped the psychological milieu in which the images of America have been formed. Exploration into the epistemological grounds upon which cumulative knowledge about America has been built is a fruitful way of studying the Chinese image of the United States. To reflective Chinese observers, America is neither unchanging nor an objective fact. Rather, they view America in the light of its relevance to their own country; they perceive America through their own historical and cultural senses. The Chinese observer often searches for a holistic view of America, even though the "reality" is forever beyond grasp.

Contrast

An understanding of the Chinese images of America depends on an appreciation of modern China as a "civilization-state" struggling to achieve respectable nationhood, as well as on a knowledge of the recent American treatment of China. The intractable realities of life in China, determined mainly by a relatively inhospitable land and dense concentration of people, has led many Western scholars to conclude that prior to the Western impact, China was a monolithic social and political entity. The salient features of traditional China, such as an agriculture-based economy, a highly centralized paternalistic bureaucracy, a family-dominated social structure, a unified written language, and an integrated value-system further give the impression that China, unlike the diversified and dynamic West, had for centuries been stagnant, if not unchanging, prior to the Opium War. The American experiment appears diametrically opposed to the Chinese permanence.

Indeed, even a superficial comparison between China and the United States reveals irreconcilable and contradictory conceptual as well as experiential differences between the two. The total area of mainland China, 3.7 million square miles within present boundaries, may appear to be larger than the 3.6 million of the United States, including Alaska and Hawaii. But more than 75 percent of China is desert, waste, or urban, and the cultivated land per person is approximately one-third of an acre. Only an estimated 3 percent of the land is reclaimable. Furthermore, the total population per cultivated square mile in China is around 2,000 as compared with 130 in the United States. While China evokes sensations of antiquity, harshness of life, and human settlements reaching a point of saturation, America seems to symbolize youth, affluence, and a land full of unlimited opportunities. Even at this level of generality, the basis for mutual appreciation of cultural values seems at best precarious.

Moreover, the Chinese revolutionary experience in the last century has been partly a reaction to the Western presence, including the American presence, and has tended to perpetuate the gap. While America, with all it symbolizes, emerged in 150 years from colonial status to become first a united republic, then a half-hearted imperial state, and eventually the strongest nation on earth, China in the same period of time had slid a long way from the glory of the high Ch'ing period to a gradual recovery from a semicolonial existence. The same historical process, known as either "westernization" or "modernization," that had made America rise to the pinnacle of wealth and power had made China the contemptible "sick man of East Asia."

The Chinese experience since the 1880s, a convulsive crisis

at all levels of human activity and consciousness, now seems more understandable. China's desperate attempts to adapt to the Western way of life, even at the expense of a total rejection of her cultural identity, can perhaps best be characterized as a complete shaking of the foundation. China simply had no precedent to guide her "response." The Buddhist transformation of the Chinese way of life in the T'ang dynasty (A.D. 618–907) and the Mongolization of China in the destruction of the Chinese polity in the Yuan dynasty (1279–1368), two historical experiences put together, might have amounted to the trauma of the Western impact. China was immobilized partly because the "shock," in the words of the statesman Li Hung-chang, was unprecedented in China's 3,000 years of history.

The breakdown of the traditional order in the economic, political, and social realms eventually led to a powerful ferment of passion in the "psychocultural world" of virtually every Chinese. As François Geoffroy-Dechaume put it:

Nothing is untouched: the self, the idea of nature, the relation to the other person, to the family, the group, the State. Love, ambition, respect, friendship, all are challenged at such intimate depths that anger becomes a protective reaction, pride a defence, hatred a strategy and contempt a reflex.[1]

And on a broader cultural and diplomatic level, the Chinese have been struggling to develop a new identity and to survive as a sovereign nation. Such a struggle cannot be understood simply in terms of China's past arrogance or as a new "Middle Kingdom" outlook in the contemporary world, but must be seen as a trauma at all levels of Chinese life. In this sense the United States played distinctive roles in initiating and defining that trauma, sometimes as a model of changes and sometimes as a military and cultural threat.

In one respect, many Chinese have seen the United States

[1] François Geoffroy-Dechaume, *China Looks at the World* (New York: Pantheon, 1967), p. 131.

as an established republic with relative stability and peace since the 1860s. American economic vitality and growth, notwithstanding occasional maladjustments, has been beyond the imagination of twentieth-century Chinese who have seldom enjoyed any sustained economic stability. In sharp contrast with the Chinese experience of tumult and war, American political institutions have worked for 200 years without losing their efficacy. In the Chinese time scale, it is as if the imperial system with all its philosophical justifications had survived to this date since the forty-first year of the Ch'ien-lung reign, more than half a century prior to the opening of the five treaty ports to the West.

Indeed, there are no centuries-old academic institutions like Harvard University for Chinese intellectuals—for such an institution would have to be a Ming dynasty academy that survived the Manchu invasion, the Taiping Rebellion, the downfall of the Ch'ing dynasty, the Sino-Japanese War, the collapse of the Nationalist government, and the development of new systems of higher education in the People's Republic. Even a relatively new university, such as Berkeley, was founded decades before the establishment of the Chinese Imperial College, which in the twentieth century eventually became the National Peking University. While numerous local papers in America can boast a record of publication for scores of years, even the most persistent journals in modern China survived for only a few years. The influential *New Youth,* for example, lasted a total of four years. The longevity of civic organizations and religious institutions in the United States should easily convey to many Chinese that America is not only a country of prosperity but also a land of uninterrupted history and impressive traditions. The Chinese sense of insecurity matches proportionately the American lack of a sense of political tragedy: "How can the Americans really know the meaning of national calamity if they have never experienced the bombing raids?"

Admiration

Students of modern China have often wondered why the
Chinese government responded to the challenge of the West at
such a slow pace. For example, although Western diplomats
began to reside in Peking as early as 1861, no Chinese
diplomatic mission functioned abroad until 1877. Of course
we could attempt to find the roots of this pattern of inertia in
the traditional Chinese tributary system. A possible explanation, involving both psychological and political factors, is simply that to the Manchu court an inequitable relationship was
worse than no direct communication at all. In this sense
Anson Burlingame's mission (1869-71) takes on symbolic
significance. Having served as Abraham Lincoln's envoy to
Peking for six years, the American lawyer from New York
was appointed by the Chinese government as her first ambassador extraordinary and minister plenipotentiary to America and
Europe. To be sure, the mission was inspired by the Irishman,
Robert Hart, who worked *for* the Chinese authorities as the
inspector general of the Maritime Custom Service and considered "the notion of a gentleman acting *under* an Asiatic
barbarian preposterous." But Anson Burlingame's cooperative and unassuming attitude toward the new assignment as
the representative of the "youngest nation" responding to the
request of the "oldest nation in the world, containing one
third of the human race, seek[ing] for the first time to come
into relations with the West" must have deeply impressed the
Chinese officials.

The emergence of America as a Pacific power after the
Open Door Notes of 1899, which advocated China's territorial integrity, was welcomed by some in the Chinese intellectual community as much as a moral force as a military and
economic presence. The idealism of Woodrow Wilson's
"New Diplomacy" was probably not intended to challenge

the entrenched imperialist privileges in China, but it seems to have underscored a major attitudinal difference between the American involvement in China and the other Western powers' encroachments on Chinese territory. The Washington Conference of 1921, which was called on American initiative, did specify the preservation of the integrity of the Chinese nation-state as a matter of principle. This, at least in the minds of some Chinese intellectuals, marked a departure from the unmitigated expansionism of Japan and the other Western powers. For such intellectuals, America, committed to the ideals of self-determination and sovereign rights and potentially a force to counter Japan's increasing threat, seemed to live up to the literal Chinese translation of its name as the "beautiful country." The symbols of General Washington and Abraham Lincoln as honest and righteous men leading oppressed people to freedom and independence were written into the Chinese textbooks of this period and provided a positive view of America for many intellectuals and revolutionaries.

Therefore, throughout much of the early twentieth century, the symbols of science and democracy as defining characteristics of American society remained powerful among many young Chinese. The polemic on "science versus philosophy of life" in 1923 can be understood as a conflict between the material West and the spiritual East as much as one between Anglo-American empiricism and German idealism. The triumph of scientism in China was thus interpreted, at least in part, as the success of the educational campaign of the returned students from the United States. This was probably also the reason why a few years previously John Dewey's trip to China (May 1919–July 1921) had generated so much enthusiasm.

Indeed, as early as 1850, a Chinese provincial governor, Hsü Chi-yü, had described the political system of the United States as a concrete realization of the spirit of impartiality reminiscent of China's legendary golden age. He also saw George Washington's selfless refusal to accept a crown and found a new monarchy as a great event in human history comparable to the virtuous abdications of the sage rulers Yao and Shun. Even the confirmed monarchist intellectual K'ang Yu-wei unequivocally stated that "of all the countries on earth, none is as prosperous and contented as the United States of America," [2] although he also noted that the republican form of government is incompatible with China's autocracy.

The reform leader Liang Ch'i-ch'ao, having committed himself to republicanism, characterized the Anglo-Saxons in America as a great people who courageously made their way with a forward-looking purpose. To the revolutionaries of 1911, the American model was particularly attractive. In Sun Yat-sen's famous "Three Principles of the People," his notion of "people's livelihood" was heavily derived from Henry George's notion of a single tax.

A cursory survey of the leading intellectual journals of the 1920s further confirms the impression that despite the contempt and condescension of many Americans toward China, many Chinese images of America were not only positive but enthusiastically favorable. For Chinese westernizers, the United States symbolized the wave of the future; and the well-known May Fourth intellectual movement can thus be understood as an appropriation of the Anglo-American model to create a new culture for China. Ch'en Tu-hsiu, the founder of the influential *New Youth* magazine, identified values basic to American society as the six guiding principles for the May Fourth movement: (1) to be independent and not servile; (2) to be progressive and not conservative; (3) to be aggressive and not retrogressive; (4) to be cosmopolitan and not isolationist; (5) to be utilitarian and not impractical; and (6) to be scientific and not visionary. The two leading intellectuals who were instrumental in the language reform which fundamentally transformed the modern Chinese mode of articu-

[2] Kung-chuan Hsiao, *A Modern China and a New World: K'ang Yu-wei, Reformer and Utopian, 1858–1927* (Seattle: University of Washington Press, 1975), p. 209.

lation, Hu Shih and Chao Yuan-jen, were both returned students from America.

In a 1905 essay, K'ang Yu-wei had observed that although the United States "had not produced a single philosopher," [3] she had made spectacular progress in science and technology. But the May Fourth intellectuals found in America not only the ingenuity of a Thomas Edison or the efficiency of a Henry Ford but also a profound sense of purpose exemplified by the personalities of Washington, Lincoln, and Wilson. Hu Shih was impressed as much by American liberalism and individualism as by American science and technology. Hu's essay on American women reveals his appreciation for the independent-mindedness of all American citizens. And one influential young writer, Kuo Mo-jo, asserted that the American that had exerted the most influence on him was Walt Whitman, though as David Roy has noted, "it did not prove a difficult step for him to move from Whitman's prophetic eloquence to the Communist version of world revolution." [4]

In the 1930s and 1940s, the Chinese images of America were not only reflections of social ideals but also manifestations of experienced presence. Many saw the establishment of Tsing Hua College at Peking, resulting from the remission to China of part of the American share of the Boxer Indemnity in 1908, as evidence of America's good will toward China. By 1936, more than a dozen influential institutions of higher learning had been established in China as joint ventures between a score of Protestant societies and several American universities. The universities of Cheeloo, Yenching, St. John, Nanking, and Lingnan, spreading from Tsinan to Canton and from Shanghai to Wuhan, were an integral part of modern China's intellectual development. Many graduates of Christian educational institutions assumed influential posts in industry, banking, trade, and government throughout China. Thus, the

[3] Kung-chuan Hsiao, *A Modern China and a New World,* p. 524.
[4] David T. Roy, *Kuo Mo-jo: The Early Years* (Cambridge, Mass.: Harvard University Press, 1971), p. 82.

Americanization of higher learning added new strength to already powerful positions held by many returned Chinese students from the United States.

Chiang Kai-shek's close association with American-trained Chinese since the late 1920s was symptomatic of a steady growth of American roots in China. After his marriage in 1927 to Soong Mei-ling, a Wellesley graduate, Chiang relied heavily upon Madame's brother T. V. Soong (a Harvard graduate), and her brother-in-law H. H. K'ung (Oberlin) in financial matters; and for affairs of the party, he later used Ch'en Li-fu (Pittsburgh School of Mines) in a top Kuomintang position. Chiang's personal conversion to Methodism significantly paved the way for American missionaries to work in conjunction with Nationalist "rural reconstruction" programs.

For some Chinese, the image of America as a great nation of democracy and science assumed a new ethical and religious meaning, partly because, as John K. Fairbank has noted, "Christian missionaries nourished the thought of a 'special relationship' between Americans and Chinese, a supra-cultural friendship based on common traits and values and mutual respect." As the Japanese encroachment upon China intensified, some Chinese leaders cherished the hope that massive American aid would be forthcoming. Indeed, the heroism of the "Flying Tigers" and the half-billion-dollar morale booster of 1942 were followed by the incredible Hump airlift. And on January 11, 1943, a new Sino-American treaty on equal terms was signed. For a couple of years, at least, many Chinese saw the coming of America as the "divine wind" and the GI's as glorious angels.

Ambivalence

Yet, behind these images of the United States of America as the embodiment of the liberal democratic ideal, as the wonder of technological achievement, as the hope for a just world, and as a trusted friend in need there was also an increasing sense of doubt and uneasiness about the sincerity of American intentions.

Images have changed—frozen images became broken ones and simple images became complex—as external conditions shifted and as Chinese expectations altered. While the United States in the 1940s appeared much more committed to saving China from foreign aggression than at the time of the Open Door Notes, Chinese positive perceptions of America had begun to fragment.

The problem was compounded by a deepening awareness among some Chinese intellectuals that the relationship was too disproportional to guarantee any true mutuality. Time and again Chinese feelings of inadequacy and inferiority were reinforced by American insensitivity and arrogance. Even the admirable Burlingame who had advocated "cooperative policy" in the 1860s prematurely proclaimed that "a new day of Westernization and Christianity had dawned in the ancient Middle Kingdom." Such arrogance began to elicit a reflexive Chinese response, a repressed energy that frequently surfaced as outbursts of anti-American and anti-Western sentiments.

The experience of the American philosopher John Dewey in China is a case in point. The emotional and intellectual intensity with which the students responded to his pragmatic message was phenomenal. Yet the students' overwhelming zealousness, more fitting to a spiritual guru than to a rationalist philosopher, seems to indicate that what they attempted to find in Deweyism was not a piecemeal solution to well-defined problems. Rather, at a time when China was engulfed in an unprecedented struggle for survival, they were desperately in need of a holistic vision, a creed that could serve as a powerful symbol for mobilizing national sentiments. The gap in sensitivity was so wide that even with his sympathy and perceptiveness Dewey never contemplated the possibility that his universal doctrine of instrumentalism, born in the comfortable academic environment of America, might be utterly irrelevant to the concerns of the troubled and divided China. In the 1920s it was extremely difficult for Dewey's followers in China to recognize that the cosmopolitan doctrine of "pragmatism" was seen by most Chinese intellectuals as a parochial escape from the deeper and more relevant intellectual battles being fought.

And Dewey himself saw his experience in China as a one-way street—expecting to contribute much to China's intellectual needs while not learning much from the Chinese in turn. It was a teacher-student relationship, a symbol of much of the American outlook on China.

The presence of American missionaries in China's interior and the American involvement in the development of modern Chinese higher education further deepened the impression that while Americans were willing to help, to educate, and to save China, they were not particularly interested in understanding either China's indigenous cultural values or her modern fate. In this respect, Stilwell's confrontation with Chiang Kai-shek, the ambassadorship of Patrick Hurley, and the mission of George C. Marshall during World War II did nothing to alter the general feeling that the American representatives presumed to know exactly how to solve China's internal problems while reinforcing the view that the China question was only peripheral to overall American concerns.

The experience of the returned students, though it varied according to time and location, reenforced the painful awareness that China had never been taken seriously by the American intelligentsia. Hu Shih noted in his Cornell diary that in a class on meteorology, the professor candidly stated that Chinese studies of meteorology could not advance on the international scale because of the deficiencies of Chinese scientists in the field; having spotted Hu Shih among the students, he urged the young undergraduate to become a meteorologist so that he could help his country to catch up with the rest of the world in this critical area of scientific research. Hu noted that he felt a profound sense of humiliation and was indeed motivated to learn the subject well.

The Chinese sense of ambivalence toward Americans was deeply rooted. Indeed the famous author Lin Yutang when asked by an American reporter about the possibility of a complete Japanese take-over in China in the 1930s, allegedly replied, "They won't get a Chinaman's chance!" Of course, some genuine and equal friendships between individual Chinese and Americans did develop in the early twentieth century. But the kind of mutual affection and respect disclosed in the correspondence between Justice Oliver Wendell Holmes and the young Chinese jurist John Wu does seem rare.

The matter was further complicated by the hostility and jealousy of returned Chinese students from Japan toward their counterparts from the United States. Some writers, like Lu Hsun, bitterly attacked the American-educated Chinese as "foreign slaves." And many American-educated intellectuals experienced psychological tension between their romantic promulgation of the liberal-democratic ideal and their painful memories of discriminatory treatment during stays in America.

The revolutionary pamphleteer Ch'en T'ien-hua, whose experience abroad was confined to Japan, effectively depicted the ambivalence of the Chinese intellectual perceptions of America. In his famous *About Face!*, published several years prior to the 1911 Revolution, he characterized America as the most egalitarian, free, and happy continent in the world. He also suggested that America, the paradise on earth with infinite potential for future development, has become what it is mainly because of its work ethic and the steadfast determination of its founding fathers to create principled democratic institutions that could be maintained. But in a different pamphlet of the same period, he listed several incidents vividly describing how Chinese students had been maltreated in America.

For instance, Ch'en described the case of a certain Mr. Sun, fortunate to have developed a genuine friendship with an American fellow student. But one day the American asked Mr. Sun not to greet him in public. The American explained that since Chinese were slaves of the Manchus and the Manchus were slaves of the Americans, he would lose all the respect of his own American friends if he was seen together with the slave of a slave. The story may be apocryphal, but Ch'en comments with all the seriousness of a confirmed nationalist that even America, the most righteous of all the foreign countries, cannot go beyond the practice of this kind of "divided equality." To many Chinese the message was clear: in this brutal world of Darwinian competition, only the strong survive with dignity; China can no longer afford to be poor and weak. Revolution is the only course of action, and by the 1920s the American revolutionary model seemed very remote in both China and the United States.

The Persistence of a Cultural Divide

Beyond the signs of admiration and ambivalence toward America, the profound differences between our societies have remained apparent. Symbolically the Sino-American treaty of 1943, in which the United States formally abandoned extraterritoriality, was the first negotiation on equal terms that the Chinese government had ever conducted with a Western power. But, as Fairbank observes, "within five months another agreement was made, freeing American troops in China from Chinese criminal jurisdiction." In fact, for a few years the massive operations of American bases on Chinese soil were "in greater volume and with greater license than Southwest China had ever seen under the unequal treaties." Fairbank continues:

At war's end Shanghai streets for many months were filled with GI's and roistering sailors far beyond the memory of treaty-port days. This ill suited China's new great-power status. China's new-found sovereignty took on a quizzical character. Right-wing chauvinists, Communists, and patriotic liberals could unite in inveighing against GI incidents connected with wine, women, and jeeps.[5]

In terms of mundane life, America seemed as topsy-turvy to Chinese as did China to Americans. Subtle differences in the perceptions of sex relations, eating habits, color, taste, space, and time all played a significant role. To a Chinese visitor, for example, everything in America is opposite. The women are aggressive and the men soft-spoken. They read from left to right in a horizontal way. Brides wear white like mourners. Real drinks come before and after dinner. The soup is served first. The food is divided in advance, and sometimes the guests are made to slice the half-cooked meat at the table. The compass points north. Taking a stroll is for physical exercise, and so on. Thus, the word *yang,* connoting novelty, strangeness, and insubstantiality, is often used to signify things American, although generically it means "foreign."

In a more serious vein, the "gut" reactions to the American presence in China may have been the result of a much more profound gap in value orientation. The American involvement in China in World War II was based on a carefully calculated policy decision to maximize the Chinese potential to resist Japanese expansionism. But it was part of a worldwide strategy based on a Europe-centered notion of world peace. Many Chinese saw this outlook as a narrow-minded and self-ish approach to international politics. They felt that a great power should assume great responsibility for maintaining "righteous principles" (*kung-li*) throughout the world. Thus the Chinese sense of American betrayal—wrapped in Open Door rhetoric—became acute in the 1940s among Chinese of

[5] John K. Fairbank, *The United States and China,* 3rd ed. (Cambridge, Mass.: Harvard University Press, 1972), pp. 305–306.

all political persuasions. And the publication of the Yalta Agreement in 1946 only confirmed their suspicions and fears.

In a deeper philosophical sense, it is clear that today as always Americans and Chinese are operating on fundamentally different value systems. There is little common ground in terms of basic beliefs about man and society that would draw Americans and Chinese together in a common cause.

The ongoing Chinese belief in the perfectibility of human nature through self-effort enables the Chinese to cultivate an inner strength without appeal to a transcendent deity. Given this commitment to the transforming power of the human will, it is difficult for the Chinese to appreciate the American insistence upon a higher law and the American demand for individual rights. In simplified terms, we frequently witness what a modern Chinese philosopher has described as a conflict between "duty-consciousness" and "rights-consciousness." While the American easily misconstrues the Chinese staying power as a form of stubbornness, to the Chinese the American sense of justice seems a sign of insincerity.

The Chinese perception of the self as a center of relationships and thus an integral part of a larger human network is quite different from the American belief in the dignity of the individual. It is not surprising that the American concern for privacy, private property, and private enterprise has frequently been misinterpreted by the Chinese as an indication of egoistic desires. In fact, the distinction between the private and the public has never been clearly made in China. The idea that private morality or personal life style is separable from public duty has not yet been fully explored in Chinese legal thought.

The concept of law in a constitutional democracy is quite foreign to the Chinese political experience. The idea of adversary relations between institutionalized centers of power in the political process can hardly be appreciated by the Chinese as a consciously and systematically designed structure of government. Since the human factor is so dominating on the Chinese political scene, the American insistence on the supremacy of law over man is certainly hard to comprehend. Just as perplexing is the positive value attached to pressure groups as healthy parts of American political life.

The Chinese view of America is further confounded by the American commitment to pluralism in economic organization, social structure, and academic institutions. The coexistence of many conflicting channels of social mobility, notwithstanding a high level of cultural conformity, is fundamentally different from the Chinese preference for a well-integrated structure of roles and functions in society. The American way of life in which a singing star or a football coach can earn several times as much as the president of a major university appears strange and unreal to Chinese (as it does to some American intellectuals as well).

Serious conflicts between American intellectuals and government officials on political as well as on ideological grounds are frequently interpreted by the Chinese as a sign of disintegration of the social order rather than as an expression of the internal dynamism of the system. The idea that an intellectual, as differentiated from the governmental functionary or business executive, should develop an adversary relationship to politics is alien to the Chinese experience. While some exceptions can be found in the divided political situation of early twentieth century China, it has generally been assumed that a Chinese intellectual should work "within the system," whether Confucian or Communist.

Confrontation

The relationship between the United States of America and the People's Republic of China since 1950 can perhaps be best described as a series of ideological, political, and military confrontations. Recent Chinese images of America have been neither admiring nor ambivalent but outright negative. The government of the United States has been considered stubbornly reactionary in its futile attempt to thwart an inevitable Nationalist collapse. It has been denounced as a staunch collaborator with the worst enemies of social progress and as a vicious conspirator against the great aspirations of the Chinese people to establish a new order. The capitalist system of American society has been perceived as a most serious obstacle in the struggle of the "Third World" for socialist transformation and thus, in the Maoist vision of continuing revolution, American imperialism is an archenemy.

The Chinese Communist commitment to change, involving a fundamental restructuring of society at all levels, has been more pronounced since the founding of the People's Republic. One might say that it has been practiced religiously. America, viewed against this background, seems to have long abandoned her substance as the embodiment of a prophetic promise. On the contrary, America is thought to have adopted a calculated policy aimed at preserving, with the backing of the most destructive military hardware, her claim of hegemony over the world's natural resources. The earlier image of America as a model of science and democracy has thus been displaced by an image of a greedy and violent nation struggling to remain the wealthiest and the strongest on earth.

The Korean War in the 1950s, where America and China brutally locked horns, was seen on both sides as both a military and an ideological struggle. In recent years the Chinese have come to see the U.S. "imperialists" and Soviet "revisionists" as two great superpowers working in collusion to establish world "hegemony." During the period of the American involvement in Vietnam, all the propagandistic images of America a decade earlier seemed to have been transformed into concrete realities by the activities near China's southern border. But as Mao often said, American malevolence is also American weakness—"U.S. imperialism, which looks like a huge monster, is in essence a paper tiger, now in the throes of its deathbed struggle." Therefore, the animosity against Soviet revisionism does not seem to have lessened the suspicion and caution with which the Chinese leadership pursues the course of normalization with the United States.

So far as "normalization" is concerned, the road ahead does seem long and tortuous, no matter how soon actual recognition takes place. The Chinese commitment to national liberation is likely to clash with the American sense of credibility in international affairs over the Taiwan issue. Here symbolism and politics are interwoven. The manner in which the U.S. government expresses its diplomatic intentions is as critical to the Chinese as its mode of operation at the level of daily routine. The matter is further complicated by China's desire to see America sincerely renounce her hegemonic claim over Asia without abdicating her responsibility as a great power in contending against Soviet expansionism in the Pacific.

The wishful thinking for "the overthrow of the two enemies," or in Mao's more graphic words "watching the tigers fight while sitting on the mountaintop," is a subtle reflection of China's self-image not only as a righteous phoenix soaring from the ashes of semicolonial status but also as the torchbearer of a revolutionary process in which "the oppressed peoples of the world will unite and defeat the U.S. imperialists, the Soviet aggressors, and all their running dogs."

The optimism of China's belief in her historical mission is clearly shown in the absolute seriousness of her commitment to the "truth" of scientific materialism. The faith in science and technology which underlies Chinese attitudes toward issues of environment and energy makes it difficult for her to appreciate arguments for the "limits to growth." The emphasis on human ingenuity pushes China to mobilize her resources for achieving the goals of self-reliance. Thus, scientism, which has obviously eroded in America, becomes a supreme value in China's quest for political and economic independence.

China's commitments to politicized collective values—

discipline, work ethic, progress, change, equality, and unity—underlie the People's Republic's goal of "comprehensive modernization" by the end of the twentieth century. In this outlook, the Americans' advocacy of environmental protection, social welfare, zero growth, conservation, pluralism, and diversity seem to reflect an America "with utter chaos at home and extreme isolation abroad," an America that has already lost her nerve and can no longer command a national consensus to confront new global challenges.

In light of what has been said, it may not be farfetched to suggest that there is still "a thousand li" ahead on the road to mutual appreciation of cultural values between the two great peoples. The Chinese misinterpretation of the Watergate affair and the American puzzlement over the recent transmission of power in Peking are only the surface manifestations of a more fundamental gap in sensitivity and value commitment. However, recalling Chou En-lai's memorable quotation from *The Doctrine of the Mean*: "the journey to a distant place must start from the nearest point," it is certain that the Sino-American talks so far have already marked a new beginning. While we have yet to find a basis for sharing common philosophical and cultural outlooks, at least we are approaching each other with a sense of equality and a greater awareness of the differences that will persist.

Part III

BILATERAL INTERACTIONS

ROBERT B. OXNAM

Introduction

As we have seen, American perceptions of China and Chinese perceptions of America have been vastly different. In this section four authors explore the various modes of interaction—diplomacy, culture and technology, trade, and military affairs—that have shaped our bilateral relationships and have expressed our shifting perspectives. Indeed, as we examine these instrumentalities and their use, both singly and in combination, over the past two centuries, we find important indications of why U.S.-China relations have been characterized by rapid shifts, unfulfilled expectations, and tensions on both sides.

First of all, while all four types of interaction are sometimes lumped together in broad explanations of our bilateral relations, it is apparent that over time each side has viewed these instruments through different perspectives. As Waldo Heinrichs observes, there has always been some form of military relationship—gunboat diplomacy in the late nineteenth century, allied expeditions in the early twentieth century, military cooperation in the early 1940s, Cold War confrontation in the 1950s and 1960s, and détente with mutual concern about the Soviet Union in the 1970s. Our diplomatic policies have been closely related to military and strategic considerations; major shifts in policies in 1900, 1941, 1950, and 1972 have paralleled such events as the Boxer Rebellion, the bombing of Pearl Harbor, the outbreak of the Korean War, and the last stages of the Vietnam War and reassessment of the Soviet Union.

But the two countries have evolved very different views of diplomatic and military relationships. The Chinese have tended to use diplomacy and armed force as defensive tools in a century-long quest for national security and international recognition. The United States, in contrast, has tended to see diplomacy and military power as concrete expressions of its role as a world power and our changing views of the strategic situation in Asia. In this sense, the 1970s offer the hope of a new era, one in which both sides recognize that we are credible adversaries, that we gain little by armed clashes and confrontation, and that we gain more by operating as diplomatic equals and seeking to negotiate issues of mutual interest.

Similarly the two countries have placed different emphasis on matters of trade and cultural relations. Lyman Van Slyke makes the observation that the Chinese have tended to envision technology as a means of protecting and strengthening ideological values whether Confucian or Maoist. In contrast to this Chinese view of "technology as technique," Van Slyke describes technology's role in twentieth-century America as more dominant, influencing all aspects of life and thus becoming "technology as culture." These conflicting outlooks help explain what Stanley Lubman sees as a persistent problem in Sino-American commercial relationships: American businessmen have long yearned for heavy involvement in a growing "China market," while Chinese have endeavored to place some limits on the trade relationship and to avoid dependency on American and other foreign technologies.

Second, looking at the relative influence of all four types of interaction, there seems to be a broad historical dividing line during the World War II era. Prior to 1941 the most powerful and sustained interactions seem to have occurred in the cultural realm if we interpret culture broadly to include ideology, education, religion, social reform, and other subdiplomatic contacts among Chinese and Americans. While economic and strategic considerations were important factors in America's becoming an Asian power in the early twentieth century, the cultural dimensions of the American vision seemed to infuse most of our interactions with the Chinese. Thus, Warren Cohen appropriately defines it as an American "era of paternalism" for China—respect for the possibility of China unifying and reforming itself in an American image. Similarly the Chinese outlooks of "admiration" and "ambivalence," observed in Tu Wei-ming's essay, arose from differing views of the applicability of the American cultural model (including "technology as culture") to the Chinese situation.

After 1941, the relationship increasingly shifted from the cultural realm to strategic considerations beginning with our mutual opposition to Japan. Indeed from 1950 to 1971, U.S.-China relations were almost entirely in the strategic realm as the two sides entered an era of mutual hostility with limited diplomatic contacts and no trade or cultural relations. And the key factors behind the era of détente in the 1970s were strategic—the desire to avert a continued collision course between the United States and China, the desire to extricate the United States from Vietnam while maintaining an American presence in the Pacific, and, most importantly, the mutual concern about Soviet expansionism. Commerce, exchanges, and even diplomatic interactions seem to have become subordinate to these global strategic calculations on both sides.

Finally, the historical record indicates that these four modes of interaction, individually or collectively, offer little leverage for either side in influencing the politics of the other's society in predictable ways. In the early twentieth century, many Americans hoped for such leverage and searched for a Chinese leader who seemed to embody stability, moderation, and progress according to American definitions. Even today some Americans advocate policies that would strengthen perceived Chinese "moderates," hoping that they would thus be more likely to support American strategic and economic interests than would the perceived "radicals." Such expectations have yielded limited results because they overlook the fact that Chinese politics has often moved in very different and unpredictable directions. Similarly the current Chinese expectation that the "American people" are likely to conduct a mass revolution against the "capitalist and imperialist American government" tells much more about Chinese ideological outlooks than it does about American realities. Fortunately, these expectations of leverage in the domestic politics of the other society appear to be subordinate themes in the era of détente. On balance, both sides generally seem to recognize that we have two very different cultures, and we should approach each other as equals, not attempting to convert or subvert the other.

In this respect, it appears that the instruments of exchange will be important indicators of the overall relationship. Culturally, the exchange of individuals, delegations, and exhibitions could enable Americans and Chinese to develop deeper understanding of our respective societies, discovering the areas where dialogue seems most fruitful, while also comprehending cultural differences with greater sensitivity. Similarly, commercial and technological exchanges test our capacities to find those limited areas where our different economic systems appear to complement each other. But these cultural and commercial interactions are tenuous links between our two societies and depend on the diplomatic and military aspects of the Sino-American relationship. In examining the instruments of exchange, it is apparent that we have entered a new era in the 1970s with potential benefits for both sides. But those benefits must be seen and explored in realistic terms, recognizing the fragility of the relationship and the frictions and unrealized expectations of our historical experience.

5

MICHEL OKSENBERG

The Structure of Sino-American Relations

Iɴ the 1800s, the political and administrative structure for ordering Sino-American relations was relatively simple. The Chinese government initially attempted to fit Americans as well as Europeans into their traditional tributary framework for dealing with peoples beyond the realm. The tribute system did not allow ongoing organized contacts with foreign nations in the Chinese capital. Only periodic missions could travel to Peking and pay homage to the emperor. Commodities were funneled into and out of China through border trading outposts.

The Chinese periodically dispatched missions abroad to attend inaugurations and other ritualistic events; they also sent military expeditions into Inner Asia. But basically external relations were conducted by staying at home and receiving foreign guests—a practice that continues. The management of tributary relations primarily fell under the Board of Rites, a name indicative of the Chinese attitude toward the whole business.

The Western penetration of Asia forced the Chinese to develop a specialized foreign affairs bureaucracy, initially called the Tsung-li Yamen. In 1860, the Western powers secured the right to station diplomats permanently in Peking, and in 1878 the first Chinese diplomat was posted in Washington. Gradually, the Chinese became enmeshed in the forms of diplomatic intercourse which grew out of Western tradition: permanent missions placed in foreign capitals and allowed in one's own capital, with a foreign ministry coordinating the wide range of contacts the structure produces. Not until 1935, however, did Western countries upgrade their missions from legation to embassy status and their representative from minister to ambassador.

World War II and Its Aftermath

World War II changed these traditional practices. All vestiges of the "unequal treaties" were eliminated and China acquired a seat on the UN Security Council. Under the Kuomintang, the Republic of China developed an extensive diplomatic system, which the Nationalists took with them intact to Taiwan. Through this network, they retained relations with a gradually shrinking number of countries. (As of 1976, the Republic of China had full diplomatic relations with twenty-four countries.)

The People's Republic of China, unable to build upon bureaucratic foundations of the ancien régime, set about constructing its own foreign affairs apparatus. Its chief architect was Chou En-lai. The Ministry of Foreign Affairs, which Chou personally headed from 1949 to 1958 while simultaneously serving as premier, has been the main bureaucracy for implementing Chinese foreign policy. To be sure, the ministry was responsive to the guidelines set by Mao, Chou, and the Politburo of the Chinese Communist Party. The ministry has the usual compliment of geographical departments—Asian, African, Soviet and East European, West Asian and North African, West European, and American and Oceanic. The United States is the responsibility of the latter department, so that American dignitaries in Peking usually meet officials from that organization. Its head—as of 1977, Lin P'ing, a former close associate of Chou En-lai—is the equivalent of the Assistant Secretary for East Asian Affairs in the U.S. State Department. The ministry also has the usual functional departments— Consular Affairs; Information; International; Organizations, Conferences, Treaties, and Law; and Protocol.

The form is similar to most foreign ministries, but embedded within the structure is the Party organization. Each embassy abroad and each department in Peking contains a branch of the Chinese Communist Party. Intra-Party directives are communicated through this network. The head of the Party group within each unit in the ministry is in many ways more powerful than the formal chief of the unit. (Frequently the same person holds the two positions.) In addition to the Party organization, the ministry has a political department that organizes the ideological study of the cadres: each member of the ministry is a member of a small study group which meets usually at least once a week, under Party supervision, to read and discuss major policy statements and speeches. Finally, it seems that in missions abroad, at least, and perhaps in Peking, one or more officials are internal security personnel charged with monitoring the behavior of their colleagues.

These internal control and indoctrination measures produce a disciplined, tightly run operation. The devotion and loyalty to Chou En-lai within the ministry was considerable, particularly among the senior officials—many of whom he had personally selected and cultivated. Within Peking, most ministry personnel appear to live in the same large apartment block, which is shared with officials from other bureaucracies in the foreign affairs system. While abroad, ministry personnel reside together, frequently living in the same building in which their embassy office is located. These foreign missions are self-contained. That is, the Chinese are their own cooks, chauffeurs, secretaries, translators, and so on. (This explains why the Chinese purchased hotels to accommodate their Liaison Office in Washington and their Mission to the United Nations in New York. They have large staffs in both places.) Spouses with different professions remain home, as do most children, but not infrequently spouses are dispatched to the same embassies abroad where they also have responsibilities. Not surprisingly, with political, social, residential, and professional life contained within one formal organization, intermarriage among younger officials within the foreign affairs system is high.

Partly for the reasons we have mentioned, partly because the standards of recruitment into the foreign affairs organizations are rigorous and partly because it is a prestigious career line, the esprit de corps of China's foreign service officers seems high. But it also seems true that, given the intensity of personal interaction within the organization and the low level of interpersonal contacts outside the units, tensions and frustrations can sometimes build up. Occasionally, at least, Americans have sensed that their Chinese interlocutors are more concerned about the effect their words will have upon their fellow Chinese than upon the American. The structure breeds caution and hesitancy.

In addition to the ministry, a number of other bodies supervise various aspects of Chinese external affairs. The International Liaison Department of the Chinese Communist Party handles party-to-party relations, an important function for an internationally minded Marxist-Leninist movement. The New China News Agency places correspondents abroad; these newsmen frequently perform quasi-diplomatic and quasi-intelligence tasks. Probably subordinate to the United Front Department of the Communist Party, the Commission for Overseas Chinese cultivates relations with ethnic Chinese communities around the world; within the People's Republic, it has its own hotels and travel service to assist ethnic Chinese who return home for visits.

High-level delegations to China—such as U.S. congressional delegations—are hosted by the Chinese People's Institute of Foreign Affairs, an organization closely linked to the ministry. Nonethnic Chinese are hosted by the China Travel Service, which helps facilitate China's "people-to-people" diplomacy. But the administrative responsibility for these people-to-people programs falls under the Chinese People's Association for Friendship with Foreign Countries. This organization attempts to encourage the founding of "Chinese Friendship Associations" in foreign countries, which it then subsidizes in conjunction with the China Travel Service by allowing the "friendly organization" to send delegations to China at discount prices. That is, the "friendship organization" charges substantially more for a visit it organizes than the organization pays the Chinese.

A number of other organizations have foreign liaison bodies. The Ministry of National Defense, for example, has a Foreign Affairs Department. Presumably among its functions is the coordination of the military attachés posted abroad. The State Scientific and Technological Commission, in conjunction with the Academy of Sciences, has a foreign affairs section which arranges scientific exchanges. The Sports Federation initiates its exchanges. And so on. But all exchanges are channeled through bureaucracy. All contacts that Chinese have with Americans, in sum, are governmentally organized and monitored.

The same is also true in the economic realm. Trade is organized by the Ministry of Foreign Trade. It primarily deals with economic relations with the developed world. Subordinate to it is the Chinese Commission for the Promotion of International Trade. This body, which has had extensive contacts with U.S. businessmen, promotes trade exhibitions, reaches trademark agreements, engages in technical exchanges, settles maritime and commercial disputes, and in general acts as a chamber of commerce. Also under the Ministry of Foreign Trade is the Chinese Export Commodities Fair, which sponsors the semiannual Canton Trade Fair to which thousands of merchants flock from throughout the world. The Ministry of Foreign Trade is the headquarters for the eight trading corporations through which Chinese trade is organized: the Machinery Export and Import Corporation, the Technical Import and Export Corporation, the Machinery Corporation, the Native Produce and Animal By-products Corporation, and so on. Finally, the Ministry of Economic Relations with Foreign Countries seemingly has primary responsibility for managing Chinese trade with the Third World and for administering Chinese aid programs.

Many of the foreign affairs bureaucracies have bureaus in the provinces and major municipalities. The Ministry of Foreign Trade, for example, has departments in almost every provincial government; the state trading corporations have provincial branches as well. Thus the bureaucratic tentacles reach not only outward but inward as well.

Since 1971, the United States has adapted itself to the Chinese bureaucratic structure. By 1976, the U.S. government and the American public—without conscious design—had changed their configuration so that every major Chinese bureaucracy had its American equivalent. Before examining the American structure, however, a brief background is appropriate.

Until World War II, American China policy was firmly in the hands of the State Department and more particularly the Far Eastern Division. Presidents took an occasional and usually uninformed interest in China; secretaries of state intervened more frequently and decisively. But the core responsibility rested with the division head, who in turn relied heavily upon the advice he received from the dispatches from his main envoy in China. The envoy, in turn, was subjected to pressures from American missionaries, businessmen, and the military on the scene. It was a relatively simple structure designed to advance and protect relatively narrow interests.

In addition, the Far Eastern Division had responsibility for Japan. A natural rivalry throve within the division between Japan and China specialists over which country was more important to the United States. But that was about the limit of bureaucratic politics in those days—mild-mannered stuff compared to more recent days.

World War II changed all that. The American alliance with the Nationalist government introduced new agencies onto the scene: the Office of Strategic Services (OSS), the predecessor to the CIA; the Office of War Information (OWI), the predecessor to the U.S. Information Agency; the Treasury Department; and of course the military services, represented by such as Joseph W. Stilwell (army) and Claire Chennault (army air force). Where bureaucracies penetrate, there they remain. Agencies that acquired a China mission in World War II and the subsequent civil war in China (1946–49) have retained them to the present day.

The only difficulty was that the bureaucracies were attached to the Nationalist government. What began as a China involvement subsequently turned into a Taiwan involvement —and therefore an anti–People's Republic activity. Indeed, through the 1950s, many agencies implemented the general policy line of anti–People's Republic "containment." Treasury and Commerce monitored the trade restrictions. Agriculture estimated Chinese food production. The U.S. Information Agency propagandized. The Defense Department beefed up American defenses and strengthened Republic of China capabilities. The Agency for International Development and its predecessors assisted Taiwan. The CIA undertook covert actions against China. The State Department built its large consulate in Hong Kong and created a new industry: "China watching." Many vested bureaucratic interests developed around a hostile policy toward China; no bureaucracy had an interest in improving relations with China. And as Robert Oxnam's essay indicates, the McCarthy era showed what could happen to an individual within those hostile structures who might argue that our national interest was not well served by all of this.

To be sure, many within the structure, particularly in the State Department, were privately critical of China policy in the sixties, but they received no institutional backing or support at the top.

Against this background, the Nixon-Kissinger cabal is understandable. It was a cabal against recalcitrant bureaucracies. Even today, the number of agencies with a vested interest in a prospering U.S.-China relationship are outnumbered by those with essentially adversarial missions. The U.S.-China relationship remains rather tenuous and without great bureaucratic support.

Nonetheless, changes have occurred. A People's Republic of China desk exists within the Bureau of East Asian Affairs at the State Department. Here is the operational core of the U.S. relationship to China. In addition, the assistant secretary for East Asian Affairs—in the Rogers and Kissinger years, Marshall Green, Robert Ingersoll, Philip Habib, and Arthur Hummel—and their deputies specializing in China have advocated improving Sino-American relations. The Bureau of East-West Trade in the Department of Commerce is charged with developing commerce. Organs with less identifiable bureaucratic interests capable of articulating broader positions, such as the National Security Council and International Security Affairs in the Pentagon, are also sources of innovation.

TABLE 1

	Chinese side	U.S. side
Government	Chairman of the Party, Premier, Foreign Minister	President, Secretary of State
	Ministry of Foreign Affairs	Department of State
	Liaison Office in Washington	Liaison Office in Peking
Semi-governmental	Chinese Commission for Promotion of International Trade	National Council for U.S.-China Trade
	Scientific and Technical Association of the PRC (People's Institute for Foreign Affairs and other designated agencies)	Committee on Scholarly Communication with the PRC
		National Committee on U.S.-China Relations
"People-to-People"	Commission for Overseas Chinese	Chinese-Americans
	Canton Trade Fair and State Trading Corporations	U.S. businessmen
		U.S.-China People's Friendship Association
	All-China Federation of Journalism	Journalists

So much for the internal lay of the land. Table 1 summarizes the way the United States has organized itself to deal with China. Periodic consultations occur at the highest levels—for example, the Nixons' 1972 visit, the Ford 1975 visit, and Kissinger's July 1971, October 1971, February 1972, June 1972, February 1973, August 1973, September 1974, October 1975, and December 1975 visits, as well as the annual visits to the United Nations by China's foreign minister and, in 1974, by Teng Hsiao-p'ing. In addition, the president or secretary of state sees the chief of the Chinese Liaison Office occasionally, and the Chinese foreign minister has contact with the head of the U.S. Liaison Office in Peking. Conversations during these visits cover a variety of important issues.

One item covered in these meetings concerns facilitated exchanges. That is, each side agrees to host a certain number of cultural, scientific, commercial, and public affairs delegations. Three nonpartisan organizations have acquired the experience and confidence of the U.S. government to handle these exchanges: the National Council for U.S. China Trade, the National Committee on U.S.-China Relations, and the Committee on Scholarly Communication with the PRC. The government-arranged exchange package also includes visits of congressional delegations to China, the composition of which is selected in the White House. All told, these exchanges have numbered between fifteen and twenty each year and account for only a small percentage of the total delegations to China. The distinctive aspect of the facilitated exchanges is that each side selects the composition of its delegation and bargaining occurs over the total package.

Outside of the governmental framework, the Chinese now have access to American society and invite delegations and individuals to China as they see fit. China also sends a few groups to the United States, primarily on commercial missions.

The relationship remains relatively thin, but the structures are now in place on both sides to accommodate an expansion into the realms of student exchanges, language programs, and joint research endeavors. Nixon's visit opened a new page in the structure of the relationship, but the chapter has yet to be written.

6

LYMAN P. VAN SLYKE

Culture, Society, and Technology in Sino-American Relations

Initial Perspectives

NOT very long ago, the combination of culture, society, and technology might have seemed rather artificial. We were used to thinking of these as separate areas of human life: culture had to do with the humanistic aspects of life, with aesthetics and morals ("the best that has been known and said in the world," in Matthew Arnold's phrase), society involved group activity, and technology was the performance of useful tasks by man-made tools and techniques.

More recently, the complex interrelationships among these spheres have become increasingly evident. A culture—any culture—may be defined very roughly as the shared patterns of meaning, values, beliefs, and symbols through which the members of that culture try to make sense of themselves and their world. Society refers to the patterns of life as actually lived by its members. It too has a certain structure, and this structure both affects and is affected by culture. But culture and society are not identical, nor does the one entirely determine the other. There is often a difference between what people believe and what they do. Indeed, this difference often explains individual or historical change, for as the gap widens, pressures build up either to change beliefs or to change behavior in order to bring the two once more into closer correspondence.

In essence, technology is the creation and use of tools in the interest of some human want or need. What things the members of a society desire, what value and meaning they place upon them, comes largely from their culture. How they go about the business of meeting these needs and distributing the fruits of their efforts is a part of the social structure. The tools men use may range from a stone axe to a spacecraft, but in every case they influence man's relation to his environment and his interactions with other men.

In our own lives, we now understand much more clearly than we once did that technology is not simply a matter of nuts and bolts, but exerts a powerful influence upon social and economic organization, life styles, values, and the arts. Where technology had once seemed a benign servant, some now see it as an impersonal master, forcing the individual to serve its needs, molding his attitudes, and altering his environment. In short, technology is inseparable from both culture and society, influencing both, just as both influence it.

Cultures and societies are not static, and both the United States and China have been changing rapidly in the nineteenth and twentieth centuries. This obvious proposition is important because we often speak of China and the United States, or even more grandly of "the West," as though these were abstract and unchanging ideas, eternally counterpoised and contrasted with each other.

It is equally common and equally misleading to think of China changing rapidly during these centuries, largely as a result of "the impact of the West," but to take our own changes so for granted that we hardly see them. In noting China's changes more clearly than our own, we often project backward into the nineteenth century our own more contemporary conditions and attitudes. To cite a single example, discussions of China's failure to embrace railway construction in the 1860s usually fail to mention that our own first efforts were failures also and that our rail development, though vigorous, was not yet much past its childhood. In short, differences viewed from the latter part of the twentieth century are often very much greater than those which existed at an earlier time.

Conversely, some of China's contemporary attitudes and policies reflect not simply cultural predispositions but also the stages of development in which she now finds herself. Indeed, many American attitudes during the nineteenth century find resonances in contemporary China. Yankee ingenuity and frontier self-reliance have Chinese counterparts today. And those American scientists and engineers who question China's commitment to basic research (some Chinese worry about this too) might recall Alexis de Tocqueville's remarks about America in the 1830s:

It must be acknowledged that in few of the civilized nations of our time have the higher sciences made less progress than in the United States. . . . In America, the purely practical part of science is admirably understood and careful attention is paid to the theoretical portion, which is immediately requisite to application. . . . But hardly anyone in the United States devotes himself to the essentially theoretical and abstract portion of human knowledge.[1]

Although the United States and China have both been changing rapidly over the period of their contact with one another, at least two differing characteristics form a persistent background to our cultural, social, and technological relations.

The first of these differences the United States inherited from the Anglo-European community, of which it was by the twentieth century the most vigorously growing member. This was a strongly outgoing quality—zeal for exploration, strong missionary fervor, and commercial ambition. China, by contrast, felt self-sufficient and willing to stay at home. Westerners, including Americans, often felt impelled to go among "the less fortunate races" in order to profit and to bring the light of civilization to them, and in so doing felt the proof of superiority. The Chinese felt no such compulsion and found legitimacy in the coming of others unto them, bearing tribute in recognition of their superiority. It is true that Chinese have migrated abroad in far greater numbers than Americans, who have rarely settled overseas in very large communities. But Americans were themselves immigrants, their oceanic travels behind them, and they had an entire continent in which to move in epic proportions. The Chinese, their land long filled, left home mainly because of poverty, overpopulation, and war—frequently as a result of misleading promises or outright coercion—and they viewed themselves as sojourners, even when there was no longer any realistic hope of returning to their native place. Though they brought their way of life with them, it never occurred to them to try to persuade others across the seas to adopt it.

The second difference can be explained largely by differences in the relation of population to resources. In China, from about the sixteenth century on, population was pressing

[1] Nathan Rosenberg, *Technology and American Economic Growth* (New York: Harper & Row, 1972), p. 34.

close to the margin of subsistence, whereas the United States was, well into the twentieth century, newly developing vast lands and the riches which lay beneath them.

In the United States, with a relatively small population and growing demand, the impetus to labor-saving innovation was powerful. Meanwhile, the newness of the continent and its people offered few entrenched social or political obstacles to the rapid diffusion of technological invention. American society, at least from the Civil War on, became increasingly one in which growth, expansion, and innovation were a part of the sociocultural pattern and seemed wholly natural, a way of life. Once this pattern had become established, each new development seemed to fit into place with little more than short-run dislocation. Although the cumulative effect of technological change on American life has been profound, such change did not until recently raise sustained controversy about its cultural, social, or environmental consequences. The utility and beneficence of our technologies were articles of faith, elements of the culture.

In China, by contrast, labor was abundant, land and resources scarce. Because so much of the population lived close to the subsistence level, there was limited mass purchasing power to create demand within the society. Capital was difficult to accumulate and was often used in ways which were rewarding in the Chinese context, but unproductive from our perspective.

Land was a secure investment. Moneylending or commerce was risky but often rewarding. Expenditures on education for official service or for other forms of cultural prestige were considerable, because such prestige also had real payoffs in society. Weddings, funerals, and festivals took some of what remained. Early efforts to raise capital for industrial development showed that such investments lacked the safety of land, the quicker and greater returns of moneylending, and the prestige of scholarship.

China was not simply primitive or simply stagnant. The fact that her agriculture was able to support an almost three-fold population increase between about 1700 and 1850 was a remarkable accomplishment. But this was achieved by more and more labor-intensive methods, by a kind of involution or increasing density, rather than by evolution to new forms of production. Once this process passed a certain point, labor-saving technological innovation was unattractive: first, because the capital costs of the innovation exceeded the labor costs it saved; second, because there was no more profitable activity in which the released labor could be employed; and third, because the margin above subsistence left little room for the stimulation of mass demand.

These conditions, along with the regionally cellular nature of the Chinese economy, help to account for the difficulty of introducing technological change in the nineteenth and twentieth centuries. Approaches which seemed eminently sensible in an American context could make only slow headway against the counterpressures of abundant labor, low demand, and scarce capital—to say nothing of opposition from those in Chinese society with vested interests in the existing system. Needless to say, the pressure of population on resources is one of the most critical legacies bequeathed by the past to the present in China.

Meanwhile, the relative security and peace achieved in China by 1700 meant that China's military capacity gradually languished. A few alarms sounded along the inner Asian frontiers, and there was always a certain amount of domestic unrest, but there was no call to exercise fully the weapons and tactics of the seventeenth century, let alone to develop them further. Both socially and culturally, China was oriented toward peace. In contrast, the Western nation-states found in their frequent conflicts both need and opportunity to forge ahead in all the arts and values of war.

It is not surprising, therefore, that the Western threat came first through the exercise of superior military technology. In 1840–42 and again in 1858–60, China suffered disastrous defeats at the hands of the British and French, including, at the end of the second of these "Opium Wars," the additional humiliation of an allied march on Peking and the deliberate looting and burning of the Summer Palace, with its huge store of cultural treasures. Out of these defeats came the "unequal treaties," extended to include all the major powers, which set the framework of China's foreign relations until 1943.

China's response to these defeats was slow and piecemeal at first, partly because her leaders were so consumed by the effort to put down the massive rebellions that broke out in the mid-nineteenth century, vaster in scope and destructiveness than the American Civil War. Thus, in the 1860s and 1870s, when a few Chinese leaders—the so-called "self-strengtheners"— began to entertain the need for certain technologies, their interest was not at all in social or cultural change. These men saw China's weakness in arms, and their concern was strategic. "What we then have to learn from the barbarians," wrote one of these men, "is only one thing, solid ships and effective guns." [2] But because of the foreign origin of these technologies, they had to be justified as defending Chinese ways, not threatening them. The attacks of critics were fended off by arguing the case for technology as technique: tools were simply tools, as effective in Chinese as in Western hands. It was to be "Western learning for practical use; Chinese learning for fundamental values."

But this slogan masked a deeper incompatibility. The technologies which these Chinese reformers wished to adopt to make China strong were among the most advanced products of the Industrial Revolution. A long history lay behind

[2] Ssu-yu Teng and John King Fairbank, *China's Response to the West, A Documentary Collection, 1839–1923* (Cambridge, Mass.: Harvard University Press, 1954), p. 53.

them, not only in hardware but also in the social organization, resource allocation, and cultural values necessary to their production and successful use.

In short, it proved impossible to make a direct graft of technology as technique from one social and cultural setting to another. Even the Chinese sponsors of "Western learning" sometimes felt an uneasy awareness of this deeper incompatibility. As the perceptive Yen Fu put it,

We cannot force the two cultures to be the same or similar. Therefore Chinese knowledge has its fundamental values and its practical uses; Western knowledge also has its fundamental values and its practical uses. If the two are separate, each can be independent; if the two are combined, both will perish.[3]

Yet another persistent concern, voiced at an early date, was the issue of self-reliance and control:

Some suggest purchasing ships and hiring foreign people, but the answer is that this is quite impossible. If we can manufacture, repair, and use them, then they are our weapons. If we cannot manufacture, repair, and use them, then they are still the weapons of others.[4]

Although these early efforts failed the crucial test of war—symptomatically against the French in the 1880s and spectacularly against the Japanese in 1894—Chinese shipyards and arsenals had turned out a substantial number of modern warships, as well as guns and munitions. Looking only at the weapons, many contemporary observers predicted a Chinese victory over Japan, herself still early in the modernization process. Problems lay less with the weapons themselves than with their adaptation and use. Flotillas were almost the personal possessions of high officials who sponsored them, coordinated training and combat tactics had not been developed, and logistics were a swamp of confusion. The failure of self-

---

[3] Teng and Fairbank, *China's Response to the West*, p. 151 (retranslated by the author).

[4] Teng and Fairbank, *China's Response to the West*, p. 54.

strengthening therefore lay precisely at the intersection of technology with society and culture.

These early experiences with Western technology reveal at least three areas of concern which, in various and changing ways, persist to the present. First was the pervasive identification of modern technology with foreigners and foreign powers. No society wishes to be thought inferior and backward, perhaps least of all one so schooled as China in the notion of self-sufficiency. That these technologies, and not only the narrowly military ones, were forced upon Chinese attention by superior firepower and unequal treaties meant that China could not ignore the fact of their alien origin. By contrast, these technologies had become so natural to life in the United States that even those originally developed elsewhere seemed distinctively American.

Second, the Chinese experience raised questions involving the social, political, and cultural consequences of technological change. In America and the West more generally, modernization had been gradual at first, and society changed along with it—a kind of "pay-as-you-go" development, whose heavy costs most of us have now conveniently forgotten. The Chinese were faced with a stark confrontation between their society and societies of superior strength with very different structures. In this confrontation, consequences of social and technological change raised unavoidable issues. In the nineteenth century, these issues involved Confucian values, the imperial system of government, and the agrarian foundation of the Chinese economy. In contemporary China, despite the revolutionary changes which have intervened, such issues are still important, only now they involve the role of technicians and experts, the use of material incentives, the relation of cities to countryside, and the balance between agriculture and industry.

The third area of concern is that of self-reliance versus dependency on others. Over the past century and more, China's experience of weakness had been painful and varied. The unequal treaties underlined it, as did the huge debts China owed foreigners during most of this period. Some of these were indemnities for wars lost or uprisings quelled, like the Boxers in 1900, by foreign troops. Many other debts were incurred for the development of railways, telegraphs, mining enterprises, and industries, all or part of the ownership of which remained in foreign hands. This memory of dependency and the determination it bred to achieve autonomy have endured to the present.

Even the Communist victory in 1949, when Mao proudly asserted, "The Chinese people have stood up," did not mark the end of this experience. One cause of the Sino-Soviet split lay in a Chinese perception that the Soviet Union was trying to keep China dependent, just as the imperialists had. The Russian response included the termination, in 1960, of all military and technical assistance programs, the recall of her nearly 2,000 technicians and engineers, and refusal to defer debt payments because of China's economic difficulties.

Americans who are unaware of this history, and for whom our science and technology seem equally relevant to all societies, often feel exasperated by Chinese sensitivities. In the light of China's experiences—experiences we have never had to cope with—these attitudes become more understandable. Among the consequences are reluctance to borrow either technology or capital unless fully justified as necessary, determination to master technologies at all levels with as little foreign assistance as possible, and the desire to diversify contacts so as to avoid being vulnerable to pressure from any one nation. Although these attitudes may be changing somewhat, they have seemed necessary to China's leaders, both psychologically and objectively, even if it means the temporary slowing of some otherwise desirable growth. China's present attitudes toward technological change and its various social consequences are thus a complex mixture of historical experience, ideology, and contemporary needs.

The Nineteenth Century

John K. Fairbank has observed that until the very end of the nineteenth century, the United States had no separate China policy, because none was needed. Instead, we remained rather petulantly under the wing of the British, accepting the gains but disclaiming the guns which had forced the unequal treaties upon China. From the Chinese standpoint, the U.S. presence was small, intermittent, and only with some effort distinguishable from that of other Western nations.

These Westerners, Americans among them, approached China from the sea, and it was along the eastern littoral of China that contacts were always most extensive and intense. This contact was focused on the treaty ports, above all Shanghai, and even after the hinterland was opened to travel and residence, the tiny and scattered enclaves of foreigners in the interiors were called "outports," expressive of their ties to the coastal treaty ports. Paul A. Cohen, discussing littoral and hinterland, draws a distinction that is at once geographical, social, and cultural. Geographically, it was along the coast that most pioneering efforts to change China were undertaken, by foreigners and westernized Chinese alike. But it was in the hinterland that these changes were adapted, assimilated, or transformed. Often enough, this involved the rejection of the pioneers and much of what they stood for, even while some of their efforts were gradually domesticated, made more wholly Chinese, less recognizably alien. One could easily list, for example, many changes for which missionaries worked—an end to foot-binding, mass education, widespread health care, individual choice in marriage—that became part of the revolutionary process, even as that same process rejected the religious message of the missionaries and in the end expelled them from China.

Americans in China during the nineteenth century were

mainly traders and missionaries. Because of their coming and going, U.S. traders had little direct influence upon China. Unlike most European nations and Japan, the United States never occupied leaseholds in China, and only rarely did U.S. nationals establish enterprises in China. Capital investments were small. The main American economic interest, and hope, in China was commercial, yet trade with China nevei exceeded about 5 percent of total U.S. trade.

Missionaries were from the start the most influential group of Americans in China, and most of them brought more than simply the word of God and the desire to evangelize the Chinese. Often they were educators or doctors as well, offering instruction in mathematics, sciences, or medicine out of the combined desire to do good, to demonstrate the superiority of Western ways, and to achieve eventual conversion.

In both the nineteenth and the twentieth centuries, education and medicine were the secular cornerstones of the American effort in China. Education was broadly conceived, aiming where possible at Chinese leadership, but more often at the humbler classes. Some of the education was provided to Chinese in the United States, but many more were reached by mission-supported schools in China, and by their Chinese graduates, who often went on to teach in "Western-style" Chinese schools that were established at an accelerating rate after 1900.

One might point to Peter Parker (1804–88), Yale-educated missionary and doctor, who opened a hospital in Canton in the 1830s and later founded the Medical Missionary Society in China. Or to Yung Wing, adopted by an American missionary and brought to the United States, to graduate from Yale in 1854. In 1872, Yung Wing's influence led to the creation of the Chinese Educational Mission, through which 120 young boys were sent to Connecticut for a fifteen-year course of education, to include such subjects as military science, navigation, shipbuilding, and surveying. This bold experiment foundered in 1881 on the shoals of conservative opposition, lack of funding, and the possibly justified fear that the boys were losing interest in Chinese ways. Nevertheless, many participants had successful later careers in government service, railway development, telegraph administration, and other fields.

The precedent of educating Chinese in America was paralleled by missionary influence on education in China itself. A unique case was the T'ung-wen Kuan ("Interpreters College"), established by the imperial government in 1863 to provide Chinese translator-interpreters for diplomatic work. Guided by the American missionary W. A. P. Martin, the T'ung-wen Kuan was soon offering instructions in mathematics, sciences, and engineering (the T'ung-wen Kuan later evolved into what was to become Peking University, the intellectual storm center of modern China). More typical, however, were schools founded and staffed by the missionaries themselves. By 1900, six "colleges"—at that time they resembled middle schools—and 130 primary schools had been set up. By the same year, 70 missionary-operated hospitals had been established.

Western science and technology were thus most frequently presented to China as foreign imports, taught by foreigners in institutions which they themselves created. Further, science and technology were embedded in self-consciously alternative ways of life, with which their representatives sought to influence China on spiritual, social, and technological planes. This effort took place under the unequal treaties which reflected China's weakness and implied her inferiority to the Western powers and Japan.

The Westerners were rarely revolutionary in the political sense of opposing the regimes which governed—or misgoverned—China at various times. On the contrary, they nearly always accepted and quite often assisted those regimes. But insofar as they aimed to change China, they were socially and culturally subversive. As one missionary wrote in 1909,

"China is a sleeping giant, and it's great fun having a tiny hand in waking her up." This was why some of the most intensely anti-Western sentiments were to be found within the challenged scholar-gentry elite, and why most of the students enrolled in these early mission schools came from the lower classes, who had no other access to education. Upper-class families disdained this heterodox and still socially useless education.

What then of Chinese influence, in culture and technology, upon nineteenth-century America? At first glance, there may seem none at all. Ralph Waldo Emerson once wrote that in the congress of nations, all the Chinese could say was "We made the tea." But Emerson and his descendants underestimated this influence, even as they overestimated the effect of the United States upon China.

In remoter times, early Chinese inventions—printing, the magnetic compass, and many others—made their way into medieval Europe, there to play a role in the quickening of life associated with early modernization. Long before America achieved independence, however, these inventions had been so domesticated and so immersed in other developments that their Eastern origins disappeared from sight. But the recognition that such remote contributions have now been forgotten does not entirely negate their significance.

In the nineteenth century, China's influence on the United States was probably greater in magnitude, though less pregnant with implications, than American influence upon China.

On the purely technological level, the China trade helped to bring into being, during the 1830s, the clipper ships—the fastest and most beautiful long-distance sailing vessels ever developed. These American and British ships, which plied the seas carrying silks, porcelain, lacquer ware, opium, and above all tea, testify to the profits to be made in this trade. Although the China trade occupied only a modest proportion of the total, it was part of a trading pattern that led to the accumulation of capital for a number of important families and firms in Boston, New York, and Philadelphia. The capital accumulated in this way was subsequently invested in domestic U.S. development both before and after the Civil War. The decline in this trade after 1850 is attributable mainly to the more profitable and safer investments then available at home, in railways, banking, and industry.

If the beauty of the clipper ships and the profits earned in the China trade graced the East Coast, Chinese labor helped to win the West. Tons of copper, silver, and gold would have lain much longer undisturbed beneath the mountains of Nevada and the Mother Lode country but for Chinese labor. Nor could Leland Stanford have driven the golden spike at Promontory Point in 1869 without Chinese railway workers. Indeed, it was often said that the American railways were built on Irish whiskey in the East and on Chinese tea in the West. In 1870, when there were about 200 American missionaries in all of China, there were more than 100,000 Chinese in the United States, all but a few west of the Rockies.

Thus, these tall ships and short men contributed to the development of nineteenth-century America. If we have not ordinarily been aware of these contributions, it was because the clipper ships and the China trade were wholly in American hands, and because Chinese labor only made existing rail and mining technologies feasible but did not influence their forms. In China, Western influence was such that Chinese were inescapably aware of its foreign origin; in the United States, Chinese influence was hardly noticed and rarely acknowledged.

The Turn of the Century to World War II

By the end of the nineteenth century, the romantic heyday of the old China trade was long since over, and discriminatory legislation backed by white labor had brought an end to the immigration of Chinese workers. "Not a Chinaman's chance" summed up the position of the Chinese in the United States. Nevertheless, the idea of China, and the image of our paternally benevolent relationship with China continued and grew after the turn of the century, and with the Open Door Notes, we came to see ourselves as China's protector, when in fact we were simply asserting the principles of free trade and equality of access by all powers to China.

The United States was willing to back up these principles when they were violated partly because its economic stake in China was small by every measure. Approximately 8,500 American businessmen in China during the 1930s participated in a trade that at no time exceeded five percent of the U.S. total, and they were always heavily outnumbered by both Japanese and British competitors. Investments finally reached about $300 million by 1936, only a tenth of the total foreign stake in China and only one-third as great as U.S. investment in Japan. Most of this activity was concentrated in Shanghai.

Until Pearl Harbor, missionaries were the second largest group of Americans in China, and America's moral stake in China was much greater than its economic interests. In the mid-1920s, Americans numbered about 5,000 of the 8,300 Protestant missionaries in China (there were about 2,000 Catholic missionaries in China, mostly from European nations). After the anti-Christian and antiforeign movements of 1926–28, the number of American missionaries fell to about 3,000 (of a Protestant total of 6,000) in the 1930s. Increasingly, however, others came to China, though their numbers were never large: teachers, engineers, economists, agricultural specialists like J. Lossing Buck, foreign service officers (some China-born of missionary parents, like John S. Service), marines, and the sailors of the Yangtze patrol. One of the most dramatic of the engineers was Oliver J. Todd, "Todd almighty" he was called, whose decade and more of work on the Yellow River failed to tame China's flood dragons but occasionally rendered them a little less fearsome. Nevertheless, most reform efforts had some connection or other with the Christian enterprise. The YMCA became a significant institution in China's major cities, and many of the American-supported efforts in rural China were channeled through the National Christian Conference. Social reform almost always carried some tincture of religion.

During and after World War II, however, generals and diplomats—often the same person—became the most prominent Americans in China, and U.S. military personnel, more than 60,000 by 1945, far outnumbered both traders and missionaries, even at their combined peak. In the 1940s, most Americans in China had an association not with Christianity or business but with the U.S. government and the war effort.

In the interwar years, education, medicine, and moderate social reform were the main avenues of American influence upon China. The flow of Chinese students to the United States was only a trickle before 1908, when the U.S. share of the Boxer indemnity was converted to a scholarship fund to bring Chinese to this country. Through this and many other channels, the number grew until, by 1949, about 36,000 Chinese students had attended U.S. schools, more than half specializing in scientific and technological subjects, including medicine. In no other foreign country except Japan, from 1900 to about 1915, were so many Chinese educated.

Meanwhile, many more Chinese were attending schools and colleges sponsored by mission boards within China, a majority of which were financed from the United States. In almost any year during this period, there were about 500,000 Chinese in mission schools at all levels, including perhaps 15,000 in Protestant middle schools, and 6,500 in Protestant-run universities. The six colleges and 130 schools of 1900 grew to sixteen colleges and 200 schools in 1930, and the quality of education was also much improved. In the same period, hospitals increased in number from 70 to 130, capped at the top by the famous Rockefeller-supported Peking Union Medical College

(PUMC), deliberately created in 1915 on the Johns Hopkins model, combining basic research and teaching—both entirely in English—with hospital-based treatment. Social medicine and mass health-care delivery were outside its sphere of interest until the mid-1930s. By 1949, PUMC's endowment was US$22 million. Except for primary schools, most of these institutions were located in the major cities of the littoral, in Peiping, Tientsin, Shanghai, Nanking, Canton.

It is impossible to accurately trace the subsequent careers of the graduates of these institutions, but it appears that more than half found employment in education or in government, the traditionally high-prestige career lines. Others were employed in medicine, industry, commerce, and journalism; some became residents of the United States. In 1937, 77 of 116 PUMC graduates were located in these five cities.

All this suggests a clustering of talent in the top layers of society, which meant also geographical concentration in the few most modern cities of China. These were the cities where they had attended school, and it was here that suitable opportunities seemed most numerous. Graduates of U.S. institutions who had studied engineering, advanced industrial technologies, or basic science often found themselves overqualified for Chinese conditions in a way that further weakened their links to society at large. The disparity in developmental stages between the United States and China therefore led to a partial misfit in the levels of training suitable to the two societies.

An unusual example of this was provided by the eccentric American missionary Joseph Bailie. In the 1920s he persuaded Henry Ford to set up an industrial training school at the Ford plant, there to accommodate annually about 100 "ethically well-conditioned" Chinese graduates of American universities. Emphasis was placed on work-study, on the practical aspects of production, and on the social utility of industry. By the 1930s, when the program fell victim to the depression, several hundred "Bailie boys" had been trained and returned to

China. Many were unable to find jobs using their unique blend of education and practical experience.

In contrast to the gradual diffusion of hard scientific and technological knowledge among a relatively small number of Chinese was the sweeping influence of the *idea* of science and material progress among Chinese intellectuals more generally. It was an idea that Americans had done much to propagate. This was part of the so-called "new culture movement" or the "May Fourth (1919) movement," which gathered momentum about 1915, peaked in 1919, and bequeathed a complex and contradictory legacy to later decades. One aspect of this intensely nationalistic movement was a radical rejection of China's traditional culture and its fundamental values. Thus, where nineteenth-century self-strengtheners had tried to justify Western science as useful in defense of tradition, these young twentieth-century intellectuals seized upon science precisely because it seemed to invalidate so much of that very tradition.

D. W. Y. Kwok has commented that "Science was an ideological entity, imported to replace the old cultural values." [5] He calls this "scientism," "the tendency to use the respectability of science in areas having little bearing on science itself." [6] For practicing scientists like V. K. Ting and for pragmatists like Hu Shih, the commitment to science remained firm, and it led these men in the direction of gradual, piecemeal reform. To those of a more radical and activist temperament, like Ch'en Tu-hsiu, scientism led in the direction of Marxist materialism, the formation of the Chinese Communist Party in 1921, and a commitment to revolution.

From 1919 to 1921, John Dewey traveled throughout China, lecturing wherever he went on the sensible virtues of education, pragmatism, and gradual change. Although very influential in educational circles, his message of step-by-step

[5] D. W. Y. Kwok, *Scientism in Chinese Thought, 1900–1950* (New Haven, Conn.: Yale University Press, 1965), p. 12.
[6] Ibid., p. 5.

reform struck some listeners as irrelevant to a China sunk in poverty, fragmented by cynical warlords, and struggling to achieve control of its own affairs.

There was also some disillusionment with the United States in these years. The Chinese had invested great hope in Woodrow Wilson's vision of world justice, and the failure of this vision—most painfully in the preservation of recent Japanese gains in China—came as a bitter disappointment. Not all Chinese agreed with Chiang Kai-shek, but he spoke for many in a 1926 interview with American reporter Lewis Gannett:

Japan talks to us in ultimatums; she says frankly she wants special privileges. . . . We understand that and we know how to meet it. The Americans come to us with smiling faces and friendly talk, but in the end your government acts just like the Japanese. . . . Your missionaries write "charity" over their doors, and I do not deny that many of them are good men who do good work. But in the end they make it easier for American policy to follow that of the other imperialist powers. So because we have been deceived by your sympathetic talk, we end by hating you most.[7]

These feelings, expressed in sometimes violent popular demonstrations during the next two years, led an American missionary to despair, "We are flotsam in a whirlpool with which we have no connection."[8]

Thus, up to the outbreak of the war with Japan, American efforts had led to the training of many, possibly a majority, of China's scientific and technological personnel, either in the United States or through educational institutions in China. American attitudes toward science—our own tendencies toward scientism—had also played a role in the broader cultural redefinition which China was seeking. A few products —kerosene, machine-spun cotton, tobacco—had found wide

[7] Cited in Harold R. Isaacs, *Images of Asia* (Cambridge, Mass.: M.I.T. Press, 1958), p. 202.

[8] James C. Thomson, Jr., *While China Faced West: American Reformers in Nationalist China, 1928–1937* (Cambridge, Mass.: Harvard University Press, 1969), p. x.

acceptance, yet the myth of the China market remained as unfulfilled in the twentieth century as in the nineteenth.

Results were not as their American sponsors had hoped they would be. First of all, the Americans—especially the missionaries—had hoped to use the appeal of science to gain a hearing for religion and other cultural values. Most Chinese, on the other hand, put up with preaching in order to get the education they wanted. Numbers of conversions always remained discouragingly small. Ironically, the idea of science, which could be used as a weapon against "unscientific" Chinese traditions, could also be used against "unscientific" Western religion, as the events of the 1920s clearly showed.

Second, the improvement of China seemed nearly as distant a goal as ever in 1937, despite thousands of dedicated lives, hundreds of millions of dollars, and some proud but limited successes. Economic development, including industries, transportation, and communications, had made progress under Nationalist rule in the 1930s, but it would be difficult to single out the distinctive contribution of the United States. Meanwhile, poverty and misery were as widespread as ever, maybe worse; famine and flood perhaps had been palliated a little, but not really alleviated; Japanese aggression was growing.

War and Civil War

The Sino-Japanese War (1937–45) did not entirely destroy this pattern, but it was seriously disruptive. Swept away or taken over were most of the Sino-American undertakings in China—schools, hospitals, rural experiment stations. The most modernized and industrialized cities of China were quickly seized by the Japanese, forcing the Nationalist government out of the lower Yangtze region and into exile behind the river's gorges in Chungking. Millions of Chinese made heroic efforts to trek inland with their government, carrying what they could of factories, laboratories, libraries. But the "big rear area," centered in Szechwan province was socially and economically backward. Americans, who were used to the littoral, now had to accommodate to the hinterland. Many were unable to do so.

One significant and revealing wartime development was that of the Chinese Industrial Cooperatives, or Indusco. The idea of decentralized local industry, owned by its operators and responsive to local needs, took shape in the spring of 1938, partly in response to the loss of China's industrial base. A cosmopolitan group was responsible for the initial idea and early planning: Edgar and Helen Snow, the New Zealander Rewi Alley, and British ambassador Archibald Clark-Kerr. Chinese government support was obtained through personal influence, money was raised abroad, and Indusco was launched with such élan that its Chinese name, *"Gung ho,"* has passed into English as epitomizing all-out effort. Yet Indusco never reached the stage of self-sustaining growth and real assimilation into local economies. This stemmed partly from the difficulties of getting machinery, training workers, securing new materials, adapting products to needs. But it also reflected political hostility and interference. Official support, never wholehearted, eroded further when early successes created opposition from vested interests in the localities where coops were functioning.

By 1942, Rewi Alley had been fired by the Chungking government as Indusco's director, and during the latter years of the war the vision of what Indusco might have become lay in ruins. Meanwhile, the Chinese Communists supported their own version of Indusco in the Yenan area, freely acknowledging the ideas of Alley and the Snows. Indeed, in the late 1940s, Rewi Alley went over to the Communist-held areas, and lives today in Peking, writing impressions and poetry about his travels throughout China.

The broader influence of the United States in wartime China was surprisingly slight. Although China received less attention than any other major theater, the U.S. presence was substantial—much greater in numbers and expenditures than all previous efforts combined. Between 1941 and 1949, the United States allocated to China more than $6 billion in credits, economic aid, and military equipment, not counting the costs of training for thirty-nine divisions, as well as for combat pilots and others. Generals Stilwell, Chennault, and Albert C. Wedemeyer worked hard, in their various and mutually antagonistic ways, for military reform. U.S. economists assisted with currency and tax problems. Eleven large air bases were built and improved, and tens of thousands of GI's brought back memories and mementos of their stretch in China. Yet, in the end, China did not become the effective combatant or the united and democratic country that the United States had hoped to create. Much of the money and equipment was embezzled, lost to inflation, wasted, or unsuitable in China. Chiang Kai-shek husbanded most of the rest for his anticipated showdown with the Communists, in which equipment and manpower was finally lost in battle, taken over by the Chinese Communist Party, or removed to Taiwan.

During the war, only a few voices, quickly silenced and removed from China, bespoke the growing strength of the Communists and the sources from which it was drawn. Disillusion with the Nationalists grew in the United States, but American support remained almost to the conclusion of the civil war in 1949.

"In the end," writes Barbara Tuchman, "China went her own way as if the Americans had never come." [9] Americans might take some comfort from the knowledge that others who had come to change China suffered a similar fate. Mikhail Borodin, the defeated Bolshevik architect of revolution in the 1920s, reflected sadly, "I came to China to fight for an idea. The dream of accomplishing world revolution by freeing the people of the East brought me here. But China itself, with its

[9] Barbara W. Tuchman, *Stilwell and the American Experience in China, 1911–45* (New York: Macmillan, 1971), p. 531.

age-old history, its countless millions, its vast social problems, its infinite capacities, astounded and overwhelmed me." [10]

The American legacy in China at the time of the Communist victory in 1949 is difficult to assess. If influence is to be measured solely by direct achievement of those goals Americans consciously set for themselves in China, then Tuchman's verdict is just. But if we look more deeply at what the Chinese assimilated to make their own, if we look at what they rejected and how the very act of rejection was part of the self-definition toward which China was struggling, then our influence was not so negligible.

Many had learned from America and from Americans, whatever their reaction. Certainly there were reservoirs of admiration and good will toward the United States in some segments of the population. On an individual level, friendships existed. As Tu Wei-ming's essay makes clear, many Chinese saw the United States as a rich and lucky land, untouched by the tragedies China had known, a land of stability and prosperity and of such technological efficiency that one could hardly imagine serious alternatives to the way things were done there.

Mixed with this admiration, however, were also deep feelings of anger and hurt. America was now incomparably the strongest Western power in Asia, and as such she inherited some of the resentments built up since the Opium Wars. America's very strength seemed a painful rebuke to China's weakness, and this too was resented. These feelings were heightened by the patronizing self-confidence of many Americans, an impatient cultural and technological condescension which barely masked contempt for Chinese impotence and inefficiency. All too frequently, the conduct of American GI's in China—among whom "slopehead" or "slopey" became a common epithet for the Chinese—was such as to inspire ill-feeling.

Finally, there was the postwar involvement of the United States in Chinese political affairs, our continued backing of

[10] Jonathan Spence, *To Change China: Western Advisers in China 1620–1960* (New York: Little, Brown & Company, 1969), p. 202.

Chiang Kai-shek's government, which was increasingly losing both its mandate and its power in China. Americans may have felt their purposes high-minded, but U.S. policy was widely seen in China as support for a bankrupt, discredited, and reactionary regime.

These mixed feelings were present, in varying degrees, among the educated and politically articulate. For millions of peasants in China's vast hinterlands, however, the United States was simply irrelevant, its existence barely known to farmers following ancestral ways, untouched by technological modernization. Americans had usually known best those Chinese most like themselves, usually in the cities of the littoral. There was a tendency to project this view to all of China, as interpreted by those Chinese who were themselves most westernized. In the hinterland, missionaries and others knew China much better on some levels, but they were more concerned to change China than to understand her. Most were preoccupied with the reality of their daily trials, and they sought to maintain American ways in a life set apart, behind compound walls. The result was a persistent overestimate of American influence, a failure to realize how superficial direct American influence had been in terms of China as a whole.

The United States, together with other foreign nations, had been partly the cause of revolutionary changes in China. But it is equally accurate to say that we were catalysts, because the changes themselves, the forces liberated by these changes, were truly China's own. They bore no trademark imprinted "Made in U.S.A."

Since the Shanghai Communiqué

The new Chinese leadership might have felt it necessary, as part of the reassertion of Chinese independence, to deprecate the United States and to eradicate the visible signs of its influence. But even had the Chinese felt differently at first, the Korean War guaranteed a prolonged and intense anti-American campaign in China. This was matched, on the American side, by a posture of hostility and confrontation which branded China an aggressor, resumed large-scale support for Chiang's government in Taiwan, and sought (unsuccessfully) to isolate China from trade with the non-Communist world.

Contacts broken in 1949 only began to be reestablished in 1971. During the interim, of course, American-trained scientists, engineers, and medical specialists were an important national resource (in the early 1950s there was strong opposition in the United States to permitting the voluntary return to China of Chinese scientists working in such fields as rocketry and nuclear physics). Access to Western technical and scientific literature was continuously available to those who required it in their work. Modern technology, some of it American, came to China from third-party nations whose policies were different from ours. Despite such tenuous influence, no direct contact existed.

Meanwhile, the Chinese had experimented with two contrasting models of technological change and industrization. The first, which lasted until 1958, was essentially the Russian model: centralized planning and control, with primary emphasis on heavy industry, capital goods, and steel production. During this period, China's technocrats were substantially in charge. The second model, seen in its most extreme form in the Great Leap Forward (1958–60), was much more decentralized. It stressed agriculture, light industry, and heavy industry in that order, and it adopted an extensive "politics-in-command" leadership. This was the era of the backyard iron and steel furnaces and of people's communes.

Since the mid-1960s, after recovery from the desperate years immediately following the Great Leap, China had been following a more mixed and balanced strategy which she refers to as "walking on two legs," that is, simultaneously utilizing modern technology and a fairly advanced scientific capacity (at least in selected fields) *and* decentralized, local development employing low and intermediate technologies, often combined with traditional methods and a high degree of labor intensivity. The latter are meant to serve local needs and to be closely integrated with agricultural development. In very general terms, this was the situation when President Nixon went to China in February 1972, and it is this mixed strategy that American visitors have seen since limited travel and exchanges began.

The metaphor of walking on two legs reflects the fact that China is not at one stage of development, but at several stages simultaneously. In China's nuclear establishment and in a few research fields China is at a high level; in major industrial centers, China is moving toward advanced production technologies; and so on down the ladder to remote areas which are only beginning the modernization process. This unevenness of development suggests that multiple strategies may not be as inconsistent with each other as they may appear to outsiders at first glance. Probably no single strategy could meet the needs of so large and diverse a society.

It is a mistaken notion, therefore, that China has a single, universally accepted attitude toward science, technology, and the modernization process in general. This diversity of viewpoint is largely masked from outsiders by official doctrine to which all must publicly subscribe. Issues are fought out behind closed doors, and the general line represents the outcome, not the debate itself. Yet only serious struggle over such issues can explain the zigzag course China has taken in policy toward science, and the modernization process generally. One can detect the outlines of such controversy even in official statements: the campaign against a certain viewpoint is evidence for its existence, and the intensity of the campaign is a rough index of its prevalence. We should not expect the Chinese to admit us to the inner halls of these controversies, but we can try to sensitize ourselves to them, as well as to the roles the Chinese must play when in contact with outsiders.

In China, one of the most persistent controversies over modernization is summed up in the phrase "red and expert." The ideal is someone who is both politically sound ("red") and technically competent ("expert"). In practice, the issue has often been "red versus expert." The issue involves questions of priorities and control of technological modernization. Should emphasis be given to political leaders even though they may have an imperfect understanding of technological and managerial requirements? Or should it be given to technicians who know their tasks but may lack a larger vision of society as a whole?

In the United States, a similar debate is sometimes heard between the virtues of the broadly trained generalist and the professional specialist. Nevertheless, professionalization is strong in American society, and there is often the feeling among professionals that their fields are too specialized to be tampered with by laymen, especially politicians, who do not understand them. In China, too, this feeling exists; if it did not, there would be no need to inveigh against it. By contrast, however, Mao Tse-tung believed that science and technology are too important to be left to scientists and technicians. Since, in China, all activity has a political dimension, the tendency of experts to step outside politics is seen as threatening to create a new elite impervious to values other than those of their profession.

Furthermore, a suspicion lingers that experts tend to be expert in foreign technology. They are thought to look down upon workers and peasants, whose indigenous methods they view as crude and unsuitable. In this stereotype, experts are said to want large-scale urban enterprises full of the most advanced imported machinery and to become so ready to accept the authority of foreign ways that they lose the capacity to improvise, to adapt, and to accept ideas from the bottom up based on working experience.

The "red" is, of course, the antithesis of all this: one with the masses, confident in their ability and their methods, unintimidated by the presumed superiority of technological mandarins and foreign authorities. The "red" will not scorn technology, but he will stress human factors and insist that motivation toward work is of crucial importance. He and not the technician will be in command.

In practice, the distinction is moderated, and emphasis has been given first to one, then to the other. It is doubtful that politics has ever been fully in command among China's nuclear scientists and among others working at advanced levels. They were among the least disrupted in their work during the Cultural Revolution (1966–68). At levels where technical requirements are not so great, the combination with politics has been more pronounced. Experts have been given a relatively freer hand in times of greatest difficulty, as in the early 1950s and just after the Great Leap Forward. In times of mass campaigns—during the Great Leap and the Cultural Revolution—"reds" are more extensively in control. Since Mao's death and the purge of "the gang of four," the stock of the experts seems to have risen somewhat.

An aspect of Chinese development which has caught the attention of Americans and other Westerners is that of small-scale industry, using low or intermediate technologies and geared closely to the needs of agricultural development. Proclaimed as self-reliant, using local resources, and depending on the ingenuity of peasants, workers, and technicians, these small plants sum up what is most characteristic in the Chinese model—a kind of Maoist guerrilla-warfare style of economic development. A rational case can be made for this approach, at least for the medium-term future.

Much of rural China is just beginning to modernize. Transportation is still too inadequate and too costly to permit full reliance on large, centralized industry; labor can be used on the spot, without swelling urban populations; local industries are flexible in the use of local resources and in meeting local needs; and relatively balanced development throughout China may be enhanced. Among a rural population with little experience in machine production, these simple technologies also have an important training function. They can quickly be felt to belong naturally in one's immediate environment, not as wonderful and exotic imports, and they are capable of being thoroughly understood and mastered by those who work with them. These technologies, of the type so long taken for granted in the United States that they hardly seem "technological" at all, can play an important role in the development of rural China, just as they did less than a century ago in the development of rural America.

On this level, the Chinese seem to feel that the United States has little to offer; what might be called the "left leg" of the walking-on-two-legs strategy is viewed as distinctively Chinese (one is reminded, however, of Indusco). Yet the weight placed on this leg should not overbalance the very great importance also attached by Chinese leaders to large-scale modern industry and high technology. Even in small-scale industry, the Chinese often state that their goals are "from small to large, from key points to overall development, from primitive to modern."

Chou En-lai's Report to the Fourth National People's Congress (January 1975) looked forward twenty-five years:

The first stage is to build an independent and relatively comprehensive industrial and economic system . . . before 1980; the second stage is to accomplish the comprehensive modernization of agriculture, industry, national defense and science and technology before the end of the century, so that our national economy will be advancing in the front ranks of the world.

These remain China's marching orders under the post-Mao leadership.

On the "right leg," there is genuine interest in American science and technology, although the pressures of experience, ideology, and the postponement of full diplomatic recognition preclude extensive publicity. Since the issuance of the Shanghai Communiqué in February 1972, there has been a surprisingly wide variety of contacts, exchanges, trade, and direct purchases. Science, high technology, and advanced industrial hardware have been central to Chinese concerns.

American interest and curiosity about China have included these areas, but have also been much broader and more intense than those on the other side. Through 1976, more than 10,000 Americans had visited China, while only about 900 Chinese citizens had come to the United States. Since the Chinese determine very largely whom they will admit as well as whom they will send, most of the control rests in their hands.

Delegations in various medical specialties, physics, earth sciences and seismology, computer sciences, entomology, plant studies, and others have visited China. Groups from China include these fields and also lasers, molecular biology, petrochemicals, industrial automation. These delegations usually remain in the host country for about a month, observing rather than doing substantive work with their counterparts. Individual U.S. citizens in fields of particular interest to China have been invited directly. A large proportion of the trade from the United States to China is in such areas as oil drilling and pipeline gear, computerized equipment for oil and gas exploration, satellite-communications components, gear- and axle-producing machinery, and large mining trucks.

China's most spectacular purchases in the United States were in 1972 for ten Boeing 707/320 aircraft and spare parts ($125 million), and in 1973 for eight large ammonia plants from the M. W. Kellogg Company, a division of Pullman Inc. ($205 million). Unlike most items of trade, these two large purchases involved technical personnel. The Chinese sent a number of aircraft specialists to Seattle to learn the 707 systems, and Kellogg has technicians in the western province of Szechwan, where the plants are being installed as key elements in very large chemical fertilizer complexes. In late 1976, Control Data Corporation sold China a Cyber computer that may have defense applications.

Nevertheless, the past continues to intrude on the present. Conditioned by its experience of foreign debt, China pays cash or accepts only short-term credits. Conditioned by her memory of dependency, she diversifies her purchases of technology among a number of advanced industrial nations, such as Japan and West Germany. Her own personnel are expected to take full charge as soon as possible (sometimes, Americans have felt, too soon). Foreign investments and joint ventures are unwelcome. One is reminded of the nineteenth century attitude: "If we can manufacture, repair, and use them, then they are our weapons. If we cannot . . . then they are still the weapons of others." In many fields of technology, the Chinese have drawn significantly on the outside world, but they have thus far sought to minimize penetration by other influences which might come along with it.

These limitations are also evident in the cultural field, which the Chinese have defined largely as the performing arts, athletics, and exhibitions, most notably the stunning exhibition of archaeological finds displayed during 1974–75 in Washington, Kansas City, and San Francisco. A few delegations in the social sciences and humanities have been sent to China—linguistics, early childhood development, art, and archaeology—largely upon repeated request by the U.S. side. From China, only delegations of librarians and language teachers fall into this category. Although most of these cultural exchanges have been warmly received, they have sometimes been troubled—just as trade relations have been—by continuing impediments in U.S.-China relations generally. The tour of a performing arts troupe was canceled by the U.S. State Department when the Chinese insisted at the last minute upon including a song about the liberation of Taiwan. A delegation of U.S. mayors was denied permission to visit China because it included the mayor of San Juan, Puerto Rico, which the Chinese regard as an imperialist colony of the United States.

Between the conclusion of the unequal treaties and 1949, the Chinese had little voice in who came to China, for what purposes, or what they did there. This is no longer the case, and whatever changes may occur, it seems unlikely that China's doors will once again be thrown open as they were in the past. China never accepted all that was presented to her; now she is choosing carefully what she will permit to be presented. Broad exposure to American culture and society are not included.

Concluding Thoughts

In uncritical moments, some observers of Chinese development fall into a faddish, trendy admiration, as though its very Chineseness conferred a special validity upon it. Part of the appeal for them lies in its perceived revolutionary critique of postindustrial, high-technology America. To some, the Chinese model embodies virtues of simplicity, frugality, and egalitarianism that rebuke the wastefulness, profit-orientation, and competitive individualism they feel characterize American life. This seems to be the latest manifestation of the idea that the spiritual values of the East are somehow superior to the materialistic values of the West—an interesting twist when the example is China, which subscribes to a doctrine of scientific materialism.

Even when these appeals exert less force, there is recognition that some Chinese methods are effective, although there may be disagreement over the reasons for their effectiveness.

Does one take Chinese explanations at face value? Or can one find in these explanations something understandable in our own terms? For example, in many American factories, incentive bonuses are given to workers who suggest practical improvements. Might this not be our equivalent to what the Chinese mean by "relying on the masses for technological innovation?" Or does one simply dismiss these explanations as ideological cant? Certainly, some observers—usually those most firmly attached to the idea that the American way is the only way—are apt to dismiss Chinese methods simply because they are different, and to view their explanations as mere rhetoric.

In the middle ground between uncritical admiration and summary dismissal is the position that Chinese examples can provide Americans with a broadened sense of question and a heightened sense of human possibility. The questions China is asking in the course of her cultural and technological modernization are in many cases her versions of the questions we ask ourselves—however different the answers may be. In this view, Chinese solutions are not seen as directly applicable to our problems, but awareness of Chinese problems and attempted solutions may give us a better perspective on our own predicaments.

In a society marked by substantial consensus concerning values, goals, and the nature of the good society, agreements are easier to reach as to the sorts of task which will help to achieve this shared vision. How to get the job done then becomes the main issue, because the value of the job itself is already agreed upon. This is the kind of society in which technology as technique is least questioned. But when there are deep disagreements over the nature of society and its goals, the value of a particular task can no longer be taken for granted. Since technology as technique is by definition goal oriented, disagreement as to goals will raise fundamental questions about its use, control, and consequence.

In short, low consensus raises problems of technology as

culture. Such consensus is lower in the United States than it used to be, and those who do not share it are more vocal than they used to be. China is trying to develop her own consensus after a century of disintegration. Postindustrial America is therefore asking some of the same kinds of questions as modernizing China.

One of the most fundamental of these questions is whether or not technological modernization and industrialization can be accomplished in China consistent with a vision of society radically different from those of other developed nations. Or does modernization carry within it an inexorable logic that ultimately must transform society in ways now familiar to Americans? It was Mao's conviction—Mao's gamble—that China must modernize differently. He sought to overcome China's backwardness, but he also saw in that very backwardness an opportunity to avoid the extreme exploitation of man by man which characterized China's past and the early stages of development in the West (recall Dickens' London, or the slavery, sweatshops, and child labor of nineteenth-century America). China is, he said, "poor and blank," and on this blankness one can "write all sorts of beautiful words."

Implicit in the Maoist vision is a society much more controlled, more lacking in personal liberties and individual free choice, than American society, but one which also seeks the wide and equitable sharing of modernization's burdens and benefits. Perhaps, in a nation of 900 million, unrestrained individualism would lead eventually to a society resembling old China or India. We might also reflect that in our own society, equal opportunities for access to the benefits of progress has been a long and tortuous struggle, incomplete even today.

The issue of modernization has been joined in China; the outcome is not yet known. In one of his most reflective moments, Mao Tse-tung remarked to Edgar Snow in 1965 that events did not always move in accordance with the individual human will, and that although he did not hope for counter-revolution, "future events would be decided by future generations."

It used to be that China was seen as exotic, strange, a place where everything was done backwards or upside down. China is still different, all right, but it is no longer a difference that defines China's irrelevance to the United States. As the late Joseph Levenson once wrote, China is worth studying "because—without making the same designs—it can be seen to make sense in the same world of discourse in which we try to make sense of the West." [11] If we can create this expanded world of discourse, our social, cultural, and technological interactions may take place in an atmosphere at once more realistic about our differences, more tolerant toward them, and more aware of what we can learn from each other.

[11] Joseph Levenson, "The Genesis of *Confucian China and its Modern Fate*," in L. P. Curtis, Jr., ed., *The Historian's Workshop* (New York: Knopf, 1970), p. 284.

7

WALDO H. HEINRICHS, JR.

The Use and Threat
of Force in
Sino-American Relations

MILITARY interaction has been one constant in the fitful dialogue between China and the United States, ever since 1844 when Caleb Cushing arrived to negotiate the first treaty with China aboard the U.S.S. *Brandywine*. Through war, police action, and sheer military presence, the United States has shaped China's relations with the West. More recently it has been substantially affected by Chinese military power. This unbroken record of military interaction illuminates patterns of Sino-American behavior beyond the depth of ordinary diplomatic intercourse.

Imperial Beginnings: 1844–1921

China and the United States approached each other with completely different conceptions of national security. For the United States, the nineteenth century provided expanding horizons. Remote from great power rivalries, shielded by a trade-minded Britain, and bounded by receding empires and weak successor states, the growing nation enjoyed an era of "free security." Only rarely and briefly before 1900 did Americans confront foreign invasion or threat to national survival. A small professional army excluded from politics, really a frontier defense force, usually sufficed. The navy, exempt from coastal defense, could roam the seas protecting commerce and assisting national growth. While for Americans the world represented boundless opportunity, for the Chinese it presented only menace. Foreign pressures along their inner Asian frontiers and 2,000-mile seacoast were unremitting, indeed intensifying, as were internal disorder and disaffection. Military strength, the foundation of alien Manchu rule, had been weakened by the nineteenth century and had to be desperately augmented to save China and the Ch'ing regime itself. Yet military force always proved insufficient to keep the foreign barbarians at arm's length, and China was left with little means of defense except resilience, cleverness, and its sheer size. For China, security became central to its perception of the world, for the United States it was peripheral.

The Sino-American military encounter began on the China coast by way of the American navy. It began not in fulfillment of a distinct American China policy but indirectly, obscurely, almost casually, in the wake of the booming East Indies trade and British men-of-war.

Britain first employed force as it led the Western penetration of China. Seeking extension of trade with least cost and political involvement, the British endeavored to protect their nationals and property and to develop a Sino-Western treaty system which would guarantee an orderly accessible market and be enforced by the Chinese themselves. The British adopted the tactic of gunboat diplomacy and occasional full-scale war—an awe-inspiring method of pressuring Peking while not intending to undercut the authority of the Ch'ing dynasty. In the Opium and Arrow Wars and local interventions of the mid-nineteenth century, Britain showed it was ready to use all necessary force. As long as Peking recognized British military readiness to intervene, the summoning of a warship and a protest at Peking usually were sufficient. A severe crisis would precipitate a large display of warships from several treaty powers, calling up of reinforcements from India, and joint regulations at the capital. But ordinarily an armed presence was enough. Garrisons, parades, ceremonial visits, and the semiannual migration of warships up and down the China coast were tangible reminders of the constraints on Chinese behavior.

In the case of the United States, the flag followed the trader, and Americans followed the British. Policy for China was undifferentiated from policy toward the outer, non-European world. The United States Navy was well schooled in the display of strength as a means of calming non-European peoples and mounted an impressive expedition to open Japan, but generally warships used their guns only in response to particular threats to American mariners and shipping. Quite apart from traditions of nonentanglement and anti-imperialism, American officials saw no advantage in sharing the burden of treaty enforcement in China when they could enjoy its fruits through the most-favored-nation clause of the treaties at no cost in risk or commitment.

In fact British and American naval activity in China differed more in degree than in kind. From 1835 onward the United States navy stationed a permanent force in East Asian waters. This East Indies Squadron, later the Asiatic Squadron, was composed of a handful of assorted vessels that cruised singly up and down the China coast. The British kept as many as nine times the number on the same station. Nevertheless, the American squadron landed marines on at least eight occasions in China before the Boxer upheaval, and its value as an enforcer of treaty rights was readily apparent to American diplomats at Peking. American commanders were ordered to use force only as a last resort, but under that order, Commander James Armstrong thought it necessary to storm the barrier forts at Canton in 1856. In 1883 the commander of an American gunboat took the lead in organizing defense of the foreign settlement at Canton. The very appearance of an American vessel among Western warships, even though it was forbidden to cooperate, suggested American participation in an international police force. From the perspective of Washington, the United States stood apart from European imperialism in China, benevolent, sparing in the use of force, and minding its own business. For the Chinese, the difference between joint Western treaty enforcement and direct protection of American interests was hardly apparent.

At the turn of the twentieth century American overseas expansion intensified great power rivalries in East Asia, and the looming breakup of the Middle Kingdom drew American attention to China as never before. China was now seen variously as the balance in a cataclysmic struggle for world supremacy, as the great untapped market, as the Gibraltar of heathendom, and as the final frontier of Western, or white, civilization. One could look forward to stability and mutual prosperity from an intact and receptive China or the grim prospect of China's immense potential harnessed by hostile powers. Most Americans continued to picture China in caricature if at all, but among those oriented toward East Asia by bureaucratic, professional, or economic interest, such new perspectives carried weight. As Warren Cohen's essay indicates, a large view of American interest in China gained currency in the Far Eastern wing of the

State Department, among army officers serving in the Philippines, and in the navy. The naval mind, bred on the seapower maxims of Alfred Thayer Mahan, shuttled easily between the idea that protection of China's future was critical for the United States and required a great navy and the idea that precisely such a transoceanic mission was necessary to secure budgets for a great fleet. Running through the differing perspectives of America's Asianists was one thread that tied them all together: the Open Door policy of Chinese integrity and equality of trade, which established the claim of the United States to a role in Chinese affairs. And at the foundation of the Open Door were the military forces that upheld it. Wilsonian foreign policy, while rejecting the old imperialist diplomacy, clung to the existing treaty order in China. The idealists simply reinforced the realists in consolidating and extending the American armed presence in and near China.

After 1898 the United States steadily became a more visible and active enforcer of the treaty system in China. The Philippines provided a secure naval base and ready reserve of troops. The Asiatic Squadron, though composed of light ships, grew to a fleet of twenty-six vessels by 1920 with a full admiral commanding to "make face" for the Americans on the China coast. Yangtze patrols began in 1891 and extended all the way to Chungking by 1928 with specially built, shallow-draft gunboats. The American commander was under orders to cooperate closely with his British and Japanese counterparts for coordinated protection of foreigners along the river. A major departure was American participation in the Boxer Relief Expedition. More than 6,000 American troops were dispatched, approximately one-fourth the total, and some 2,000 marched to Peking under foreign command to lift the siege of the legations. In 1912 the Fifteenth Infantry Regiment landed at Tientsin to secure the railroad from Peking to the sea and remained as a permanent garrison.

It was a one-sided encounter. The only time American

troops confronted organized forces—Imperial bannermen and Boxers in the relief of Peking—the Chinese repeatedly fell back in disarray. Usually violence was local and spontaneous, furious mobs setting on helpless missionaries, each outburst bringing deeper, more settled American intrusion. Such was the pattern of Sino-American military interaction from the turn of the century to the twenties. Fair words about democracy and self-determination might encourage Chinese diplomats, but the reality spoke otherwise. In 1923, when the Nationalists at Canton seized foreign-controlled revenues, the United States responded with a display of force. The Americans might have sent a Lafayette, Sun Yat-sen bitterly commented, but instead sent an admiral "with more ships of war than any other nation in our waters." A China incapable of organized resistance and engaging in wanton brutality elicited American contempt. For Chinese, the Stars and Stripes multiplying in port cities and inland waterways sharpened the image of America as a Western imperialist.

Glancing Encounters: 1921–50

Before World War I, American Far Eastern policy had a speculative, theoretical quality. It related to international standing, future opportunities, and possible contingencies. In the 1920s the Nationalist phase of the Chinese revolution and then Japanese imperial expansion tested that policy and its military underpinnings against the hard facts and immediate necessities of vital interest and national security.

The Northern Expedition of the Kuomintang in 1926–27 threatened Western lives and property throughout China and the entire treaty system. The Chinese revolutionary movement, which had foundered from 1900 to 1924 for lack of a strong military component to contain domestic warlords and imperialist forces, had developed a potent army with Russian advice in the mid-1920s. Now confronting Chinese forces capable of sustained attack with modern weapons, marching in the vanguard of intense Chinese nationalism, the treaty powers found themselves divided. During the Nanking incident of 1927, British and American destroyers laid down a curtain of fire to cover escape of their nationals and threatened bombardment of military objectives unless foreigners were permitted to evacuate the city. This far, protection of lives, the Coolidge administration was prepared to go, but no farther. In the face of public opinion strongly opposed to intervention in the Chinese civil war, the U.S. government denied protection to property and refused cooperation with other powers in enforcing the treaty system as a whole. By 1928, bowing to Nationalist success, the West was prepared to go far in conceding China equality of status by extending diplomatic recognition to the Nationalists' Republic of China at Nanking. Even so, treaty revision was gradual. The Nanking government found a community of interest with the treaty ports in the capital resources they commanded and the Western stake in China they represented in the face of Japanese encroachment. So the old imperial sway was gone, but American gunboats and garrisons were allowed to remain.

Indeed, they remained until Pearl Harbor, hostage to an ambivalent Far Eastern policy. As American military planners grappled with the geographic, political, and strategic determinants of war with its most likely East Asian enemy, Japan, they found again and again, indeed from decade to decade, that Asiatic defense was a dubious proposition. Many military strategists assumed that Japan would precipitate war, most likely from a clash of interests in China. The United States, an isolationist nation investing meagerly in armed forces, would be on the defensive initially and would need time to marshall its fleet for a thrust into the Western Pacific and decisive engagement with the Japanese fleet. In the meantime, Japan would pounce on the Asiatic Fleet and the Philippines. Given this dismal overture, American armed forces in Asia seemed not only anachronistic with respect to the emerging China but also a liability in case of war with Japan. Meanwhile, the Chinese Nationalist forces were fighting a losing cause against Japan, the most aggressive imperialist power they had confronted. By the mid-1930s Japan had conquered Manchuria and portions of North China, and in 1937 the Japanese imperial army invaded China in force, taking the major coastal cities and forcing Chiang's armies to their southwestern retreat in Chungking.

The Franklin D. Roosevelt administration was determined not to scuttle and run, but it was equally determined to avoid war with Japan. "In no circumstances should we indicate any intention . . . to weaken ourselves in the Orient," White House strategists concluded in 1934. When the question of pulling out the China garrisons came up in 1936, the State Department insisted that withdrawal would further break down the treaty system which legitimated collective action to uphold the integrity of China. Thus, American armed forces in China emerged as a symbol of the position in principle which Cordell Hull was carefully constructing as a basis for opposition to Japan. American garrisons at Shanghai, Tientsin, and Peking constituted, according to a State Department official in 1941, "the keystone to the whole structure of the Occidental position in Japanese-occupied China." Withdrawal would be taken as a sign of American intention either to employ armed force on a large scale or to abandon China. The last contingents remained until the eve of Pearl Harbor and indeed some were trapped in China by the war.

The Chungking interlude, 1941–45, was a world turned upside down. Westerners had come to China by sea, with the mobility and firepower to secure footholds where they chose along more than 2,000 miles of coast. Now General Joseph Stilwell's command was locked in the interior of China eking out a war with matériel flown over the Hump, and, like the Chinese, confronting the foreign barbarian on the coast. Formerly the American military had been confined to strategic enclaves, now it drilled Chinese armies and planned frontal warfare. Before, China had been the favorite of the United States Navy while the army held out for perimeter defense in the eastern Pacific. Now generals ran the China theater while admirals fought blue-water battles.

In spite of great American hopes for postwar China—as a market, a democratic protégé, a stabilizing force in East Asia—its importance to the United States during World War II always boiled down to its usefulness in prosecuting the war on Japan. As a theater of war China was virtually inaccessible and initially appeared less critical than defensive campaigns in the Pacific, aid to Russia, opening the Mediterranean, and preparing for the invasion of Europe. Still, Chiang Kai-shek, warning of collapse, demanded massive assistance, and the president dared not call his bluff. More difficult than preventing China's capitulation, however, was gaining its active participation. Fighting had practically ceased on the China fronts, permitting Japan to draw off reinforcements for the Solomons, New Guinea, and the central Pacific. Roosevelt wanted the Chinese armies to pin down the Japanese by offensive action, and he wanted air bases from which to engage the Japanese air force and destroy shipping.

Two strategies for prosecuting the war in China competed for presidential favor in 1942 and 1943. The first, championed by General Joseph Stilwell, envisaged slow, solid, painful conquest and development of a long route to China through north Burma. Chinese divisions in Yunnan, trained by Americans and supplied across the Hump, would first assist in opening the route and then constitute the main force for an advance into East China to secure air bases for the assault on Japan. The Stilwell approach promised, ultimately, wide-ranging results in territory retaken, the effectiveness of the Chinese army, the power base of Chinese politics, and the strength and stability of the Chinese state. It would involve the United States intimately in China's future. The second approach, that of the air force commander in China, General Claire Chennault, worried less about land routes and base security and allocated the bulk of Hump tonnage to an early air offensive. The Chennault approach emphasized strategic focal points such as Calcutta, Ledo, Kunming, and the cluster of airfields northwest of Canton. It treated China like a vast terrestrial extension of the Pacific Ocean and sent American power island-hopping across it. It entailed far less American impact on China, keeping Chinese and American operations distinct and leaving Chiang's armies and regime largely untouched.

Roosevelt, as usual, rejected neither approach, but he put the emphasis on Chennault's. Chiang resisted the Stilwell strategy because it threatened to upset the delicate equilibrium of warlord power on which the Generalissimo's authority rested. Roosevelt was disposed to conciliate Chiang during the first desperate years of the war, but he had his own preference for quick results. He likened Chennault's air strategy to Operation Torch, the seizure of North Africa, and the analogy is significant, for Torch too was more concerned with the geographical advantages of the territory in relation to ulterior military objectives than with its intrinsic political significance. When Chennault promised to sink or damage more than a million tons of Japanese shipping, the president banged his fist on the desk and chortled, "If you can sink a million tons, we'll break their backs."

With the Teheran Conference in late 1943, the military significance of China began to fade. There Roosevelt was encouraged to believe that he could gain Soviet cooperation in the defeat of Japan; at Yalta in 1945 he secured a commitment. In 1944 the American drive in the Pacific finally gained momentum. In July, Saipan fell, and in January 1945 the B-29s in China moved to the Marianas for more effective prosecution of the air offensive against Japan. The tortuous pace of the Burma campaign, the apathy of the British, the obstructionism of Chiang, his outrageous demands, and the Japanese seizure of the east China airfields all contributed to the sense that the China war was hardly worth the candle. China simply did not provide sufficient military advantage in time and slipped into a backwater of American strategic thinking. At the Cairo Conference in 1943 during one of Chiang's innumerable tiffs, Stilwell pleaded for American combat troops in China, and the president, perhaps sardonically, offered him a brigade of marines for Chungking.

One casualty of the swift ending of the war was the idea advanced by foreign service officers in China, among them John Service and John Davies, of military assistance to the Communists as a means of increasing the Chinese effort against the Japanese, inducing Kuomintang reform, and preventing Yenan from falling back on the support of the Soviet Union. Roosevelt policy makers were dubious; it seemed a risky involvement in Chinese internal strife. Interest in assisting Yenan rose briefly in the wake of the Japanese offensive in China of 1944 and the ensuing Kuomintang political crisis but waned in the spring of 1945 when the Japanese pulled back their armies into North China for a last stand.

The idea of assisting China to become a unified, secure, stable, modern nation always came out second best with Roosevelt. He wished for that end, but in truth, that objective was less important than the defeat of Germany and Japan and postwar relations among existing great powers. During World War II, China held for the United States essentially a functional military significance.

The critical American role in the Nationalist recovery of China at the end of the war can be partially explained by the sheer momentum of American military assistance. Operations already under way for opening a south China port were easily shifted for northward deployment of Kuomintang armies. The landing of 53,000 American marines with air support in north China was a different matter. This powerful combat force denied the Communists control of vital territory until Nationalist troops could be ferried in. The American aim here was in line with the larger Truman strategy of establishing stakes for hard bargaining with the Soviet Union. An American armed presence in China would be a counter to ensure Soviet withdrawal from Manchuria as well as a means of preventing division of China between the Kuomintang and a Communist regime in the north dependent on the Soviets. This major intervention in Chinese internal affairs seemed justified as a temporary expedient, honorably assisting America's Asian ally in taking surrender of the Japanese invaders on its own soil. American expectations of postwar collaboration with the Soviet Union within the Yalta framework were in any case based on the legitimacy of the Chungking government and the unity of China.

By late 1945 the United States was fast sliding down the slope of intervention in the Chinese revolution. Having established the marines in north China, Truman faced the embarrassing problem of getting them out. It became evident that Nationalist troops would be unable to hold the north without American help. To withdraw the marines the United States would have to carry in more Nationalist armies and plunge deeper into the struggle for the north. This dilemma precipitated the mission of General George Marshall, which sought a political settlement on the basis of an enlarged and reformed Kuomintang government. Marshall was instructed to keep secret the plans for transporting the Generalissimo's troops as a means of inducing him to reform, but the decision was taken nonetheless to ensure ultimate Kuomintang control of China. Lacking leverage and constrained to finding a solution only on a basis Chiang was willing to concede, Marshall had no possibility of success. Upon his failure, the last marines were withdrawn and the United States left Chinese internal forces to find their own equilibrium, not without first weighting the balance with arms and money in favor of the Kuomintang.

American policy in China had a profound effect on Chinese history in the aftermath of the war. Denial of aid to the Communists, massive military assistance to the Kuomintang, indirect support for it during the Marshall mission, and direct military intervention in north China made the outcome of the revolution slower and more painful. In Communist eyes, tank landing craft carrying the First Marine Division across Taku Bar in September 1945 simply extended a consistent pattern of American imperialism in China. To the Americans, China remained an inchoate state at the margins of American strategic concerns. Disillusioned in their hope for a unified China as a stabilizing force in East Asia, they sought at least a neutralized China that would not be a bone of contention among the great powers. Failing that, the United States still rested secure in its conquest of the Pacific and its carriers, atomic bombs, and island bases rimming East Asia. What appeared as persistent military intrusions to the Chinese were, in the American global perspective, mere glancing encounters.

Confrontation and Adaptation: 1950–71

During World War II and its aftermath most American observers in China and almost all back home had missed a crucial military development in the Chinese revolution—the growth of a potent Chinese Communist army, using both conventional and guerrilla tactics, based on popular support in much of north China by the mid-1940s. Relying largely on its growing numbers and captured weapons rather than outside support, the Communist forces moved rapidly into Manchuria and north China in 1945–47, and then in 1947–49 began pushing the Nationalist forces southward, and eventually forcing Chiang's retreat to Taiwan and providing the military strength behind the establishment of the People's Republic of China. For the first time in almost two centuries, China was unified and had a potent military arm capable of defending its borders.

The confrontation soon came in Korea when China felt called upon to defend itself against onrushing American troops approaching the Yalu River. Against North Korea and China, American forces reached 300,000 and suffered 142,000 battle casualties, the Chinese losing perhaps four times the number. The United States sought to contain China and East Asian communism with an encircling alliance system, air and missile bases, naval patrols, client armies, and economic sanctions. It supported overflights and clandestine missions to the mainland. Both sides engaged in heated invective and propaganda and fostered sinister public images of the adversary. Yet the militarized relationship of 1950–71 was profoundly different from previous encounters because the United States now respected China's will and capacity to fight. Furthermore, governing elites on both sides developed an awareness of the constraints on military action, sensitivity to each other's interests, and deliberation, caution, and sophistication in signaling intentions and managing crises.

A complacent attitude about China prevailed in Washington in the spring of 1950. By then the United States pursued a global Cold War strategy which cast the People's Republic in a Moscow-directed Communist conspiracy for world domination. China would provide a "springboard" for Communist expansion into south and southeast Asia. But hopes for Chinese Titoism persisted and Americans saw the new Communist state as too weak and disorganized to present any immediate threat. Subversion in Indochina gave more concern than Korea, and Communist threats in Europe and the Middle East more concern than both. Taiwan might succumb to the Chinese Communists, but its loss was bearable. With the North Korean attack in June 1950, President Harry S. Truman swiftly sent the Seventh Fleet into the Taiwan Straits, but as much to leash Chiang's Nationalists as to protect them, as well as to avoid the political embarrassment of an ultimate "loss of China" while Korea was being defended. General Douglas MacArthur was not leashed. After his troops crossed the 38th parallel he was ordered in case of major Chinese intervention to continue the campaign as long as it offered reasonable chance of success.

In spite of, or rather more because of, a century of military involvement in China, the United States was completely unprepared for the Chinese onslaught in Korea on November 25, 1950. In 1945, Secretary of War Robert Patterson had boasted that the American marines in north China "could walk from one end of China to the other without serious hindrance." The contempt for Chinese military capacity reflected in that remark permeated the American military outlook, as did confidence in air power and superior military technology. Given American disgust with Kuomintang inefficiency and corruption, the American verdict on the civil war was that the Nationalists lost it, not that the Communists won it. Viewing China as a new dimension of Soviet power, Truman policy makers gave little weight to purely Chinese interests and security concerns. In spite of a carefully orchestrated attempt by Peking to warn the United States not to cross the 38th parallel and a limited intervention in October to permit American reconsideration, MacArthur plunged north for the Yalu River. Only with the humiliating retreat of American forces out of the North Korean mountains and down the peninsula did the United States begin to grapple with the idea of China as a significant, independent factor in world affairs.

During the first year of the Korean War the tide of battle

swayed up and down the peninsula in steadily smaller swings. In the spring of 1951 the front stabilized at a halfway point, intersecting the 38th parallel but mostly north of it. For two years thereafter bargaining in the truce tent set the rhythm of battle. Both sides fought intensely, but intermittently and selectively, in a conflict of trenches and terrain features—Old Baldy, Heartbreak Ridge, the Punchbowl—to strengthen defense lines, prove determination, and inflict casualties. The object became the coercion not the destruction of the enemy. Each side recognized that the further the enemy was pushed back, the greater his advantage from shortened supply lines and the greater the risk of wider war. The Chinese weighed success in protecting their frontiers and a neighboring Communist state and fighting their chief imperialist foe to a standstill against awesome casualties and debilitation of their meager resources. The United States, having proven its will to resist aggression, recognized the upper limits of conflict as well. Public opinion and the demands of global containment made it impossible to keep seven divisions pinned down in Korea indefinitely, let alone mount a knockout punch. Thus, strategic stalemate satisfied the minimal requirements of both sides. The line of battle was accepted as the prospective truce line as early as November 1951. The antagonists confined ground combat to the waist of Korea and air actions to North Korea while the negotiators wrangled on remaining issues. Separately China and the United States had pursued the same logic and come to accept the same determinants of their encounter, an entirely new experience in their relationship. For complicated reasons, fighting continued for twenty bitter months after agreement on a truce line. Stalin's death in March 1953 unlocked the negotiations at Panmunjom.

The negotiations at Panmunjom were a bleak beginning to the era of equality in Sino-American relations. It was a frigid encounter: no small talk or amenities, rarely a moment of humor, mostly acerbic exchanges and incessant Communist harangues. On one occasion both sides stared at each other in silence for more than two hours. After signing the armistice, the delegation leaders simply "locked glances for a moment" and left. Nevertheless, when policy permitted, the negotiators engaged in brisk horse-trading and compromise. The Americans shifted from perceiving their adversaries as "Orientals" who should be allowed a "golden bridge" of retreat to "save face" to taking them as hard-bitten Communists. Rigid insistence on equality by the Chinese–North Korean team, even to the point of erecting equally fancy lavatories, made an impression. Altogether the Korean War resulted in profound changes of attitude. The Chinese, in spite of their success, reflected on their inferiority. Revolutionary élan was not enough by itself in confronting the withering firepower of the Eighth Army; the People's Liberation Army had to be professionalized and modernized. The change in American military attitude is reflected in an intelligence report of the Second Infantry Division which concluded that the Chinese soldier was tactically proficient, well led, brave, resourceful, and "tough."

The keystone of the Sino-American military encounter for the balance of the 1950s was deterrence. The image of monolithic Communist menace persisted, but with Red China now seen as a particularly unstable, aggressive element. The strategy devised by Eisenhower policy makers to meet this threat was a nontheoretical and more militant form of "containment." The United States should not conform to Communist initiatives, they insisted; there must be no more Koreas. In a struggle of indefinite duration, the nation should husband its resources and stand free to resort to massive retaliation with means and at places of its own choosing. It should not try to match Asian with American armies but play from its strongest suit, sea-air-nuclear capability. The "New Look" strategy called for withdrawal and reduction of ground forces, arming of client states on the Communist periphery, development of tactical and hydrogen nuclear weapons, and expansion of the air force to fifty-five strategic bomber wings. B-47 jets with a combat radius of 2,000 miles would bring all China's great cities within range of Okinawa, the Philippines, and other bases. B-52s coming into production could reach 1,500 miles farther. Carrier task forces would provide roving bases for additional nuclear might. It was a strategy tailored for the air force and a carrier-minded navy. Needless to say, the army dissented. Eisenhower and his principal advisers believed that such awesome destructive power together with the explicit intention of using it would convince the Soviet Union and China that armed adventure was too dangerous.

The threat was entirely apparent to Peking, which intently studied American pronouncements and military deployments. More than ever American power seemed to encircle China like a "stretched-out snake," setting off pure resonances in the Chinese historical experience and Marxist-Leninist-Maoist view of the world. Lacking nuclear weapons and delivery systems, the People's Republic faced an adversary ever lengthening its lead in sophistication and destructiveness of weapons.

However, there were grounds for encouragement. So long as Peking could count on the support of its ally, Soviet nuclear weapons provided a counterdeterrent. Furthermore, the American threat was ambiguous. Eisenhower's atomic warnings in the final phase of the Korean negotiations, when peace was at last within grasp, must have seemed irrelevant and therefore mere bluster to Peking. Since China had secured a friendly covering state in North Korea without crossing the nuclear threshold, probes beyond existing frontiers were still conceivable. Chinese leaders would act with means and at times of their own choosing. They had many objectives: recovery of Chinese territories, protection of buffer states and zones, securing international acceptance, and acquisition of regional leadership, world revolutionary influence, and great power status. Both revolutionary and nationalist values were fundamental to Chinese foreign policy, but they often conflicted and the nationalist tendency prevailed. Protection and advancement of interests, especially those touching on sovereignty and security, made more immediate and vital demands and consistently received higher priority. Americans eyeing revolutionary rhetoric alone had their Cold War images confirmed while in fact China behaved rather more like Western states, pursuing national power and interest.

As Korea receded, the seven-year Franco-Vietnamese struggle in Indochina moved toward a decisive outcome, drawing Peking and Washington into a new confrontation. Each stepped up its investment of assistance and prestige, particularly Washington. The United States threatened "grave consequences" in case of overt Chinese intervention and then during the climactic siege of Dien Bien Phu warned against Communist take-over "by whatever means." Additional carriers moved to the South China Sea as administration leaders canvassed the possibility of American air strikes. Publicly they stressed the transcendent importance of Indochina: a Communist breakthrough in southeast Asia would have profound consequences, like "falling dominoes," all along Pacific–East Asian defense lines.

Behind this militant posture lay doubt and discord. American policy makers recognized that the conflict was essentially a colonialist war largely immune to outside manipulation. Threats of massive retaliation would probably deter the Chinese from open intervention, which they had no reason to consider as long as the Vietminh were winning, but would hardly force them to desist from supplying the Vietminh. Air strikes proposed by navy-air enthusiasts could not alone turn the tide, warned General Matthew Ridgway, army chief of staff and former commander in Korea. Large American ground forces would be required as well, opening another Korea. If the United States intervened and tipped the balance against the Vietminh, Korea suggested the Chinese would intervene anyway, regardless of threats. These sobering probabilities as well as reservations of congressional leaders and allies led President Dwight D. Eisenhower to decide against any combat intervention. The "New Look" simply did not mesh with the hard facts of Indochina, but at least these hard facts and not abstract imperatives determined American action.

In spite of this American marching and countermarching, the Indochina crisis had a stabilizing effect on Sino-American relations. It extended the demarcation of spheres, at least temporarily, to that volatile region. The United States was more deliberate and calculating than in Korea in communicating its intentions to Peking. Secretary of State John Foster Dulles' warning at the height of the crisis was carefully phrased to reflect American constraints so as to avoid Chinese overreaction: he predicated American action on joint intervention with allies and used the hortatory "should" rather than the imperative "must." Later, to make his threats more credible, he allowed that retaliation did not necessarily involve use of nuclear weapons, opening the range of conflict, to be sure, but providing room for maneuver below the nuclear threshold. Nevertheless, Dulles was playing a dangerous game which depended on intimidation. Circumstances in this instance permitted his adversaries to be cautious and fashion a Geneva settlement tolerable to the United States.

The next confrontation, shortly thereafter in the Taiwan Straits, pitted the United States directly against the People's Republic. On September 3, 1954, the People's Republic began shelling the Quemoy Islands, a Chinese Nationalist outpost two miles from the port of Amoy, opening eight months of artillery, air, and naval exchanges with the Nationalists, centering on these and other offshore islands held by Chiang Kai-shek. Taiwan then as now posed a fundamental challenge to the integrity and legitimacy of the People's Republic. The occasion for the assault was the particularly menacing cast of American policy in the wake of the Geneva Conference, reflected in the marshaling of the SEATO alliance, talk of liberation of the mainland to the accompaniment of raids from the offshore islands, and discussions pointing toward a Taiwan defense treaty and perhaps a Northeast Asia replica of SEATO based on China's inveterate enemy Japan. A carefully controlled probe now might uncork the trade of Amoy and Foochow, discredit the Nationalists, and test the limits of American support for Taiwan and other potential Asian client states.

Gingerly at first and then more firmly the United States picked up the challenge. Eisenhower reaffirmed orders to defend Taiwan, solidified that commitment with a defense treaty, and secured congressional authorization to use American forces to protect Taiwan and related positions. As a counterpoise to massing of troops on the mainland, Eisenhower concentrated sea and air forces in the Taiwan area, withholding American forces from the offshore fighting while sustaining Quemoy and Matsu logistically. He practically guaranteed Taipei defense of these islands against all-out attack but let Peking know that secret understandings attached to the defense treaty precluded a Nationalist attack on the mainland. At the culmination of the crisis in March 1955, Secretary Dulles construed further Communist "open armed aggression" as a decision for general war in Asia, which, the president added a week later, would entail American use of nuclear weapons against military targets. In the face of these risks, Peking backed off and called for talks, to which the United States acceded, and the fighting petered out.

It was a businesslike crisis. Unlike the runaway escalation of Korea, it built stage by stage with direct exchange of warnings and signals at each stage. Responsiveness, flexibility, and caution were in evidence on both sides. Nevertheless, in pursuit of militant containment the United States again intervened in the Chinese civil war, this time with a permanent and inflatable commitment to the Nationalists. Chiang Kai-shek stuffed 55,000 of his best troops into the offshore islands which then drew in American protection like a magnet. Their loss, it was feared, would be an intolerable blow to Nationalist strength and morale. Since Peking could not limit its public intent to the offshore islands without damaging its claim to Taiwan and Washington believed it could not defend Taiwan without extending its commitment to the offshore islands, the two issues fused. In place of an ocean buffer 100 miles wide, the Sino-American confrontation settled on a line alongside the beaches of the mainland. That precarious American commitment, publicly sanctioned only by ambiguous language in the Formosa (Taiwan) Resolution, formed the basis of a chilling nuclear threat. Diplomacy was frozen out of the Taiwan problem; confrontation was built in.

The Chinese military power in this confrontation grew rapidly in the 1950s. The Chinese People's Liberation Army (PLA) had developed an infantry force of 2.7 million well-drilled troops led by a highly professionalized officer corps—a far cry from the guerrilla armies of the 1930s and early 1940s. The PLA was also equipped with light and medium weaponry including artillery and tanks developed on Soviet models. And in 1956, Mao committed the People's Republic to the development of nuclear weapons within a decade (the first Chinese atomic bomb was detonated in October 1964).

Crisis resumed in the Taiwan Straits on August 23, 1958, when the People's Republic began sustained shelling of Quemoy with a two-hour barrage of 41,000 rounds. This second crisis was basically a replay of the first, with certain distinguishing features. Peking's resumption stemmed from the revolutionary militancy of the Great Leap Forward, confidence in enhanced Soviet nuclear capability after Sputnik, and probably too from the provocative effect of American deployment to Taiwan in 1957 of Matador nuclear missiles capable of reaching mainland coastal areas. Nevertheless, this probe was even more careful than the first, limited to starving Quemoy by artillery siege, thereby placing on the United States the onus of escalating to save the island. Eisenhower, no less determined to hold fast, ordered a heavy concentration of strength on Taiwan, including a buildup to five carriers, installation of Nike surface-to-air missiles, and arming of Nationalist planes with the deadly heat-seeking Sidewinder missile. This time, however, his warnings were more muted and vague, reflecting growing sensitivity to the risks and domestic liabilities of "brinkmanship" over an isolated outpost. On September 4, while rallying the home front with visions of disaster in case of the loss of the islands, worse even than the "loss" of China in 1949, Eisenhower and Dulles suggested resumption of the U.S.-People's Republic ambassadorial talks at Warsaw, and Peking agreed.

During the following two weeks, the United States, matching Communist tactical innovation with technological innovation of its own, succeeded in reversing its unfavorable position at Quemoy. The trick was preloaded, tracked amphibious craft manned by Nationalists. After American convoying to the three-mile limit, these debouched from landing ships, darted through the shellfire, and scurried ashore to inland unloading areas. The scheme worked. By September 21 the siege was lifted and Peking soon deescalated to a temporary cease-fire and then intermittent shelling. The second Taiwan Straits crisis, tightly and jointly managed, demonstrated how far the two sides had come in adapting to confrontation. By reaffirming and reinforcing the existing order in that sector, it had a stabilizing effect. It was an order providing a shaky foundation for peace, however, and one now all the more impervious to diplomacy.

The eruption of the Sino-Soviet dispute in 1960 fundamentally altered the international political terrain but not Sino-American relations. So deeply set was the preconception of a dichotomous world engraved with lines of containment that polycentrism barely penetrated New Frontier thinking.

Peking's attack on India in 1962 and support for revolution in Laos and Vietnam reinforced the image of Chinese aggressiveness. Strategic missions and hence budgets of the air force and navy were based on the premise of a monolithic Communist bloc; China's arrival as a nuclear power in 1964 simply justified enlargement of nuclear capability for deployment to the Pacific. The U.S. Army, a restraining force in the confrontations of 1954–55, developed "hawks" of its own, some pressing for a counterinsurgency mission, others contending that Korean-type wars could be won by highly mobile forces. Realistic appraisals of the dangers posed by the People's Republic contended with exaggerated estimates from military information networks fed by self-interested defense communities in client states like Taiwan.

The People's Republic of China was not in fact disposed to conciliation in the decade after 1957. This period from the Great Leap Forward through economic crises of the early 1960s to the Cultural Revolution was one of dissidence, disaffection, and acute leadership struggles within China. Internal troubles made China feel more vulnerable externally. Encircling enemies were suspected of aggressive collusion. Short of Soviet support, exposed to threats from all quarters, at times isolated and introverted, China assumed a defiant and revolutionary posture in world affairs. Yet throughout this forbidding period, as before, frontier security received first attention, and in this area the Chinese were never adventuristic.

Vietnam tested that caution to the utmost. Rapid American escalation in 1964–65 brought Peking to the brink of war. Indeed, when acute warnings of the type used in Korea failed to deter the United States, the People's Republic resorted to limited intervention. The Chinese air force assisted North Vietnam with sanctuary airfields and coordinated defense of the border zone. These measures could not prevent devastating bombing of the north but influenced the American decision to extend the air campaign northward step by step, giving

Hanoi time to prepare, and for most of the war spared a buffer zone in the far north, easing movement of Chinese supplies southward. Of greater effect was Peking's dispatch of 50,000 construction and antiaircraft troops into North Vietnam to keep open roads and railroads and its development of a large base complex northwest of Hanoi for use in case of intervention. These actions were taken without disguise but without publicity to make the warning more credible and less provocative. The People's Republic made it clear that invasion of the north would bring China fully into the war—a fact that was accepted by President Lyndon Johnson's most hawkish advisers. In 1962 the Americans had shown their desire to avoid war with China as well. Chinese Nationalist threats of invasion prompted massing of troops on the mainland and a new Taiwan Straits crisis brewed. President John F. Kennedy quickly informed Peking through Warsaw that no such invasion was contemplated, and the tension subsided. The modes of confrontation developed in the 1950s persisted through the 1960s —to the brink of war but with increasing restraint on both sides.

In this era, under the twin impact of the American threat and the dramatic growth of the Soviet military influence on the border, Chinese military expenditures increased significantly. Considerable efforts were made to develop nuclear and military capability, efforts isolated by the turmoil of the Cultural Revolution. And the People's Republic initiated the development of a naval modernization program.

Old Paths, New Directions

Whether Vietnam ended a phase or an era of Sino-American confrontation remains to be seen. New crises may occur over Taiwan or Korea. Nevertheless, the promise of open, active, equal relations between China and the United States is tantalizing. As the two nations seek to define a new relationship, an understanding of past military interactions can be helpful.

Far beyond American public awareness and contrary to American principles, the United States has been a persistent intruder in China. Since the beginning of relations, American forces have always been on Chinese soil or hovering nearby. American interventions have seriously affected China's self-development and at least from Peking's perspective American power has menaced China's existence. However, the United States has not been the deepest intruder. That was Japan. On occasion American forces have served the Chinese as counterweights to other aggressors (Japan in the 1940s and the Soviet Union in the 1970s). The United States does not overshadow China territorially as the Soviet Union does. Sea and recently sea-air power is less incursive, tangible, and settled than land power. The American intruders kept to treaty port enclaves, ships, or strategic bases, exhibiting little hunger for land and rule. Ground-force interventions were usually transient or peripheral. These factors place American power in a somewhat less threatening perspective.

Chinese weakness facilitated intervention but did not inspire it. Rather it tended to put China out of mind. American policy makers developed no coherent, distinct China policy that took into account American priorities as well as China's emerging significance, character, and interests, but instead fitted China into broader schemes and policies to serve ulterior American objectives. Thus, China was viewed as part of the non-European backdrop of American commerce, an element in the Western mechanism of trade protection, a pawn in the Japanese-American confrontation, a springboard for defeat of Japan, and a sector in the Soviet-American Cold War. The result has been a bewildering transiency in American military activities, casualness about their consequences for China, and in 1950 a head-on collision. Lack of direction from Washington left broad discretion to the field, and from Armstrong in 1856 to MacArthur in 1950 aggressive commanders in East Asia often pressed the Chinese harder than Washington deemed necessary after the event. Equally this lack of balanced purpose has permitted the central bureaucracies, especially the navy, to stake out large missions with respect to China for budgetary purposes, resulting in further policy confusion. A final effect of random purpose was fragmentary military interaction whether in circumstances of cooperation or confrontation. New officers with new missions arrived before old sets were familiar with each other. Only in the ominous confrontation of the Korean War did we begin to interact as equal powers, each respecting the might of the other.

The era of confrontation has encouraged rather than discouraged the idea of a stable, broadened relationship. The People's Republic of China has displayed circumspection, consistency, and rationality in the definition of its objectives and the manner of carrying them out. It has clearly indicated the supreme importance it attaches to frontier protection. Equally important, though more amenable to tactical considerations, is its aim to recover territory it considers legitimately its own. These are goals the international system is designed to accommodate.

8

STANLEY B. LUBMAN

Trade and Sino-American Relations

TRADE between the United States and China, despite its relatively rapid growth since it was revived in 1972, still remains relatively small and faces an uncertain future. The overall Sino-American rapprochement on which it depends is fragile. Commercial relations between the two Pacific giants are also overshadowed by painful recollections of the past on both sides. Memories still rankle in Peking, where the United States has been viewed not only as imperialist and exploitative, but as having fomented and led a campaign of economic warfare against China since 1950. The historical legacy combines with Peking's uncertain economic development policies and limited foreign trade to place strong constraints on Sino-American commercial relations.

Today, as during the century from 1850 to 1950, American business and banking interests desire increased trade with the world's most populous country. But the highly touted China

market remains elusive. During the 1970s, China has made
modest compromises with its policy of economic self-reliance
—exporting some consumer goods and agricultural products
in return for imports of food grains, capital goods, and high-
technology items—but total U.S.-China trade amounted to
only $336 million in 1976 (a minuscule portion of total world
trade). And Chinese-American trade at its height in 1974
amounted to a total of less than $1 billion.

The future of Sino-American trade will be determined by a
combination of economic circumstances with more important
political factors and cultural values. The influence of those
forces in the past must be understood before we look at current
conditions and future prospects.

Historical Perspectives: 1800–1949

The past hangs heavily over Sino-U.S. trade, particularly from
a Chinese perspective. Confucian China viewed commerce
with distaste and placed the merchant at the bottom of the
social hierarchy. The traditional Chinese tributary system
permitted the "barbarian" countries around China's periphery to trade only when they presented tributary gifts and
homage to the Chinese emperor. The system gratified the Chinese sense of superiority while satisfying the foreigners' desire
for trade with the Middle Kingdom. Sometimes, around the
frontiers of the empire, exceptions were tolerated and trade
without tribute was permitted (often with a rake-off for the
imperial coffers). At the southern city of Canton, for instance,
from 1760 to 1840, Western merchants were permitted to
trade, but under severe restrictions and only with specially
licensed Chinese merchant organizations. The Chinese had no
interest in going beyond these traditional systems, but the
Western barbarian was persistent in his passion for free trade
on the Chinese coast from the sixteenth century onward.

The Westerners could not be restrained, particularly British merchants who expanded their trade in the early nineteenth century to sell Indian opium, which was an easily transported product, with an ever growing demand among Chinese addicts. The opium trade mushroomed in the 1820s and 1830s, causing a serious drain of Chinese silver currency, precipitating a moral crisis in Peking, and eventually leading to the Opium War. As we have seen earlier, the Opium War led to the system of unequal treaties, to Western enclaves on the China coast and later in the interior, and to the principle of extraterritoriality. The treaty port system also set the context for trade over the course of the nineteenth and early twentieth centuries. Tariff rates were fixed by the treaties, and the Imperial Customs Service (under the Chinese government but supervised by the Irishman Robert Hart) oversaw the trade with the West. Under the favorable circumstances, Western trade with China expanded considerably in the nineteenth century, though it never lived up to the dream of "400 million customers." The American share of this trade was small, though some American merchants did a thriving business in Chinese tea, silks, and ceramics in return for American cotton (and sometimes opium). Russell and Company of Boston became one of the leading China trade organizations, using their swift fleet of clipper ships to transport goods.

Not until the 1880s and 1890s, however, did a substantial segment of the American commercial community begin to take an interest in the China trade. The economic panics and depression of those years pushed some prominent businessmen to worry about "overdevelopment" and to look beyond the West Coast for trading opportunities. These pressures, heightened by the hope of a great China market, were important factors behind the development of the "Open Door" policy and its emphasis on an "equality of commercial opportunity" in China. But American commercial hopes proved unfounded and the great China market never materialized, mainly because Chinese domestic production, in the growing industrial sector and the handicraft industries, tended to satisfy most needs.

Before 1949 the United States was involved in China trade principally as a buyer of raw materials or semifinished goods, especially wood oil (tung oil), sheep wool, skins and furs, raw silk, gum rosin, bristles and tea, and as a major supplier of tobacco, oil, kerosene, and timber. U.S. firms had also begun to sell small amounts of sophisticated manufactured products such as sewing machines, radios, typewriters, and vehicles. At no time, however, was China trade of real economic consequence to the United States. (Total U.S. foreign trade with all countries has only been a small fraction of the U.S. gross national product.) Nor did foreign trade possess great importance even for China before 1949. China's total foreign trade "never exceeded 1½ percent of the total value of world trade . . . . in per capita terms, it remained negligible," [1] according to one leading student of the pre-1949 Chinese economy. Despite its low economic value, trade with the West had great cultural impact and also stimulated the development of Western-type business organization in China, as in banking, shipping, insurance, and transportation. And yet, although the China trade stayed small and its quantitative importance should not be exaggerated, the idea of protecting a mythical China market became a cardinal principle of American policy throughout much of the early twentieth century.

From the perspective of many Chinese revolutionaries and reformers, the American commercial presence, however limited, was part of a larger Western economic imperialism. Significantly, in 1905 many Chinese boycotted American goods to protest U.S. discrimination against Chinese immigration. Again in 1919 and 1925–26, two periods of widespread anti-imperialist protests, American firms were included in the demonstrations. Indeed, some of the organizers of these protests

[1] Rhoads Murphey, *The Treaty Ports and China's Modernization: What Went Wrong?* (Ann Arbor, Michigan: Center for Chinese Studies, 1970), pp. 46–47.

went on to become leading figures in the Chinese Communist movement. At the same time, another smaller but influential segment of the Chinese community, particularly industrialists and bankers, many educated in the United States, developed close ties with American merchants. Some of these Chinese entrepreneurs also established ties with the Nationalist movement—the classic case was the family of Charlie Soong, whose son became economic minister and whose three daughters married Sun Yat-sen, Chiang Kai-shek, and H. H. K'ung, forming a political-commercial complex of great importance. Much of the American China trade shifted to Taiwan after Chiang Kai-shek's defeat in the civil war. U.S. trade with Taiwan has grown since then, to $4.8 billion in 1976, more than ten times the U.S.–People's Republic trade.

The current situation in Sino-American trade echoes the historical experience reviewed above. U.S. business would like to expand commerce (though few continue to entertain illusions of a huge China market), while Chinese want to limit the trade to maintain economic self-reliance and achieve a favorable balance of payments. As for Chinese resentments about the past, they persist and should be viewed in light of John K. Fairbank's assessment: "The West expanded into China, not China into the West. The foreigners even in their best moments were in this sense aggressive; they were agents of change, and the destruction of the old order." [2]

The Cold War and Its Legacies: 1950–71

If the history of Sino-Western trade before 1949 is important, the most recent twenty-one years, 1950–71, in which there was virtually no Sino-American trade, are critical for understanding

[2] John King Fairbank, *The United States and China,* 3rd ed. (Cambridge, Mass.: Harvard University Press, 1972), p. 147.

both recent developments and future commercial prospects. After the People's Republic was established in 1949, American actions convinced the Chinese Communists that the United States used aid and trade as weapons against the Chinese revolution. The United States organized and led a multilateral system aimed at carrying on economic warfare by denying Communist countries, including China, strategic goods. In 1950 the United States was instrumental in bringing about the creation of the Coordinating Committee (COCOM), composed of representatives of the NATO countries and Japan, to supervise the embargo of certain items and to monitor the sale of others. COCOM continues to exist today. Until 1957 the level of control over trade by COCOM member nations with China was even more severe than that applied to the European Communist countries. The list of goods embargoed or monitored has been reviewed from time to time, and, especially in recent years, the United States has been under pressure from the other COCOM members which wish to increase their trade with Communist countries and reduce the number of embargo items. In 1975, for instance, the United States did not block the sale of Rolls Royce Spey jet engines to China, engines that could be put to military use by the Chinese air force.

The United States has also maintained its own extensive controls over exports of U.S. goods and technology to Communist countries. Until 1972 the United States maintained a total embargo on sales to China and a near-total prohibition on purchases of Chinese-origin goods. Since 1972, American citizens have been permitted to make purchases from China and pay for them in dollars, and exports, instead of being under a total embargo, are under the same export control restrictions as sales to the Soviet Union. Under the Export Administration Act, the president has unlimited authority to limit exportation of any commodity to any country. U.S. policy has been stricter than COCOM; a Commodity Control List considerably longer than the COCOM list enumerates commodity categories which require validated export licenses. These are granted by the Department of Commerce only after other agencies, particularly the Defense Department, have approved the proposed transactions.

The Chinese regard these U.S. policies as part of a strategy intended to undercut Chinese economic development, and indeed they are the the outgrowth of a policy of economic warfare. Goods and technology *were* denied to China in order to make the tasks of the Communist leaders more difficult. The embargo, it should be stressed, continues to exist, and although it is selective rather than total it inhibits Chinese purchase of products in which they have evinced considerable interest. Thus, even today China necessarily sees some U.S. economic policies as continued outgrowths of Cold War hostility.

On the American side most businessmen probably shared the general anti-Chinese Communist hostility of the 1950s, although a small number opposed the embargo and wanted increased contact and trade before trade reopened in the early 1970s. Since then, many businessmen have sought to visit China, mainly for their commercial interests but also because of a sincere desire to see the country firsthand. Some businessmen have become fascinated by the mystery of "New China" and by the drama of a new era in U.S.-China relations.

At the same time many businessmen lack perspective on China's history, on Sino-Western trade in the past, and on the organization and structure of Chinese society today. Suggestive in this regard were some of the Americans who went to China in 1972 in the first group of American businessmen to be invited, and who returned with sentiments which, although understandable, then and now seemed extravagant. Illustratively, one was quoted by the *New York Times* as speaking of the "strong residual [*sic*] of the genuine Chinese affection for Americans"; another claimed that he had been made the "liaison man" between one sector of Chinese industry and its American counterpart. The *New York Times* (on the family page, where such flippancy is perhaps acceptable) spoke of the Americans as " '72-style Marco Polos," as if other Westerners had not been going to Canton for sixteen years before Americans arrived. Americans such as these, busy in attending to the present, tend to disregard the long history of Sino-American economic relations as well as the differing interpretations of the past which exist in the two countries.

Trade in the 1970s: Chinese and American Outlooks

China's trade with the rest of the world is conducted within severe limits imposed by both practical circumstances and ideological dictates. Under the policy of "self-reliance," emphasis is laid on the need for China to use its own resources, to develop its own innovative solutions to the many problems of modernization, and to use as little foreign trade and aid as possible. Mao Tse-tung argued that "socialist construction" of China can only be correctly accomplished through the exertion and self-sacrifice of China's mobilized masses. The success of the Chinese Communist Party in leading peasant armies to make a great revolution without foreign assistance reinforced the belief of Mao and many of his colleagues that if a new China was to be built only Chinese could do it. Economic relations with the West might not only revive Western exploitation, but also, to the extent that they encouraged Chinese reliance on imported technology and equipment, they might contribute to weakening the Chinese revolutionary spirit. The hazards of dependence were bitterly emphasized when the Soviet Union abruptly withdrew its technicians and assistance in 1960. Since then, China has redirected its trade so that over 80 percent is now with non-Communist countries.

Self-reliance is a policy based not only on ideology, however, but on necessity. China, denied easy access to embargoed Western goods and deprived of Soviet aid, had self-reliance thrust on it during the 1960s. A combination of pressing circumstances—the dislocations caused by the Great Leap Forward, a series of natural disasters, and, later, the Cultural Revolution—kept China's foreign trade from increasing.

The 1970s have been notable for the increase in China's foreign trade. In 1971 and 1972, under Mao and Chou's leadership, a noticeable shift from strict self-reliance was signaled by large Chinese imports of machinery, equipment, and whole plants. Between 1972 and 1975, China signed contracts for more than $2.6 billion of whole plants and for more than $2 billion of machinery and equipment, which exceeded all such purchases during the preceding decade.

Why did Chinese foreign trade rise dramatically after the Cultural Revolution? Technical and economic concerns seem to have been paramount. China needs technology to modernize. In nonmilitary sectors of the economy such as agriculture, for instance, China has made large purchases of fertilizer plants (including eight from the M. W. Kellogg Company), which will reduce dependence on fertilizer imports; in petroleum and petrochemicals Chinese leaders have realized the need for foreign equipment and technology to accelerate the growth of new but burgeoning Chinese industries. Imports have also been made for military use; in late 1975, China agreed to purchase the know-how to manufacture Rolls-Royce jet engines. At the same time China's exports have also increased in order to generate foreign exchange. Chinese sellers, formerly not very concerned about varying the design, packaging, and labeling of their products for sophisticated foreign importers, have begun to show greater interest in adapting to the requirements of markets abroad.

However, compromises with the policy of self-reliance brought about by the need to purchase foreign technology and equipment and to plan and stimulate exports have led to political controversy in the People's Republic. The late Premier Chou En-lai championed the cause of "comprehensive modernization" and urged imports of high-technology products and whole plants from various developed countries, including the United States and Japan. Chou seems to have won a considerable following for this policy in the military and state bureaucracies—and his outlook has been endorsed by the new Chairman, Hua Kuo-feng. But many of the so-called "radicals," led by the purged "gang of four" including Mao's widow, Chiang Ch'ing, are now accused of trying to undercut industrial and agricultural modernization policies in the early 1970s. These controversies involve the issue which Mao called "red versus expert," the conflict between emphasizing ideology or technology as main social forces in China's development. These concerns recall the dilemma of some nineteenth century Chinese who strove for a balance: "Chinese learning as the essence, Western learning for its practical use."

The past is evoked not only by China's doubts about how to mesh foreign technology with Chinese society, but by the way the Chinese deal with the foreign businessmen who can be agents for transferring technology and products to China today. The Chinese have used some special methods to deal with Westerners, often quite different from the Westerners on the other side of the negotiating table, and sometimes even recalling the Canton system 150 years ago. When U.S. or other foreign businessmen go to China they deal almost exclusively with representatives of China's state trading corporations, the only agencies authorized to engage in foreign commerce for China. These bodies, supervised by the Ministry of Foreign Trade, divide responsibility functionally for machinery, chemicals, metals, and minerals, textiles, cereals, oils and foodstuffs, light industrial products, native produce and animal by-products, and the purchase of whole plants and licensing of foreign technology. The corporations are independent legal entities which represent Chinese production units and economic enterprises which ultimately receive imported goods. Because they stand between the foreign businessmen and Chinese enterprises, they also insulate the foreigners from contact with Chinese society.

The trading corporations, as constituent parts of a large bureaucracy, are often slow to make decisions. The bureaucratic caution of Chinese trade officials is exacerbated by their apparent distrust of foreign capitalists. Chinese negotiators often seem wary and uncommunicative, because although the Westerners seem to be expected to tell all—about prices, market conditions, and their margin of profit—they also find it difficult to elicit answers to their own requests for economic information in return. Information supplied by Westerners seems to be distrusted and double-checked. Thus, it seems as if the Westerners have to justify themselves, while the Chinese act as if their own sincerity and purity of motives must be regarded as unquestioned from the beginning. Difficulties of communication and of establishing trust are subtly compounded for the foreign business visitor to China who, although he is given elaborate and attentive hospitality, nevertheless finds himself unable to move about freely.

Other difficulties flow from Chinese reluctance to transact business on terms other than those derived from Chinese practices in foreign trade in the 1950s and 1960s, long before Americans appeared on the scene. Terms derived from widely used international banking and contractual practices—admittedly strongly shaped by the customs of developed Western nations—are eschewed in favor of terms which are bargained for between the Chinese and their trading partners. Chinese foreign trade officials have made a point of saying that international practices "will be taken into consideration," but even when the Chinese adopt a common Western practice they do so selectively and regard the decision as entirely within Chinese discretion. Foreign businessmen sometimes have the impression that the Chinese are compelled to prove that today's China cannot be treated as a helpless object of Western commercial exploitation. When representatives of the American Arbitration Association discussed the settlement of international trade disputes with Chinese "legal specialists" in 1975, the Chinese stated that the most important principle was "the policy of independence and keeping initiative in our own hands," which crucially modifies the other principles they mentioned, "equality and mutual benefit" and "the policy of taking into consideration international practice."

In recent years experienced European, American, and Japanese sellers of products and technology much desired by the Chinese have been able to negotiate adequately specific contracts. Today the larger number of sellers negotiating with the Chinese has produced an increase in requests for changes in standard Chinese contract terms. For example, since 1971 in contracts signed with large sellers of capital goods, the Chinese have shown an increased willingness to agree to protect a seller's know-how, arbitrate trade disputes in third countries, and occasionally even to apply a third country's law to resolve questions arising under the contracts. Long-established international business customs thus impinge on strong Chinese desires to dictate the terms of trade, although the tension between them will undoubtedly continue as a characteristic of Sino-Western trade.

Americans bring to their encounters with Chinese trade officials their general lack of concern with the past, mentioned above, as well as their own cultural values, which lack the uniformity of Chinese values. Some American businessmen, aware of their own lack of knowledge, have tried to gain perspective by consulting officials in the U.S. Departments of State and Commerce, who are often able to be helpful. The National Council for U.S.-China Trade, a nonprofit organization which publishes an excellent magazine, *U.S.-China Business Review,* and generally assists American businessmen, also has helped to demystify China for businessmen.

But Americans often bring to the China trade a mischievous combination of insularity and self-confidence—which coincidentally reinforce Chinese recollections of the exploitative aspects of the Sino-Western trade of an earlier day. American importers may present a special case. Because much American importing is of consumer goods in which fashions and markets change quickly, U.S. importers must be both aggressive and agile, particularly in the intensely competitive garment trade. In this regard, the mismatch between New York's Seventh Avenue and the understandably less nimble bureaucracy of the Chinese textile industry and foreign trade apparatus has helped to provoke misunderstandings with some rather suggestive implications.

Importers of garments have for years flown around Asia, bargaining hard and impatiently with manufacturers and agents in Japan, Taiwan, South Korea, and Hong Kong who usually operate on a narrow margin of profit, who depend heavily on obtaining orders for their wares from the world's largest market, and who are accustomed to entertaining, flattering, and sometimes bribing their powerful guests. The U.S. buyer is usually in a hurry, expects to be wooed, and may exhibit demanding, if not downright callous, traits which are not likely to be appreciated by Chinese trade officials sensitive about the wrongs done to China by Western imperialism. Unlike many exporters elsewhere in Asia, the Chinese expect to negotiate with buyers as absolute equals. Some European veterans of the China trade, and some Americans as well, would say that the Chinese expect to be treated as *more* than equals.

If importers are sometimes impatient, so too are representatives of U.S. exporters. These are often employees of large corporations who often seem to expect deference to be shown to them by foreign customers because of the prestige of their corporation, their rank, or both. Their employers are usually large enough to be able to afford a long view of their prospects for sales to China. Thus, busy executives may be piqued when they are kept waiting for a day or two before an appointment can be arranged with a Chinese negotiator in Canton, a city which their employers may have spent much time and money trying to obtain an invitation for them to visit. Their impatience may grow when they do meet with a Chinese who barely identifies himself, says little of substance in response to their presentations, and lacks the power to do more than accept the sales literature thrust upon him. But the Chinese invite relatively few would-be exporters, and, when they do, some time generally elapses while they are trying to form an impression of the seller. Furthermore, it is in Peking and not Canton where final decisions on exports are made, and thus the exporter at the biennial Canton Trade Fair is only in the first step of his negotiations. Moreover, Peking negotiations, if the exporter gets that far, can be very time-consuming and arduous. Often misunderstandings can be avoided if Americans inform themselves about the rudiments of the Chinese economic system, including the slowness with which purchasing decisions are made. Sellers with experience in Eastern Europe and the Soviet Union are least likely to be surprised.

The impatience of U.S. corporate salesmen in Canton or Peking can be traced to sources that have nothing to do with China. Exporting has historically been much less important to the U.S. economy than to the economies of Western Europe and Japan. Only very recently did U.S. foreign trade increase even to 10 percent of the gross national product of the United States. With some very prominent exceptions, such as manufacturers of vehicles and electronic instruments, many U.S. companies have not sold their goods on a large scale to most of the rest of the world, let alone to China.

If the past experience of Western European and Japanese

predecessors in the China trade offers any lessons, U.S. businessmen who impress the Chinese as "sincere"—and this does not mean reliance on flattery or failure to insist on their own interests—can, if they return frequently and work hard to establish solid relationships, come to be regarded as "old friends" and be considered particularly reliable. The knitting together of durable commercial relationships requires considerable patience and time.

As we have observed earlier, U.S.-China trade historically remained small, and the 1970s has been no exception. And indeed the historical pattern of fluctuating trade patterns has also been perpetuated. The figures are as shown in Table 2.

TABLE 2
U.S.-China Trade, 1970–76
(in millions of U.S. dollars)

Year	Total Trade	U.S. Exports	U.S. Imports	Imbalance
1970	—	—	—	—
1971	5.0	—	5.0	–5.0
1972	95.9	63.5	32.4	31.1
1973	805.1	740.2	64.9	675.1
1974	933.8	819.1	114.7	704.4
1975	461.9	303.6	158.3	145.3
1976	336.4	135.4	201.0	–65.6

In the peak year of 1974, some 81 percent of U.S. exports to China were agricultural commodities (wheat, $234 million; cotton, $185.9 million; soybeans, $138.2 million; and corn, $95.7 million). Apart from the sales of ten Boeing aircraft ($150 million) and eight fertilizer plants from the M. W. Kellogg Company ($215 million), no other major purchases of whole plants have occurred, and relatively few purchases of machinery and equipment have been consummated. Since 1973 the Chinese have reduced their purchases of agricultural commodities. They canceled contracts for grain purchases in 1974 and apparently intend to treat the United States as a residual supplier, with Canada and Australia serving as principal sources. In 1974, China placed new orders for only $14 million of machinery from the United States; in 1975 the figure more than doubled, chiefly because of purchases of equipment for use in the petroleum industry. Sales by Japan and Western Europe to China have been much larger. For example, U.S. whole plant sales to China constituted only 8 percent of such Chinese purchases from 1972 to 1975.

Recent years suggest, then, that China has not rushed to buy from the United States. At the same time, the Chinese have expressed a continued interest in American technology and the late 1976 purchase of a sophisticated Control Data Cyber computer indicates that the selective importation of such goods may continue in the post-Mao era. Chinese imports of aluminum, steel scrap, and chemicals can also be expected to continue, depending on the competitiveness of U.S. sellers in the light of world market prices.

In some other areas selective Chinese purchases can be expected. They are continuing to seek computers, in which U.S. companies are preeminent, and they show interest in equipment and technology used in the petroleum, natural gas, and petrochemical industries. Purchases of equipment for use in mining coal and nonferrous metals and in steelmaking are also likely. If earlier patterns are any guide, however, Chinese purchases of capital goods will probably be spread among various sellers so that China will not become overly dependent on any particular foreign suppliers. Thus, the United States in 1975 was the source of only 3 percent of China's overall trade, a percentage which probably shrank in 1976 and is not likely to increase dramatically in the immediate future.

Among the most important Chinese exports to the United States have been cotton cloth, chemicals, tin, antiques, bristles, fireworks, raw silk, and bamboo baskets and bags. The Chinese have shown considerable interest in increasing their exports of light manufactured articles and garments and have sent trade delegations to the United States to promote sales of these products.

As noted earlier, U.S.-China trade resumed just when Chinese trade with the West and Japan grew. Yet, although imports have a high demonstration value and can serve as conduits for advanced technology to China, China's foreign trade remains quantitatively unimportant. China's total foreign trade turnover in 1975—a record year—was $14.3 billion, or less than 5 percent of China's gross national product of $299 billion. Chinese purchases from the West and Japan during 1974–75 slowed because of a large trade deficit, suggesting that China will be reluctant to expand imports greatly unless exports can be enlarged or financial assistance obtained by purchasing capital goods on credit, as China began to do in 1973.

Even the availability of foreign credit, however, may not prompt the Chinese leadership to enlarge exports as long as the policy of self-reliance remains important. However, China may have the capacity to generate sufficient foreign exchange earnings to finance large-scale imports while maintaining a trade balance by increasing exports of one important commodity—petroleum. In the 1960s and early 1970s, China was remarkably successful in developing a petroleum industry where none existed before. Major oil resources have been located and are being developed in north, northeastern, and southeastern China, and approximately 90 million metric tons of crude oil were produced in China in 1976. Pipelines have been built, refineries enlarged, and port and terminal facilities expanded to permit large tankers to load crude oil.

China has also become a petroleum exporter. In 1976, China sold 6.8 million metric tons of crude oil to Japan and smaller amounts to the Philippines, Thailand, and Hong Kong. The extent of China's commitment to expanding petroleum exports is unclear, and some problems have arisen to complicate Chinese planning. Crude oil from China's major Taching field is extremely waxy, requiring special processing, and Japanese and Philippine refineries have not been eager to purchase it. Also, world demand for crude oil has fluctuated in recent years and oil prices have not continued to rise. In addition, if the Chinese made a commitment to increase oil exports they would have to make additional investments in the oil fields and petrochemical industries, which in turn would necessitate considerable purchases of foreign equipment and technology, particularly from the United States, a world leader in this area. The Chinese have shown interest in purchasing offshore drilling platforms and purchased approximately $25 million of U.S. oil-field equipment in 1975, but they have not yet moved ahead with offshore drilling so intensively as to create the prospect of enormous sales. The internal disputes over development strategy mentioned above doubtlessly affected Chinese purchases in this area during 1975–76.

Present and Future Problems

Although China is a potentially sizable market for certain U.S. capital goods and technology mentioned above, relatively little has been purchased from the United States. The slowness with which the Chinese have placed orders with U.S. firms may signal the importance which the Chinese attach to establishing a full diplomatic relationship. The experiences of other trading partners suggest that the Chinese prefer to direct their trade to nations with which they are on good terms.

To some extent closer trade relations must wait upon the settlement of the financial problems presently outstanding between the United States and China, and China apparently wishes to postpone such settlements until full diplomatic relations are established. Thus, the Chinese have so far avoided establishing direct commercial banking relationships with U.S. banks. Approximately $80 million of Chinese assets have been frozen in U.S. banks since Chinese intervention in the Korean War. Although the United States and China announced in 1973 that the future disposition of these assets had been decided "in principle," no further movement has occurred. A likely solution would be to link settlement of this question to a decision on the private claims against China by U.S. citizens and organizations for property nationalized by the Chinese government, assets which have been fixed at approximately $197 million by the U.S. Foreign Claims Settlement Commission. An earlier U.S.-Soviet agreement on similar problems may offer a precedent: the frozen assets could be assigned to the United States to be used to satisfy at least part of the claims, which could then no longer be asserted against China. No final agreement has yet been reached, and in any event complex legal questions will have to be sorted out. Until a settlement is accomplished, Chinese flagships and planes cannot visit the United States without fear of being attached by a private claimant. When these problems are rectified, commercial links can be strengthened.

Other serious problems include Chinese desire to prevent an unfavorable balance in U.S.-China trade. The imbalance rose to more than $700 million in 1974 because of large Chinese purchases of agricultural commodities. But because the Chinese have slackened purchases from the United States while increasing exports to the United States, the imbalance fell to around $145 million in 1975 and disappeared by 1976, when Sino-American trade was in China's favor by about $65 million. However, the total volume of trade has fallen considerably.

Other problems are caused by certain U.S. trade policies toward Communist nations, which presently inhibit expansion of trade with China in a number of respects. In order to change these policies, however, the United States will have to

make decisions that would either treat China equally with the
Soviet Union or favor one over the other. Although the list of
products for which licenses are required has been reduced and
China and the Soviet Union are now treated equally, the U.S.
list of goods and technology for which licenses are required is
still longer than the COCOM list. NATO member nations
and Japan deny fewer products to China and the Soviet Union
than the United States, and U.S. exporters have long desired
reduction in the list. Unfortunately, the United States lacks a
clear policy on trade with Communist countries, and indeed
individual agencies have different policies—the Commerce
Department seeks to promote exports, the State Department
sometimes links trade with political issues, and the Defense
Department wishes to restrict sales of products or transfer of
technology which might give Communist countries undue
military advantages.

Recently, some specialists on Communist affairs have suggested that to signal opposition to Soviet ambitions, the United
States should permit the export to China of U.S. weapons
which could be used to defend China against Soviet attack. It
may be that this view influenced the attitudes of U.S. policy
makers who restrained U.S. objections to the sale of British
jet engines and an American computer, both of which could
be put to defensive military use.

But even if Washington and Peking characterize some
weapons systems as "defensive," would the Soviets agree? On
the other hand, if the United States refuses to sell weapons to
China which it also refuses to sell to the Soviet Union, does
not the greater industrial power of the Soviet Union mean that
"evenhandedness" favors Moscow? Trade with China clearly
may have more than bilateral implications and may raise
issues of global and strategic significance.

Distinctions between China and the Soviet Union may be
important in the dismantling of trade barriers to Chinese imports. In 1950 the United States decided to deny all Commu-

nist countries most-favored-nation treatment. It has since been granted to Poland, Yugoslavia, and Rumania, but it is denied to all other Communist nations. As a result the tariff duties imposed on almost all Chinese and Soviet goods are higher than those on imports from nations to which the United States accords most-favored-nation status; some cannot be imported at all because of the level of the discriminatory tariff duties.

To compound matters, Congress in the Trade Act of 1974 established rigorous standards which must be met by a presidentially negotiated bilateral trade agreement with a Communist country. The so-called Jackson-Vanik Amendment to the act prevents the president from entering into an agreement unless he can certify that the country in question does not unreasonably hinder emigration. Directed at the Soviet Union's hindrance of Jewish emigration, the act is broadly drafted enough to apply to China as well. Although the suggestion has been made that the act be repealed partially to apply only to the Soviet Union, little support has appeared in Congress for such a move. Here again, as in the argument in favor of relaxing export controls so that China would be favored slightly over the Soviet Union, a decision would have to be made whether to vary a policy directed generally at Communist countries in order to treat China more favorably than the Soviet Union.

The same type of issue might arise under the Trade Act in a related but slightly different connection. The act sets forth the general criteria which a bilateral trade agreement with a Communist country must meet, including willingness on the part of the Communist nation in question to make concessions in return for securing most-favored-nation treatment, such as adopting means to facilitate trade, to protect Americans' industrial and literary property, and to arbitrate trade disputes. Again we must ask: by what standard would a Sino-American agreement be judged, as compared with a Soviet-American agreement?

Finally, in considering obstacles to trade with China we should note that certain general U.S. policies affecting imports have had considerable impact on trade with China. For example, regulations for the protection of the consumer have been particularly important. Food and Drug Administration regulations on labeling and purity of foodstuffs have often caused Chinese imports to be denied entry into the United States. In the largest single case known, $800,000 of frozen shrimp from China had to be reexported after FDA inspectors refused to allow the goods to enter the United States. The Chinese have shown considerable interest in exporting canned and frozen pork. However, under U.S. regulations, the plants at which such products are processed must be inspected regularly by U.S. Department of Agriculture personnel. The Chinese will have to take U.S. legal requirements into consideration if they wish to increase their exports of foodstuffs to the United States. Chinese foreign trade officials, though they originally thought the U.S. was singling China out in a discriminatory fashion, now understand that federal food and drug legislation applies to all exporters and to domestic products in interstate commerce as well. In some cases the Chinese have moved to meet requirements set by U.S. law, and in others they have expressed willingness to consider making necessary adjustments.

Other questions of trade policy will affect U.S.-China trade. More serious problems await U.S. importers of Chinese products which compete with goods manufactured in the United States. The Trade Act not only left intact previous measures created by earlier legislation which assist U.S. industries threatened by foreign competition, but also created new means of slowing or altogether ceasing imports from Communist countries, including China. Quite apart from the act, in other areas such as textiles, which are of considerable importance to China, domestic producers have succeeded in pressuring the executive branch to negotiate "voluntary" restraints by other exporting nations. Domestic U.S. protectionism invoked in the past against imports of Asian goods could again affect imports from China.

As with all other matters surrounding current Sino-American relations, the problems of diplomatic "normalization" and the related issue of Taiwan affects U.S.-China trade. The establishment of formal diplomatic relations would promise some increase in trade with the People's Republic, although it is difficult to predict just how much. At the same time, a new stage in the relationship with Peking would require the United States to develop a new set of economic and legal protections for American trade with Taiwan. It may be difficult to arrive at a solution that will balance Peking's desire to isolate Taiwan, a commitment to Taiwan in Washington which is not entirely clear, and the desires of some U.S. commercial interests to maintain a relatively profitable trading relationship.

Conclusion

The growth of Sino-U.S. trade will depend partly on whether the will exists on both sides to clear away at least part of the web of trade-related policies which presently limit trade. More, however, will depend on whether deep uncertainties in the political relationship between the two countries are resolved. Economic realities alone suggest that neither nation needs the other's trade so badly that commercial interest could propel the two closer together politically.

In the absence of dramatic developments, trade will most likely develop slowly, with China making selective purchases— the amount probably varying with the intensity and warmth of the overall relationship—and U.S. buyers seeking out products which they can import profitably through the interstices of the discouraging U.S. tariff and nontariff barriers. The uncomfortable heritage of the past and the wide divergence between Chinese and American perceptions of trade will also continue to make more difficult the expansion of the still insubstantial Sino-American commercial dialogue.

Part IV

MULTILATERAL INTERACTIONS

MICHEL OKSENBERG

Introduction

THE next two essays focus on the impact of the Soviet Union and Japan upon Sino-American relations. As we have already seen, the bilateral ties between China and the United States are weak. Indeed, with the exception of the war years and America's Taiwan connection, links always have been weak. The commercial, military, and intellectual interests of the two countries have never been sufficient in and of themselves to determine the relationship.

Rather, Sino-American relations today as in the past largely have been the product of the broader strategic setting in East Asia and the world more generally. In an earlier era, the Sino-American relationship derived from the British role in East Asia. Then, the Anglo-Japanese alliance set the context. The 1940s saw Sino-American friendship emerge from the conflict of both with Japan. The Sino-American hostility of the 1950s reflected the importation of the European cold war to Asian shores, as the United States decided to confront the Soviet bloc globally. And the Sino-American détente of the 1970s stems from common concerns about the Soviet Union.

Both the Soviet Union and Japan loom larger in the eyes of Washington than does Peking. We are engaged in a costly arms race with the Soviets and compete for strategic advantage almost everywhere. Japan is our close ally and second largest trading partner. In a sense, Tokyo and Moscow also loom larger in Peking's eyes than does Washington. Both are near neighbors. The Soviet Union poses an immediate military threat which the United States no longer does. The Russians are also bitter ideological foes. And Japan is China's largest trading partner. Thus, both China and the United States approach with a calculation of how their dealings with each other affect their relations with the Soviet Union and Japan. It is a complex quadrangular relationship.

The linked nature of the relationships also means that the United States can improve its ties with China *through* the way it deals with the U.S.S.R. and Japan. This is a crucial consideration. Precisely since our bilateral connections are weak, perhaps the most effective way to pursue a better relationship with China is through our policies toward the Soviet Union and Japan.

Allen Whiting and Steven Levine address this issue, again in historical perspective. Whiting notes that the era since 1971 is virtually unheralded. Heretofore, we have always had to choose between China and Japan. Now however, we have the opportunity—perhaps only a passing one—to build a firm relationship with both. We can use our alliance with Japan as part of our China connection. Levine counters conventional wisdom in asserting that manipulating the Sino-Soviet conflict to establish links with China may have reached the point of diminishing returns. His reading of history suggests that if China felt more secure—for example, if its tension with the Soviets had diminished—the Chinese would find it easier to engage in cooperative ventures with the United States on Korea or to work toward arms control. Levine's insight is well worth pondering.

9

ALLEN S. WHITING

Japan and Sino-American Relations

Introduction

AMERICAN preoccupation with the Soviet Union as a determinant of U.S.-China relations, first in the Moscow-Peking alliance and then in the Sino-Soviet split, has obscured the historic role of Japan in framing Chinese as well as American policy. From 1895 to 1940 Japan's power compared to that of other countries in the region steadily grew, as did its hegemonic threat. China's vulnerability to penetration and conquest offered no counterweight. America's fitful involvement in East Asian politics offered sympathy to China but did not substantively confront Japan until World War II. Washington's public rhetoric raised Chinese hopes of offsetting Tokyo but the realities of power repeatedly destroyed this illusion.

Then from 1949 to 1971 a new configuration of relations emerged in East Asia. China, in alliance with Russia, became the dominant military force on the continent while the United States established itself as the protector of the periphery extending from South Korea to Thailand. Japan was pivotal to the new American role, both as a strategic base and as an area to be denied to the Communist bloc. Historic relationships were reversed. China, long the object of Japanese policy, now became a major actor while its traditional enemy was reduced to a dependent ally of Washington. Historic ties were broken; America was no longer China's friend, but a major force threatening to intervene in the Chinese civil war and in the Korean conflict.

Suddenly in 1971–72 a third configuration emerged with détente between Peking and Tokyo. The Soviet factor was critical in both instances, on the one hand forcing Peking to compromise its Taiwan position so as to improve relations with the United States, and on the other hand prompting Chinese acquiescence in the Japanese-American security treaty to forestall greater Russian influence in Northeast Asia. Nevertheless, the historic question of Japan's role in Asia and its potential military threat continued to weigh in Chinese calculations. Moreover, as the United States searched for an alternative to American power for protecting the status quo, the prospect of Japanese "equal partnership" won recurring attention.

Thus the strategic interactions of China, Japan, and the United States bear examination for their effect on Sino-American relations. These interactions do not determine policy in a mechanistic manner. They are mediated by perceptions and interests of sub-national groups and individuals. Bureaucratic factions, economic interests, and influential personalities affect the definition of "national interest" and "strategic threat."

Surveying these dynamics of domestic politics and foreign policy in the context of changing power relationships permits a more prudent projection of probable future developments, more so than is possible either from a narrow focus on Sino-American relations or a simplistic weighing of objective factors.

Pre-World War II

From the 1905 Portsmouth Conference that ended the Russo-Japanese War to Pearl Harbor in 1941, United States policy in East Asia was intermittent and largely impotent. It lacked consistency, unity, and a commitment of adequate military resources for any appreciable length of time. The dichotomy between American public opinion and official policy, whether over Oriental immigration or the merits of China compared to those of Japan, further confounded any rational pursuit of clearly defined goals. Considerations of power, profit, principle, and prejudice produced varied outcomes depending upon the mix of interests and individuals that determined policy at one time or another. Central to most policy debates, however, was the sense of a need to choose between China and Japan.

In terms of pure power, of course, Japan steadily improved its strength over that of its two Asian neighbors. Russia's defeat in 1905, China's submission to the Twenty-One Demands in 1915, and Tokyo's expanded control over Manchuria and North China between 1931 and 1937 mocked any pretense at a balance of power in East Asia. The United States could counter with limited force, as during the Siberian intervention of 1918–20. Russia could inflict local border defeats in 1938–39. China could fend off total collapse in 1939–

45, but basically Japanese military power dominated the Asian scene. Against this power Washington could seek bilateral diplomatic constraints such as the 1908 Root-Takahira and 1917 Lansing-Ishii agreements, and multilateral naval limitations through the Washington and London accords of 1922 and 1930. However, neither approach could be effective without deployable power in the region.

Objectively then, Washington had little choice but to acquiesce in Japanese hegemony. Yet the subjective hope of economic profit through trade and investment in "the vast China market" repeatedly tempted the United States to intervene on behalf of "the Open Door." Repeated affirmation of this alleged principle persuaded important audiences in the United States, Japan, and China that commitment to "China's territorial integrity" meant a willingness to protect the weaker against the stronger. The failure to so act at the Versailles Conference and after the establishment of Manchukuo in 1932 did not end American illusions, Japanese fears, or Chinese hopes that Washington could deter Tokyo from further expansion. Thus, both the shadow and the substance of Sino-American relations turned on Japan's posture and power.

Religious principle also argued for favoring China against Japan. The ascendancy of Christian convert Chiang Kai-shek in 1928 seemed to climax a half century of missionary effort to win the world's largest population to God's way. To be sure, mission interests in Japan competed for attention just as the substantially greater American trade with Japan logically dictated a policy of appeasement. However, the editorial appeal of a "Christian democratic China" far outweighed that of "imperial militaristic Japan." The combination of missionary and media messages worked against a cool calculation of interest and capability in the East Asian confrontation.

Racial prejudice was initially directed against Chinese laborers imported for railroad construction across the western plains, but subsequently focused more intensively on Japanese migrants in California. Local discrimination and Oriental exclusion legislation aroused political passions in Tokyo despite Washington's efforts to explain states' rights and to negotiate compromise agreements. By comparison, positive Chinese stereotypes symbolized by Pearl Buck's classic *The Good Earth,* won a favorable response, predisposing Americans to sympathetic support for the plight of Nanking and beleaguered Chungking under the assault of rapacious troops and indiscriminate bombing.

These various considerations became manifest through policy pressures from naval interests, church groups, labor unions, and public affairs associations, and were aided by astute Chinese lobbyists. Within the State Department, policy toward East Asia consistently fell under the control of China specialists. At the top no president after Theodore Roosevelt devoted much attention to East Asia as compared with Europe. The result was a policy of intermittent posturing in support of China without sufficient power for any basic effect until 1941.

The dismal record of American ambivalence in East Asia did not deter Chinese advocates from exploiting the United States as a potential makeweight against Japanese or Russian hegemonic threats. At different times between 1905 and 1945 the use of the more distant barbarian to control the nearer one proved persuasive in Chinese policy councils. The bait of Manchurian railroad development failed to lure New York bankers at the end of the Ch'ing empire, and Sun Yat-sen's appeal for American support to the fledgling Republic fell on deaf ears. Nevertheless, both Chiang Kai-shek and Mao Tsetung competed separately for Washington's favor during World War II, simultaneously struggling with Japan and with one another for control of China. American military and economic aid was seen as important for both endeavors. In addition it might offset Russia, which was about to replace Japan as China's most powerful neighbor. Neither Chiang nor Mao, however, anticipated Yalta and Roosevelt's acquiescence to Stalin's demands in Northeast China.

It is important to note that for most of this period substantial differences in objectives separated Chinese and American advocates from a common, joint approach to Japan. Chinese policy sought the specific goal of security. American policy encompassed a wider framework of interests and expectations that embraced both economic and ideological goals. Chinese nationalism meant anti-imperialism, espoused by both Nationalist and Communist elites. American expansionism sought to penetrate, if not dominate, China's social and political development. This disparity of goals could be muted for the more immediate need of meeting the commonly perceived threat of Japan, but removal of that threat would reveal the underlying differences bedeviling "Sino-American friendship."

Post-World War II

Calculations of power, profit, and principle continued to affect American and Chinese policies after the defeat of Japan, ultimately altering the key roles and relationships during the period of 1949–71. Now the United States hegemony in East Asia was unchallenged on the periphery while the newly born People's Republic of China quickly emerged as a major power in its own right. Not only had decades of civil war and warlord rule ended, but in late 1950 the Chinese People's Volunteers threw General Douglas MacArthur's United Nations force from the Yalu River back to the Thirty-Eighth Parallel. Japan lay devastated and stripped of all its empire, including Taiwan. The Sino-Soviet alliance carried Cold War bipolarity from Europe to Asia, at least so far as American perceptions of Peking were concerned.

This simple summary of the new postwar configuration of power obscures, however, the complex underlying relationships that affected the interaction between China and the United States. Our focus illuminates one such relationship, namely Chinese Communist assumptions about Washington's intentions as reflected in the handling of Japan. By 1945–46, for instance, armed Japanese troops were used to protect communications lines vital to the movement of Chinese Nationalist armies into areas contested by Mao's forces—a signal of the rapid change from enemy to ally and perhaps vice-versa. At the same time General MacArthur's personal monopoly of control over the occupation of Japan, to the virtual exclusion of any allied influence—including the Soviet Union—brought into question America's long-range designs.

This question was at least partially answered by the time Mao made his historic trip to Moscow in December 1949 to negotiate the Sino-Soviet alliance. Increasing constraints on extreme left wing and particularly Communist activity paralleled by a gradual reemergence of conservative business interests, foreshadowed America's intent to secure Japan as a power base. Occupation measures changed from assuring Japanese weakness, military and economic, to rebuilding a viable financial and political system that could relieve Washington of a patron's responsibility, while reducing the likelihood of a socialist evolution, much less a communist revolution. The prospects of a separate peace treaty, or at least one offered on a "take it or leave it" basis to China and Russia, increased steadily.

It is often forgotten that the Sino-Soviet alliance specified an attack by "Japan or any state allied with it" as the determinant of mutual military assistance. By comparison, the 1945 Sino-Soviet treaty addressed only the question of an attack by Japan. Foreign Minister Chou En-lai made the "any state" allusion more specific in his Moscow speech which was directed against "American imperialism." This highlights the pivotal role assigned to Japan and the importance of its relationship to America in Chinese perceptions. In this context, President Truman's response to North Korea's attack on June 25, 1950, and his interposition of U.S. military force in the Taiwan Strait on June 27, 1950—both made possible through the use of bases in Japan and Okinawa—proved Peking's calculation of the new threat to be correct. Washington hammered the point home in 1951 by forcing Tokyo to sign a separate peace treaty with Taiwan, thereby foreclosing any positive relationship with Peking.

For its part Washington's postwar expectation of a friendly, united, and democratic China as a stabilizer, if not ally, in Asia collapsed with the rapid shift in power from Chiang to Mao. Nor was Washington sensitive to China's reaction to steps taken to prevent Japan from falling under Communist (read Soviet) control. Thus the emergence of a formal alliance between Moscow and Peking reinforced American assumptions of monolithic Communist unity under Russian domination, and it accelerated the transformation of Japan into a secure American power base. The Korean War put the final cap on this process. Without the Japanese developments as a catalyst, however, there is a genuine question as to whether the Sino-Soviet alliance would have ever emerged.

American security interests won gradual economic reinforcement as Japan quickly moved from reconstruction to rapid growth, expanding trade and investment opportunities by annual leaps of unprecedented magnitude. As Japan's new democratic political system emerged in sharp contrast to China's harsh totalitarian image—reflected in China's public executions and mass mobilization campaigns of 1950–53—ideological principle paralleled economic profit in reorienting American attitudes. Most important, of course, were the lurid Korean War reports of "human wave" attacks and "brainwashing" of POWs that evoked fears of "yellow hordes" and their age-old threat to "civilized mankind." Thus, political developments reactivated latent prejudices so as to reverse traditional American attitudes of hostility toward Japan and sympathy toward China. In this way the same considerations that had set American-Japanese relations on a collision course before 1941, and had thereby created a Sino-American alliance, now produced an American-Japanese alliance ready to confront a hostile China.

From the perspective of Peking, this development could be explained within the Marxist framework of analysis, which defined capitalism in general and imperialism in particular, as necessarily dedicated to the destruction of communism. Therefore an alliance between Japanese monopolistic capitalism *cum* militarism and American imperialism was to be expected. However, it was not to be feared because the omnipresent contradictions, both within capitalist states and between them, weakened the enemy's strength and provided opportunities for splitting his ranks and eventually destroying him.

Moving from this general framework to specific policy implementation, however, raised questions of perception and interest analogous to those encountered on the American side. For example, we now know that Mao's concept of the "intermediate zone" posited Japan more as an unwilling victim of American hegemony than an active accomplice with aggressive designs. His unpublished speeches and informal comments reveal that relatively little fury lay behind the virulent Chinese propaganda of the 1950s that attacked Japanese "militarism" and American "imperialism" propaganda that emanated from Chinese media. Moreover, Mao's personal reservations about the Soviet developmental model and the Soviet alliance coincided with Peking's persistent probing for an improvement in Sino-American relations from 1955 to 1957. The contrast between these private views and postures with those manifest in public suggests divided counsel on how to cope with China's international relations.

Additional policy conflict appeared latent in Peking's mili-

tant support for the radical Japanese Communist Party line and
the anti-government posture of the Japanese Socialist Party
on the one hand, and on the other hand a steady expansion
of trade that implied limited economic dependence on conservative capitalist interests. Increased tourism and trade between
Japan and China was more conducive to rapprochement between the two governments than to revolution in Japan. These
conflicts between ideological and state interests were probably exacerbated by the emotional residue of past aggression
and continued suspicion over the implications of a Japanese-
American alliance.

These inner policy tensions may account for some of the
apparent inconsistencies in Peking's position that stalemated
its potential gains in Japan, although insufficient evidence is
at hand to prove the point. Certainly the provocative incident
involving the Chinese flag at the Nagasaki trade fair in 1958,
the abortive effort to apply pressure through Japanese steel
exporters by cancelling contracts, and the militant rhetoric in
response to the 1960 Security Treaty debate with the attendant
downfall of Prime Minister Kishi all tended to reinforce those
critics in Japan and the United States who argued that China
posed an expansionist threat in East Asia. At the same time
the increased Japanese ties with South Korea and Taiwan
strengthened the hand of those in Peking who took Secretary
of State Dulles' extreme anti-Communist statements at face
value, seeing a Northeast Asia Treaty Organization as a potential counterpart to SEATO.

In this context the expansion of Japan's Self-Defense Force
in violation of the constitutional renunciation of military power
takes on added significance for Sino-American relations. Implicitly linked to Washington's alliance and base system in Asia,
it posed the prospect of an eventual replacement of American hegemony in the West Pacific by a restored Japanese power,
albeit in tandem with the United States rather than independent as prior to World War II.

To leap ahead, Chinese sensitivity to perceived collusion

between Tokyo and Washington against Peking's interests seemed confirmed by the Nixon-Sato communiqué of September 1969 which linked Taiwan's security with that of Japan. The resultant propaganda campaign against "Japanese militarism" mounted in intensity over the next two years, reaching unprecedented heights at the same time that Mao and Chou were secretly communicating with President Nixon and Henry Kissinger over a prospective summit meeting. A virulent speech by the chief of staff along these lines after the first Kissinger visit in July 1971 evoked a somewhat lame explanation from Chou when questioned by James Reston, suggesting differences over any softening of policy. A few months later the fall of Lin Piao, Mao's chosen successor and top military figure, reinforced this sense of internal differences within China regarding détente with Washington and Tokyo.

At another level, the depiction of Japanese villainy through the artistic media of opera, film, plays, and literature vividly recalled the rape and pillage that had begun back in 1894–95 and had ravaged much of China. The linkage with "U.S. imperialism" during the civil war provided historic precedent for contemporary attacks against the security pact. The virulent campaign against "American aggression in Vietnam," with direct or indirect support from bases in Okinawa and Japan, seemed to foreclose any possibility of reduced tensions in East Asia as far as Sino-American and Sino-Japanese relations were concerned.

Developments Since 1971

Suddenly the situation changed. The surprise announcement of the Kissinger visit and the forthcoming Nixon trip to China came without advance warning or consultation between Washington and Tokyo. Subsequent "Nixon shocks" that rocked Japanese politics included devaluation of the dollar and imposition of a 10 percent surcharge on imports. Prime Minister Sato's support crumbled and the Japanese-American alliance suffered its worst strain since 1960.

Almost immediately the image of "Japanese militarism" began to fade from Chinese newspapers and radio broadcasts so that a year later Prime Minister Tanaka could be welcomed by Chairman Mao without embarrassment to either side. In fact, Sino-Japanese relations improved faster than Sino-American relations because Tokyo broke its ties with Taipei to establish an embassy in Peking, whereas Washington only reduced its military presence on Taiwan and by summer 1977 had yet to transfer diplomatic recognition to the People's Republic of China. Nevertheless, Peking compromised its own position in 1973 by proposing the establishment of liaison missions by both China and the United States. Washington agreed with alacrity since it could maintain the Taiwan treaty without impairment.

Not only did Chinese propaganda do an about-face with respect to Japan, but Chinese officials privately assured foreign visitors that it was for the Japanese and American peoples to define their own security relationships. In effect, this sanctioned the U.S. troops there and the defense pact as well. Travel and trade between China and Japan quickly surpassed that between China and the United States. Economic and strategic interests meshed in the growing export of oil to Japan —only eight million tons in 1975 but foreshadowing a potential supply of considerable importance ten years hence. Meanwhile the Japanese-American defense relationship deepened in the aftermath of the Indochina War with favorable side effects in South Korea that further safeguarded Seoul against fear of abandonment in the face of threats from the North.

Several questions, however, plagued the analysis of this striking change of relations. To what extent was Sino-American détente simply a function of Sino-Soviet tensions and undertaken by Peking merely to offset the perceived threat of attack from Russia? How much was Sino-Japanese normalization a tactical exploitation of Tokyo's backlash to Washington's unilateral actions in 1971? How much were both of these Chinese policies linked to the hope of collapsing Taiwan's morale by isolating the regime there from its two principal supporters? Would an easing of the Soviet threat together with frustration over Taiwan's continued inaccessibility prompt a return to the former anti-American and anti-Japanese postures? Or had short-term tactics gradually hardened into a longer-term strategy that reflected a basic reassessment of a new power balance wherein a semi-permanent *entente* juxtaposed a potential Sino-Japanese-American bloc against the Soviet Union?

A further dimension of difficulty for outside observers lay in the uncertainty over what forces or factions held which policy preferences in the ongoing debate over China's proper posture toward all three of its major East Asian neighbors. While Mao and Chou pushed successfully for détente with Washington and Tokyo in opposition to Moscow, their understanding or expectations with respect to Taiwan appear not to have been fully realized. This left détente vulnerable to attack from those who argued for greater intransigence toward all of China's enemies, present and potential, and perhaps from some who favored a balanced détente with Moscow as well. Efforts to categorize these alternative points of view as "radical" or "moderate" fail to capture any credible or consistent positions that can be identified with specific individuals or groups. Even less useful are such terms as "pro-Russian" or "pro-American" which imply that genuine rapprochement rather than limited détente was advocated. These analytical caveats to the contrary notwithstanding, the fact remains that circumstantial evidence reinforces logical assumptions that Sino-American and Sino-Japanese relations were the subject of controversy in Peking during 1968–75. This should not be any surprise in view of the previous record of selective memory, experience, and actual behavior that posited Japan and the United States as potential enemies.

Chinese perceptions of Japan are not wholly based on the past. One present grievance concerns the ownership of small, unoccupied islands that lie one hundred miles northeast of Taiwan, called the Senkakus in Japanese or Tiao Yu Tai in Chinese. This issue flared up briefly in 1970 with anti-Japanese demonstrations in Taiwan, Hong Kong, and the United States and an official statement from Peking, all directed against Tokyo's interference with Chinese Nationalist fishing in the area. Subsequently Peking indicated privately it was willing to shelve the issue for the sake of advancing other negotiations with Japan; the matter remains unsettled. On at least one occasion Vice-Premier Teng Hsiao-p'ing told overseas Chinese visitors it would come up again in the future.

The islands have no intrinsic value but provide access to the continental shelf where large undersea deposits of oil are believed to exist. In this regard the U.S. Department of State publicly adopted a neutral position and cautioned American oil firms against accepting a Japanese invitation to explore the area. This raises the larger question of ocean resources that could cause friction between China and Japan. Peking has already protested an agreement between Seoul and Tokyo that formally divides ownership of the ocean bed equally between the two countries, and specifies that expenses and profits accrued in drilling that will occur on either side of the line are to be shared. Contracts went to oil companies to begin exploration, and the Diet ratified the treaty in June 1977.

The issue is further complicated by the problem of Korea. Peking defines Pyongyang as the only legitimate regime there and is committed by treaty to its defense in the event of war. Tokyo and Washington, of course, recognize Seoul as the sole Korean government, and while the United States is its only formal military guarantor, Japan has steadily increased its informal pledges of interest in South Korean security. Furthermore, Japanese investments in and financial assistance to South Korea during recent recession setbacks guarantee a dominant interest and influence there.

After the Tanaka trip to China in September 1972, Peking stopped echoing Pyongyang's strident attacks against "Japanese militarism and aggressive U.S. troops" allegedly planning war in the peninsula. However, the issue remains potentially explosive, literally as well as figuratively. Past events contribute to present apprehensions. The Sino-Japanese war of 1894 arose over the question of hegemony in Korea. Japan's seizure of Manchuria in 1931 was launched from Korea. China fought the United Nations forces from 1950 to 1953 because General Douglas MacArthur ignored Peking's warnings and drove his forces from the Thirty-Eighth Parallel to the Yalu River.

This history is not forgotten in China, particularly its most recent manifestation. Illustrated children's booklets graphically depict heroic "Chinese People's Volunteers" bayonetting and grenading the "American devils" who "sought to attack China" in 1950. The distribution of such pamphlets by the millions since the celebrated Shanghai Communiqué that ended President Nixon's visit to China in February 1972 demonstrates the persistence of past perceptions that might constrain future attitudes. It is obviously impossible to predict precisely how these attitudes will affect policy, but as long as they are reinforced by official media the problem deserves attention.

Future Factors

In attempting to project the parameters of probability within which Japan's role is likely to affect future Sino-American relations, our emphasis will shift from the negative to the positive aspects. This is not to deny the relevance of the recurring animosity and conflict that marked Sino-Japanese relations from 1894 to 1945, and its revised appearance in the confrontation between new China and the Japanese-American alliance from 1949 to 1971. Instead we will focus on those favorable factors that have begun to erode this confrontation heritage so that we may appreciate the dynamics of change. We will also examine how policy in Tokyo and Washington can affect this process.

First and foremost is the fundamental change in Japanese political attitudes and behavior. In contrast with the militaristic system that produced an aggressive foreign policy in the 1930s, there is no foreseeable likelihood of a strong rearmed Japan seeking to dominate its neighbors. No nuclear threat is feared as long as the American security treaty remains operative and Japanese public opinion is overwhelmingly opposed to the acquisition of nuclear weapons. With the Self-Defense Force level remaining under 300,000, despite China's acquisition of a nuclear capability and a growing surface fleet, there is no reason to anticipate any sudden or dramatic change in this posture.

Moreover, Japanese relations with China have stressed conciliation and compromise since the normalization of relations in 1972. Agreements on shipping, fishing, and aviation have successfully maneuvered around the sensitive problem of Japan's continuing involvement with the Taiwanese economy. High level delegations have made amends for past aggression. At the risk of arousing Moscow's wrath, Prime Minister Miki declared in 1976 that Japan would not take sides in the Sino-Soviet dispute but neither could it remain "equidistant" between its two Communist neighbors. In short, it would tilt toward China. Miki proved his point by stressing his desire to sign the treaty of peace and friendship with Peking, including some variant of the pledge against "hegemony" to which Moscow had repeatedly voiced strong objection.

Thus mutual political and strategic interests have emerged

in the Sino-Japanese relationship to reinforce, over time, a changed role for Japan in Sino-American relations. What may have begun as a tactical ploy for Peking in 1971 has taken on longer-term significance as China seeks to keep Japan's level of armaments low while persuading it not to align with the Soviet Union. For economic as well as political reasons, Tokyo has no desire to increase its military expenditures nor to associate itself more closely with Moscow. Both sides find their goals mutually served by the Japanese-American alliance and the Sino-American détente. Even if the ruling Liberal Democratic Party suffers sufficient setbacks to cause another coalition to be formed, which would include some present opposition elements, there is no likelihood of change either with respect to rearmament or the triangular relationship with Peking and Washington.

These strategic and political interests are reinforced by economic ties. China's need for Japanese steel, chemical fertilizer, and industrial equipment should expand in pursuit of the industrialization and modernization goals articulated by the late Premier Chou En-lai in addressing the National People's Congress in January 1975. Reciprocally, the Japanese need for petroleum provides a significant opportunity for barter in an exchange that can reverse the present heavy imbalance of payments in Tokyo's favor. Although this is unlikely to exceed one-fifth of Japanese petroleum imports before 1985, it nonetheless offers a conveniently located source of energy not subject to the hazards of Middle East supplies. A greater expansion of the symbiotic relationship could come if China were to accept longer term credits and greater dependency on foreign technology in either its industrialization or its exploitation of onshore and offshore oil reserves.

In Korea a *modus vivendi* might mitigate traditional Sino-Japanese competition, although admittedly this is a less promising possibility because of local attitudes, both North and South. Kim Il Sung has built a seemingly monolithic, regimented society with a major emphasis on military strength and an unrelenting exploitation of twin sentiments against Japanese domination and in support of national unity. Uncertainty about his ultimate intentions is compounded by a total lack of information about his successor; at present it appears his son will accede to his office. Meanwhile Park Chung Hee has developed a similar personal system in the South that relies on a blend of economic prosperity, political repression, and anti-North fervor. Here, too, an uncertain future threatens internal stability with domestic dissidence that could invite intervention from the North. In short, Korea is primarily subject to domestic developments on either side of the Demilitarized Zone and only secondarily affected by the policies of larger powers.

Within this framework, however, all concerned countries share a common desire to avoid military hostilities in the peninsula. The precedent of 1950 and the prospect of three nuclear-armed allies of the two Korean states in direct or indirect confrontation provide a basis for some common understanding, if not a formal agreement, on the transfer of weapons and the level of armament to be tolerated. Tokyo's gradual improvement of relations with Seoul, accompanied by subtle signals of its willingness to communicate with Pyongyang, has set the stage for an incremental increase in the expression of Japanese interest in the security of South Korea. However this has prudently stopped short of actual involvement with any joint defense planning or commitment of armed forces to the peninsula. Thus there is no objective basis for alarm in Peking or Pyongyang, but there is an appreciation of Japan's concern which may further serve to caution against provocative or aggressive action.

Obviously these developments are recent and remain subject to various hazards. An American demand for reduced military expenditures could lead to increased pressure for a major strengthening of Japan's military capability, perhaps including greater responsibility for the defense of South Korea. Should this win support in Tokyo and Seoul, a fresh debate would undoubtedly begin among Mao's successors as to the implications for China's relations with Japan and the United States, not to mention relations with North Korea and possibly the Soviet Union as well. At this point much would depend on the state of Sino-American relations, and in particular how United States policy toward Taiwan has evolved. Japan's vulnerability as a possible whipping boy for Chinese propaganda may be heightened by succession struggles in Peking that invite the exploitation of foreign policy for domestic politics.

Another contextual variable that could emerge independently or coincidentally with an increase in Japanese military capability concerns the competition for ocean resources in general, and conflicting claims to the Senkaku Islands in particular. China has made a fine art of winning concessions in principle and granting compromises in practice. At times, however, this makes agreement impossible because the implications of conceding the principle are unacceptable to the other side, as in negotiations over the Sino-Soviet border. It is conceivable that this formula, which facilitated Sino-Japanese normalization and subsequent bilateral agreements, will run afoul of future Japanese politics. Should the Senkaku Islands issue become active, or should Peking press its claim to the continental shelf by the use of force, a stiffened Japanese posture could seriously strain relations.

These prospects are unlikely but they do fall within the range of reasonable possibility. As such they pose problems for American policy. On the one hand the Japanese alliance is deservedly the cornerstone of our East Asian strategy, and it is reinforced by strong political and economic ties as well. On the other hand our still fragile relationship with China is more readily subject to strain, and it may eventually face competition for influence with Moscow should a Sino-Soviet détente follow the passing of Mao from the active political scene.

We are unlikely to know the full range of factional disputes in Peking, much less their constituent elements and their respective power. However, we can be sensitive to clues of controversy, particularly when they correlate with past positions and perceptions that hark back to decades of Sino-Japanese and Sino-American confrontation. In continuous consultation with our Japanese ally, we can coordinate policy so as to lessen the risk of unnecessary friction and increase the possibility of mutual compromise. Symbolic politics cannot substitute for substantive solutions to problems that involve conflicting interests. Nevertheless considerable harm or good can result from the timing and content of public statements, high level meetings, and demonstrations of intent. For instance, the systematic visits to Tokyo by Secretary of State Kissinger while going to and from Peking set a useful example of how we view our relations with both capitals, even though we are an ally of one and a partial adversary of the other.

The prospect for a permanent defusing of East Asia as the cockpit of war that has wracked the region for nearly a century does exist. It is an uncertain prospect at best, but it remains a feasible goal provided that decision makers are farsighted not only with respect to their own national objectives, but also concerning the reactions as well as the actions of other powers in the area. In terms of inherent strength, both Japan and the United States enjoy an immensely superior advantage over China. This should permit them to evolve flexible policies and practices that will strengthen bilateral and possibly multilateral cooperation in managing the region's affairs. At the very least, confrontation will hopefully remain confined to propaganda postures and will not escalate to serious tensions. Only in this way can 1971–72 become a benchmark in time worthy of the hyperbole attributed to it—having allegedly introduced "a generation of peace."

10

STEVEN I. LEVINE

The Soviet Factor in
Sino-American Relations

For present-day Soviet school-children the names of Erofei Khabarov, Nikolai Muraviev, and Sergei Witte—great figures from the tsarist past—evoke the era of Russia's eastward expansion across the continental land mass of Eurasia which parallels America's westward thrust across the Pacific. More often than not, the resultant of these two great historical vectors has been competition and conflict in Northeast Asia. The history of Sino-Russian relations is a long one, dating back to the early seventeenth century. From a historical perspective, contemporary Sino-Soviet relations form but a brief era in the difficult long-term process by which two giant empires reconcile themselves to each other's existence.

Long sensitive to the historic threat to their security from across the northern frontier, for more than a hundred years the Chinese have lived uneasily with the knowledge that a stronger power faced them from this direction. For the last twenty-five years, the Russians have realized to their discomfort that China is determined to repair this power deficit. The present exaggerated fears on either side, the toxic by-product of this adjustment process, could be the catalyst of a war that would be extremely dangerous in this nuclear age.

The interaction among the United States, China, and the Soviet Union is a central strand of contemporary world politics and presents crucial policy choices to these states. But even a cursory glance at history reveals that the politics of this triangle is an old story in East Asia. In the years since World War II, American and Chinese preoccupation with the Soviet Union has had an important effect on U.S.-China relations.

Sino-Russian Relations: A Historical Overview

In the 1680s, Manchu and Russian troops at the outer edges of their respective empires clashed in a no-man's-land thinly peopled by local tribes. In 1689, with the aid of Jesuit priests, the Treaty of Nerchinsk (Nipchu), the first treaty between China and a Western state, was signed to define parts of the border between the two empires. Since that border and the character of the settlement are now matters of dispute, the imprint of history on contemporary Sino-Soviet relations is obvious.

Since the dawn of China's imperial age more than 2,000 years ago, the sedentary agricultural society of the Chinese has been prey to armed nomads from the north. Imperial China's basic defensive orientation was toward this northern menace even after the arrival in southern waters of armed European merchant-seamen in the sixteenth century created an alternative locus of anxiety. Like their contemporary successors in

Peking, the Chinese emperors presided over a vast state and faced the intractable problem of trying to cope with this dual threat. A key defensive strategy has been to gauge which threat seemed more severe and to seek alignment with the other in order to counteract the danger.

Immense changes in world politics and technology have altered the character of China's present strategic concerns, but the Soviet Union (from its Siberian bases) and the United States (from the Pacific) may still be perceived in terms of the historic continental and maritime threats to Chinese security. Chinese leaders must still judge which is the more pressing danger and how best to counter it. Moreover, the historic buffer zone of nomadic peoples between Russia and China no longer exists. From Sinkiang in the west through the disputed Amur and Ussuri River region in the east, Han Chinese and Great Russians have moved in and striven to incorporate the old pastoral minorities into their own state machines. The nomadic cushion has collapsed.

Straddling the divide between Europe and Asia, the tsarist empire looked both east and west. Peter the Great, who "opened a window to the West," also saw a continental destiny for Russia across the eastern steppe. While many Russians, especially from among the westernized elite, viewed Orientals with fear and contempt, others sensed a real or imagined kinship with these people. St. Petersburg often argued that its actions in and around China would counteract the aggressiveness of Western and Japanese imperialism, thus protecting China while promoting Russian goals.

In 1860, for example, the Russian minister played a devious role at the Chinese court. He promised to deflect an Anglo-French attack on the capital, and on the strength of this promise (which he had neither the intention nor the capability of fulfilling), extracted a treaty ceding a large chunk of Chinese territory to the tsar (the present Maritime Province where Vladivostok is located). Similarly, in 1895, Russia proclaimed itself as "a friend of China" and pressured Japan into returning part of its wartime spoils (the strategic Liaotung Peninsula guarding the Po Hai gulf and Peking). Then, in 1898, Russia occupied this Chinese territory after wheedling permission to build the Chinese Eastern Railway across Manchuria to Vladivostok. Chinese officials, naturally, viewed the Russian record as no different from that of the other imperialists who were threatening Chinese sovereignty. From the turn of the twentieth century, we can trace a competitive alternation between American and Russian influence in Northeast Asia.

Russia correctly perceived a threat to its position in Manchuria and staunchly opposed the "Open Door" initiatives of American Secretaries of State John Hay and Philander Knox. The Russian and American competition for influence in China intensified after the Bolshevik Revolution of 1917. The Soviet Union presented a revolutionary model of development and provided both the Chinese Nationalists and the Chinese Communists with organizational and material support. Meanwhile, the United States, less consciously, presented a model of nonrevolutionary change culminating in a democratic capitalist system. But America's major impact came through the work of thousands of nonofficial persons—missionaries, businessmen, journalists, and adventurers—while the Soviet effort was an exclusively official enterprise which was much easier to coordinate and control. (Even in tsarist days there had been very little official Russian activity in China.)

Taking a very broad perspective, one can see that in the library of ideas from which Chinese reformers and revolutionaries of the twentieth century freely borrowed Jefferson and Bakunin, Whitman and Tolstoy, Wilson and Lenin uneasily shared the same shelves. By the late 1920s the experience of the Russians in revolutionizing a backward country by means of a disciplined party organization and a unitary ideology seemed more relevant to many politically aware Chinese leaders than did the American experience. But most Chinese leaders remained wary of Moscow's meddling in key decisions affecting revolutionary strategy and the safety of the Chinese state. And many leftist leaders maintained their admiration for American culture, efficiency, and power.

The history of relations between the Chinese Communist Party (CCP) and the Soviet Union gives ample evidence of continued tensions in spite of a common Marxist heritage. The Soviet Union helped establish the CCP, but from the 1920s onward Chinese Communist leaders debated whether the Russian experience was directly relevant to China and whether Soviet nationals and Moscow-trained Chinese should be entrusted with the exercise of revolutionary leadership. Broadly speaking, a major CCP trend from the late 1920s through the 1940s was to align the party with the U.S.S.R. on international political issues while jealously preserving the authority to chart the course of the Chinese revolution itself. There was a clear though unstated realization that Soviet state and Chinese revolutionary interests might not always coincide, a lesson learned from the 1920s.

Despite their reservations, the Communist leadership which proclaimed the establishment of the People's Republic in late 1949 encouraged a dramatic intensification of Sino-Soviet ties in the political, military, economic, and cultural fields. Lacking experience in the administration of a complex state machine and the development of a backward agricultural economy, the CCP welcomed thousands of Soviet technicians, engineers, scientists, and administrators who helped set China on the path toward industrialization and state power. A mammoth Sino-Soviet Friendship Association served as the main conduit for the rapid influx of Soviet cultural influences in music, literature, film, education, and so forth, while the Resist American Aid Korea campaign of the early 1950s attempted to extirpate certain pro-American legacies among some of the older educated elite.

The massiveness of the Soviet involvement in China coupled with the deep-seated Chinese ambivalence toward foreign influences (confirmed by Chinese discontent with Soviet economic and military aid) combined in the late 1950s to initiate a rapid reversal of Sino-Soviet relations and to bring about a period of hostility which has not yet abated.

From this historical outline, we can see some of the origins of current Sino-Soviet polemics. Now we can turn to the post-1949 triangular politics involving the United States, China, and the Soviet Union and see how each has viewed the other two in developing its policies.

Chinese Approaches to the Soviet Union and the United States

In July 1949, Mao Tse-tung enunciated his principle of "leaning to one side," and explained that the structure of world politics was such that "all Chinese without exception must lean either to the side of imperialism or to the side of socialism. Sitting on the fence will not do, nor is there a third road." At the time, this statement seemed to confirm the inevitability of a Peking-Moscow link based upon the subordination of Chinese leaders to Moscow. To Americans at least, China appeared as Russia's largest satellite.

This American interpretation of Mao's "lean to one side" statement missed the peculiar and precarious nature of the Sino-Soviet alignment of the 1950s. Unlike the East European Communist leaders whose "power" derived from their unprincipled loyalty to Stalin, the leaders of the CCP were men of ability and independent political authority whose leadership qualities had been tested over twenty years. Moreover, the fierce intraparty struggles of the 1930s and the early 1940s in the

CCP had isolated (though not eliminated from the ruling coalition) precisely those leaders who might have filled the roles of a Chinese Bolesław Bierut, Klement Gottwald, or Mátyás Rákosi. Chinese leaders had persisted in their revolutionary course despite Stalin's low estimate of the Chinese Communists at the end of World War II. Yet it was these same Chinese leaders led by Mao himself who sought alignment with the Soviet Union in 1949.

Necessity dictated the alliance. Long before his final victory in 1949, Mao had thoroughly considered his options in the postwar international system and concluded that China had only a Hobson's choice to make. From 1944 into 1946 the Mao-Chou leadership made persistent efforts to forge an American "connection" in order to gain military aid, neutralize American support for the Kuomintang, and probably also avoid exclusive dependency upon the Soviet Union. But American policy was unresponsive to Chinese initiatives. Even as late as the late spring of 1949, the CCP sought to engage the American ambassador John Leighton Stuart in discussions which they probably hoped would lead to American diplomatic recognition, but these efforts were rebuffed at the presidential level because of the preponderant evidence of Communist hostility and the Cold War atmosphere in the United States. Whatever slim chance had existed to avert two decades of Sino-American hostility was lost.

To the CCP leaders, the Stalinist thesis that the world was sharply divided between the socialist camp and the imperialist camp must have seemed only too accurate. In a hostile world environment, the fledgling Communist government in China needed protection which only the Soviet Union was willing to provide.

In addition, ideology doubtless played a vital role in predisposing China's new leaders toward seeking alliance with the U.S.S.R. Some Chinese were more trustful of the Soviets than Mao, but even Mao appears to have believed that the shared ideology of Marxism-Leninism created a congruence if not an identity of interest between Soviet and Chinese Communists. Soviet aid could make China strong and a strong China would reduce Soviet vulnerability to American power and hasten the decline of imperialism which threatened them both.

The neo-imperialist security and economic arrangements which Stalin extracted in Manchuria and the paucity of Soviet aid undoubtedly caused Mao himself discomfort, but the 1950 Treaty of Alliance against Japan and the United States may have seemed worth the compromised national pride. Moreover, in 1952 while Stalin was still alive and in 1954 after his death, the Soviet leadership showed its willingness to give China more aid and accord her a higher status in the Communist camp. Yet shortly thereafter the Sino-Soviet alliance began to suffer from a fatal dry rot. What went wrong?

Central to its decline was the increasing divergence in foreign policy. The death of Stalin led to a thaw in the Cold War, as the Khrushchev-Bulganin duumvirate signaled its desire for a reduction of international tension. Khrushchev also tried to improve Sino-Soviet relations by increasing aid and showing respect for the Chinese leadership, but his gestures seemed insufficient to the Chinese. Significantly, at this very time the Chinese leadership made a new approach to the United States hoping to negotiate directly to remove the American-imposed blocks to Chinese unification and the threats to her state security. While seeking to achieve a better working relationship with its Soviet ally, China was also trying to take advantage of the atmosphere of détente to widen its international contacts, but the United States again proved unwilling to respond meaningfully to Chinese initiatives. Unable to make a breakthrough to the United States and beginning to chafe within the tight-fitting jacket of their alliance with the U.S.S.R., Chinese leaders began to look for new ways to regain their autonomy and achieve their goals.

Chinese displeasure was compounded by the increasing

Soviet unwillingness to support China's foreign policy goals in the Taiwan Straits and the Sino-Indian border region and by conciliatory Soviet policies toward the United States. (By 1965 the Chinese openly chastized "Soviet-American collaboration," perhaps recalling the example of Yalta, where a Soviet-American deal had sacrificed Chinese national interests.) Peking's leaders again confronted a difficult choice. They could swallow their pride and defer indefinitely the pursuit of their goals while tagging along after the Russians. Alternatively, they could inscribe the Soviet revisionists on their lists of enemies and choose to defy both superpowers by constructing new coalitions from the countries of the "intermediate zones" —the Third World nations and such disaffected alliance partners as France.

Although Mao chose defiance, many Chinese leaders believed that the severe imperialist threat to China and the entire socialist camp necessitated continuing at least a partial alignment with the Soviet Union. But Mao prevailed and the "dual adversary strategy," articulated by Lin Piao, lasted until late 1968 when Chinese leaders perceived that the Soviet threat urgently required a counterweight, which the United States was finally willing to supply. (Again, there is evidence of conflict within the elite on this issue.) But the new Chinese diplomacy avoided any exclusive dependency relationships. Continuing Soviet-American competition in an era of declining bipolarity enhanced China's ability to play its own hand.

This brief narrative suggests that Chinese perceptions of the Soviet-American relationship act as a critical factor to constrain the foreign policy choices of the Chinese leadership. Although Chinese leaders prefer to avoid exclusive alignment with any single element in the international system, their preferences are strongly modified by the existing environment. In addition, there has been significant diversity within the Chinese elite on questions of policy toward the United States and the Soviet Union.

Soviet-American Relations as a Factor in America's China Policy

American policy toward China in the years since World War II has been largely determined by global concerns of the United States, particularly its strategic relationship with the Soviet Union. Yet in examining the immediate postwar period we confront a paradox. Most American policy makers viewed the Chinese Communists as loyal members of the international Communist movement centered in Moscow, but while the United States pursued a policy of containment in Europe, it did very little to prevent the Communist victory in China. Massive American aid which might have prolonged the Kuomintang's hold on power was withheld even when it began to appear that Chiang Kai-shek was losing badly in his struggle with the Communist forces.

Two decisive considerations explain the apparent inconsistency. First, Americans were slow to realize that not only were the Nationalists losing but the Communists were winning! Like almost everybody else (including the Chinese Communists themselves), a generation of American officials accustomed to political chaos in China was ill-prepared to comprehend the rapidity and totality of the Communist triumph. Even when the Communist victory was in hand, sober analysis suggested that the tasks of consolidation and recovery were so immense that China would add little of consequence to the serious Soviet threat. And it was also feared that U.S. intervention in China might lead to a direct Soviet-American clash.

Second, Secretary of State George C. Marshall, probably because of his firsthand experience in China, doubted that the United States possessed the political influence and military capacity to have a significant effect on the outcome of the civil war. The advocates of intervention were stymied by the unavailability of American troops and the negative mood of the public. Marshall's influence within the administration proved decisive. There would be no threat to American interests: the political incapacity of the Chinese and the "democratic individualism of China" would complicate the Communist consolidation of power.

While continuing to slight the importance of China, American policy paid greater attention to the strategic importance of the Western Pacific, and the United States sought to rebuild Japan into a bulwark of security. Meanwhile, Washington sought to block its allies from extending diplomatic recognition to the new government in China, and with the outbreak of the Korean War in June 1950, the United States became reengaged on the Asian mainland. The underlying assumption of American policy—which the Sino-Soviet Treaty Alliance of February 1950 and the Korean War both appeared to confirm—was that the Chinese Communists had solidly aligned themselves with the U.S.S.R. However, Secretary of State Acheson, among others, entertained the hope that in the longer run divergent national interests would pull Russia and China apart.

American belief in the monolithic unity of the Communist camp thus set the stage for Sino-American confrontation in Korea. Dismissing the indigenous Korean origins of a conflict which American policy in that country had helped to precipitate, the United States concluded that the Soviet Union, as in the earlier crises in Czechoslovakia, Berlin, and the Balkans, was testing American resolve. President Harry S. Truman and Secretary of State Dean Acheson declared at once that the Seventh Fleet would be dispatched to the Taiwan Straits to prevent a Communist attack on Formosa, although there was as yet no firm commitment to support Chiang Kai-shek's exiled regime itself.

U.S. policy was too cocky by half. Swayed by General Douglas MacArthur's assurances, the administration could not believe that the Chinese Communists, with their primitive army, would dare to intervene in Korea no matter how jittery MacArthur's northward drive made them feel. The administration was wrong.

After Stalin died in 1953, the new leadership in the Kremlin encouraged the belief that the major problems in world politics could be solved along a direct Soviet-American axis. Until about 1960 the Chinese gave no obvious indication that their overall international strategy and goals diverged from those of their senior allies. Since China appeared to be following the Soviet lead in world affairs, the United States had little incentive to devise a separate China policy.

The divergence between Chinese and Russian policy became unmistakable by the early 1960s as Peking criticized the "craven capitulationists" and "revisionists" in the Kremlin who had supposedly abandoned their revolutionary perspectives and sold out to imperialism. American policy makers drew an important conclusion from the Sino-Soviet split. The zeal of the Maoist leadership and its commitment to transforming the status quo was a function of its own lifetime experience of struggle. But just as successive generations of Soviet leaders were less "ideological" and more pragmatic, so the Chinese would undergo the same mellowing as the mainsprings of revolution wound down. Thus, after abandoning John Foster Dulles' belief that Communism in China was a "passing phenomenon," Secretary of State Dean Rusk overrode those within his department who advocated new policy initiatives toward China and adopted the notion of "waiting out" the older generation of Chinese leaders behind the shield of the alliance system which Dulles had created. Once more the upshot was to defer serious reconsideration of China policy. The Soviets, who had nothing to gain from Sino-American rapprochement, themselves widely advertised the notion that the Peking leadership was composed of unstable and dangerous men. The Cultural Revolution did nothing to allay such suspicions.

Finally, of course, it was two men of the old guard—Nixon and Mao—who broke up the logjam in U.S.-China relations. As the Cultural Revolution receded and the notion of a multipolar international system replaced Cold War bipolarism, China began to appear as a desirable counterweight to the Soviet Union which was rapidly gaining strategic nuclear parity with the United States. Moreover, Kissinger believed that a Peking-Washington rapprochement could lever the suspicious Russians into agreements at the strategic arms limitation talks and elsewhere. After viewing China as an appendage of the U.S.S.R. in the high Cold War period, the United States now saw China as a key element in the attempt to contain Soviet power and construct a stable world order.

Recent Chinese Perspectives on the Soviet Union

As suggested above, a paramount concern of most Chinese leaders since 1949 has been to avoid excessive dependence upon any single element in the international system, that is, to maximize China's freedom of initiative within the limits of its power. To the extent that Chinese leaders perceive a direct security threat from the United States or the Soviet Union they have felt constrained to compromise their autonomy in order to avoid disaster.

The political struggles of the past decades confirm that deep differences divide the CCP leadership on foreign policy as on other issues. What options have Chinese leaders discerned vis-à-vis the Soviet Union? Undoubtedly, the broad issue of policy toward the U.S.S.R. can be analyzed into many sets of subissues—military threat, party affairs, cultural relations, international Communist affairs, and so forth—but it may be worthwhile to suggest certain general tendencies within the leadership. Adapting the broad view which Michel Oksenberg and Steven Goldstein suggest in their analysis, "The Chinese Political Spectrum," one can propose four perspectives within the CCP vis-à-vis the Soviet Union. These perspectives may be defined as (1) emulation/cooperation, (2) limited partnership, (3) opposition, and (4) isolation.[1]

The first perspective—*emulation/cooperation*—assumes that China should not only follow the Soviet lead in international affairs, but also in such areas as party matters, state organization, economic development, and culture. The Twenty-eight "Old Bolsheviks," the Moscow-trained young Communists who took over party leadership in the early 1930s, may be identified with this position. (This group was fatally weakened by the *cheng feng* campaigns of 1942–44). Kao Kang, the Manchurian regional leader purged in 1954, may also be identified with this view.

The second perspective—*limited partnership*—places a much lower value on emulation of the Soviets in domestic affairs (although seeking military and economic aid), but asserts the utility of cooperation with Russia in international affairs in order to oppose imperialism, expand the domain of communism, and reduce China's vulnerability to imperialist attack. China's military professionals in the late 1950s, Lo Jui-ch'ing in 1965–66, and perhaps Liu Shao-ch'i as well may have adhered to this position. A contemporary version of this position might distrust the utility of the Sino-American rapprochement, argue the need for a reduction of Sino-Soviet tension, and manifest less concern for the threat to revolutionary values which Soviet revisionism ostensibly poses.

The third perspective—*opposition*—not only rejects the relevance of Soviet developmental experience for China but also views the U.S.S.R. as the direct and prime threat to the security and revolutionary values of China. In external affairs, policy preferences appropriate to this perspective include

[1] Michel Oksenberg and Steven Goldstein, "The Chinese Political Spectrum," *Problems of Communism* 23 (March–April 1974): 1–13.

active struggle for leadership in the international Communist movement, active involvement in international organizations, pursuit of better relations with Western states including the United States, and relations with the established governments of the Third World. (The precise policy mix would depend, of course, upon the external environmental conditions as well.) Chairman Mao and Chou En-lai may have represented this tendency.

The fourth perspective—*isolation*—likewise rejects the Soviet developmental experience and views the Soviet Union as a threat to revolutionary values. However, it minimizes the danger of a Soviet attack and in any case believes that the Maoist people's war is the best instrument for dealing with any such eventuality. A focus on domestic rather than foreign affairs distinguishes this perspective which, however, supports foreign revolutions through largely rhetorical and symbolic means. The Cultural Revolution radicals may be identified with this perspective.

In China as elsewhere broad agreement on long-range foreign policy goals does not exclude sharp disagreement on the means toward these ends. Three of our four perspectives reject the notion that isolationism is an effective means for attaining Chinese goals vis-à-vis the Soviet Union. However, both the limited partnership and opposition perspectives share the view that China must avoid exclusive dependency upon any single element in the international system. (Isolationists would assert that the best way to avoid dependency is to remain uninvolved.) The emulation/cooperation position, however, would see no danger in identifying China with the Soviet Union. While the isolation position disdains both the United States and the Soviet Union, among the other groups only the limited partnership perspective favors roughly equal ties with the two superpowers. But because this position is now in eclipse, it is difficult to discern any partisans of equally balanced diplomacy in the People's Republic.

During the long course of his pre-1949 struggle to consolidate his personal authority in the CCP, Mao fought against the emulation/cooperation option within the party. The purge of Kao Kang was the death blow to this tendency. Since about 1960 the advocates of limited partnership with the Soviet Union have also been put on the defensive as Mao tried to deprive this position of legitimacy within the Chinese political arena. The ferocious and unending public attacks on Soviet revisionism and Soviet social imperialism may be viewed as Mao's attempts to raise the political cost of advocating a limited partnership position so high that no one will dare to speak forth in China. Only opposition and isolation remained open options in Mao's lifetime, and limited partnership is another alternative for the post-Mao leadership.

Soviet Hopes and Prospects in China

What hopes do the Soviets have for either short-range or long-range improvement in Sino-Soviet relations? What action do they contemplate in China to affect political outcomes?

Soviet analysts of Chinese politics and society do not speak with a single voice, but they differ in degree much more than in kind. In general, for them China represents a bleak and inhospitable political landscape. In this view, after a lengthy struggle within the CCP, the national chauvinist forces led by Mao completely routed the "internationalist" forces loyal to socialism and bloc solidarity (our category of emulation/cooperation). Despite widespread discontent, only fragments of opposition survive among the military, the Party and state apparatus, the economic managers, and the working population. China, say the authoritative Soviet analysts, is ruled by a military-bureaucratic dictatorship which brazenly flaunts the banner of socialism to which it has no legitimate title, for China is no longer a socialist state.

The Chinese political system, however, is anything but stable. Soviet analysis perceives the existence of two levels of political conflict. Popular discontent, manifested through sporadic strikes and wall-poster *samizdat,* is brutally repressed by the regime. At the very apex of power, the Soviets see an ongoing battle between "moderate pragmatists" and "extreme leftists," a battle exacerbated by the process of succession and the purge of the "gang of four." Although such a regime cannot survive in the long run, as the Soviet Communist Party theoretical journal *Kommunist* commented, "it would be unrealistic to expect a radical change in China's domestic and foreign policy only as a result of one or two more crisis phenomena or other events in the political life of the country."

What are the policy implications of such a view? To interpret these Soviet analysts is like trying to decipher a double palimpsest inscribed with invisible ink. Let us begin by focusing on what is left unsaid. Although the Soviets repeatedly attacked Mao, they usually avoided attacking other leaders or identifying the composition of the competing groups within the Maoist elite. Also, the Soviets are careful not to compromise any Chinese leader by intimating that he is viewed with greater favor or even lesser hostility in the Kremlin. To do so would be to damage him severely and possibly jeopardize whatever hope he might offer of improving Sino-Soviet relations. However, might Soviet silence on this point not also reflect an unstated assumption that many if not most leaders or leadership coalitions in a post-Mao China will favor an amelioration of relations with the U.S.S.R.? In such a case, it is wise to offend no one and maintain maximum flexibility.

Actual Soviet hopes for an improvement in relations with China rest on the expectation that the limited partnership tendency is a workable option in Chinese politics in this post-Mao era. Mao was seen as personally responsible for the uncompromising character of Chinese policy toward the U.S.S.R. even when other Chinese leaders loyal to him were willing to be more flexible. But over the long term several possible benefits may lead the post-Mao leadership to seek a limited détente with the U.S.S.R. A reduction of Sino-Soviet tension would allow the partial diversion of funds budgeted for the military into vital economic development purposes. It would increase pressure on the United States to yield on the Taiwan issue in order to check the drift of China toward the Soviet Union (unless a solution to this issue in Sino-American relations has been reached already). More generally, it would enhance Chinese bargaining capacity by more nearly equalizing the sides of the Sino-Soviet-American triangle. Finally, it would open the Soviet Union as an important market for Chinese light industrial goods as well as an additional source of modern technology.

The actual modalities of Sino-Soviet tension reduction need not detain us very long. A partial drawback of Soviet troops from the disputed border might well lead to rapid progress or to a postponement of the stalemated border negotiations, and it might open the way to a mutual nonaggression pact such as both sides have proposed at different times. Expanded cultural and scientific exchanges might also serve as a primary means of improving the relationship.

American Interests in the Sino-Soviet Relationship

Finally, let us return to the area of Sino-Soviet-American interaction. What type of Sino-Soviet relationship is most conducive to the attainment of American policy objectives? Should the United States seek to block the easing of Soviet-Chinese hostility?

I suggest that we should differentiate between short-term *power-maximizing* and long-term *problem-solving* approaches.

There is no doubt that Sino-Soviet hostility short of war divides the attention of the Soviet leadership, ties up Soviet political and military resources, and weakens Soviet pressure in the West. At a time of declining American willingness to utilize power in world affairs, the Chinese function as a tacit partner with strong parallel interests in curbing Soviet expansion throughout the world. This fact has led a number of American commentators to advocate a definite U.S. "tilt" toward China. This might involve a decision to provide military-related technology in order to strengthen Chinese defenses. The critical deficiency of this perspective is that it looks at best toward an indefinite perpetuation of the present status quo without focusing on the dangers inherent in such a policy.

By adopting the alternative perspective of long-term problem solving, we may suggest two key areas where a reduction in Sino-Soviet tension might be of benefit. The first broad area is that of arms control and disarmament. Partly because of its felt need to augment its defensive capacity against the U.S.S.R., China has refused to participate in serious arms control and disarmament negotiations. A limited Sino-Soviet rapprochement might provide the added security which would encourage Chinese leaders to engage seriously in such negotiations, rather than simply seeking to perfect their nuclear deterrent capabilities. Bilateral Sino-Soviet negotiations on the prevention of accidental warfare would also be of wider benefit and would contribute to stability in Northeast Asia.

The potential for achieving a multilateral solution to the Korean problem might be enhanced by Sino-Soviet rapprochement. One can imagine a Moscow-Peking agreement, in response to sufficient incentives from the West, to deny North Korea support for reopening the suspended war on the Korean peninsula. North and South Korea might thereby be induced to find a solution to the political stalemate. Finally, the denuclearization and "neutralization" of Southeast Asia might become possible as Sino-Soviet competition in the area abated.

In brief, the prospects for improving world security might be measurably advanced to the benefit of the United States and most other nations.

A second area of benefit (though not to a narrowly defined U.S. interest, perhaps) might be the accelerated transformation of the international economic system in the direction of greater equity. The acrimonious wrangling which now characterizes Sino-Soviet interaction at the United Nations and other international organizations might give way to cooperative efforts which the United States could join to confront problems of population, energy, natural resources, trade, and so on. Should this occur, the explosive potential of economic injustice which casts a shadow over the future of the United States and other wealthy industrialized nations might be dissipated. While such hopes may seem visionary, they represent a worthier objective than that of merely striving to build a tacit Sino-American alliance as a buttress against Soviet power.

The effect of Sino-Soviet rapprochement upon American interests will depend very much upon the state of Sino-American relations at such time as Moscow and Peking draw closer together. If at that time Peking perceives that Washington is still engaged in supporting the separate statehood of Taiwan, for example, then a Chinese move toward Moscow could be seen as directed against the United States. But a newly powerful China need no longer choose between a Soviet or an American protector.

One thing is clear. Although Sino-Soviet relations may improve, the operational unity of the Sino-Soviet alliance of the 1950s is highly unlikely to be restored. The "normalization" of Sino-Soviet relations would not eliminate differences between the two countries on matters of ideology and internal development, nor on many questions of international politics. Nor would Sino-Soviet competition for power and influence disappear. A sensible American policy should avoid a panicked reaction to signs of Sino-Soviet détente and should not seek to impede such a process.

Conclusion

As suggested above, long-term secular changes have brought Russia and China into closer geographic and strategic proximity. The Chinese have developed Manchuria and more recently the Northwest; the Russians have developed the Trans-Baikal region, eastern Siberia, and the Maritime region. The technological revolution in weaponry has reinforced this trend, linking the fates of Khabarovsk and Shenyang, Vladivostok and Peking, Irkutsk and Lanchow, and a host of other cities. Marxism-Leninism, which brought Russia and China together in the 1950s and now divides them, may still prove a long-term bond. In Northeast Asia and the Pacific, Southeast Asia, the South Asian subcontinent, and elsewhere, Soviet and Chinese objectives presently clash. And in all of these areas, American interests are also present to one degree or another.

In the short run, the United States and China can cooperate to check any expansionist tendencies of the Soviet Union which (for very different reasons) neither is presently able to contain by itself. But American hopes to perpetuate Sino-Soviet discord are misplaced and ill-advised. As China approaches parity with the United States and the Soviet Union in the critical indicators of power, it will be the most effective guardian of its own independence. Both the United States and the Soviet Union would be wise to recognize this emergent reality.

Part V

INTERACTIONS AROUND CHINA'S RIM

MICHEL OKSENBERG

Introduction

CHINESE and American interests are intertwined in three regions: Korea, Taiwan, and Southeast Asia. These were the scenes of the Sino-American confrontation from 1949 to 1971. In the bleakest outlooks, it is possible that conflict in these areas could recur and threaten confrontation again in the future.

On the other hand, the three areas offer the opportunity to engage Chinese and American interests in more cooperative ways. Cooperation in the maintenance of stability on the Korean peninsula is a realistic goal for U.S. policy. Rather than Taiwan as a bone of contention, one could envision Taiwan as a prosperous entity with which the United States retains a full range of economic and cultural ties and which contributes to rather than threatens Chinese security and economic interests. And in Southeast Asia, a cooperative relationship particularly among the ASEAN countries, China, and the United States would bring stability to the region and prevent an outside power from achieving a position of dominance. In a different but related view, Jerome Cohen's concluding essay asks in hardheaded fashion how international law might be used to bind the United States and China more firmly.

The conclusion of these papers is guardedly optimistic: providing we have a sense of ourselves and a sense of history, we may be able to construct a better relationship with China. And providing our policies in Taiwan, Korea, and Southeast Asia and on international law are not designed for an American audience alone, perhaps we can look forward to greater stability in Asian affairs.

11

PETER VAN NESS

Taiwan and
Sino-American Relations

THE issue of American policy toward the island of Taiwan—perhaps the central obstacle to improved Sino-American relations—has remained essentially unchanged since Richard Nixon signed the Shanghai Communiqué at the conclusion of his precedent-breaking journey to China in February 1972. In a more fundamental sense, the question of Taiwan has been a major point of contention between Peking and Washington since June 1950, when Harry Truman ordered the U.S. Seventh Fleet into the Taiwan Straits between the island and the Chinese mainland following the outbreak of the Korean War.

How did this situation come about? What are the key dimensions of the Taiwan problem?

I would like to thank several people for particularly helpful criticism and suggestions during the writing of this chapter: Hong Che-sheng, Hsieh Shan-yuan, Penelope Prime, Tien Hung-mao, and Ellen Van Ness.

Taiwan, an island about the size of the Netherlands lying 100 miles off the southeastern coast of China, is today the home of 16 million Chinese, of whom about 85 percent are native Taiwanese. The island is ruled by the Republic of China government, the Kuomintang regime, which was nominally established on the mainland in 1912 and which unified China under the leadership of Chiang Kai-shek in 1928. Defeated by Communist revolutionaries in 1949, the government fled to Taiwan where since that time it has governed under martial law, never giving up its claim to being the rightful government of China and continually insisting that it will reconquer the mainland and overthrow the Communist People's Republic of China.

Taiwan has become an issue in Sino-American relations in several important respects. First, Taiwan represents the fact that there are two competing Chinese governments. Since 1949 each government has sought international support and recognition as the sole legitimate government over all of China (both the mainland and Taiwan) and has demanded that other countries choose between them, both refusing to maintain formal diplomatic relations with any country which had established relations with the other.

Second, Taiwan constitutes a special problem for the United States because of President Truman's decision in 1950 to send the U.S. Seventh Fleet to intervene in the Chinese civil war, thus deterring a planned Chinese Communist assault on the island and preventing the completion of a Communist victory over the Chiang Kai-shek regime. During the years since 1950, the United States has sustained the Republic of China through military and economic aid and diplomatic support. In the United Nations, for example, the United States insisted that the defeated Republic of China government was the rightful holder of China's seat in both the General Assembly and the Security Council until October 25, 1971, when the membership of the United Nations finally overruled the American position and seated Peking in the place of Taipei. If the United

States is to establish formal relations with Peking, it must decide how recognition will affect its long-term relationship with Taiwan and how it intends to withdraw from almost three decades of involvement in the Chinese civil war.

Third, Taiwan raises two related problems; irredenta and self-determination. The People's Republic insists that Taiwan is part of China and, therefore, that the island must ultimately be placed under its jurisdiction. However, many Taiwanese demand that the people of the island should have the right to choose their own future. The Taiwanese claim to self-determination embarrasses those Americans who are eager to wash their hands of the entire Taiwan affair, especially since self-determination is a political principle which American administrations have long enunciated as fundamental to American foreign policy.

Finally, an American decision to shift its formal diplomatic recognition from Taipei to Peking, as in the case of any major policy change, must also be assessed from the perspective of the implications which the new policy would have in relationships with other countries, particularly in Asia. For example, would a change in China policy be costly or beneficial regarding U.S. relations with Japan, the Soviet Union, or non-Communist countries of Southeast Asia?

In an effort to shed some light on the various dimensions of the Taiwan issue in Sino-American relations, let us examine in turn the different perspectives taken on the question of Taiwan by those parties most deeply involved: the People's Republic of China, the Republic of China government and the Taiwanese population, and the United States.

China's View

Ever since Chiang Kai-shek's attempt to destroy the Chinese Communist Party in 1927, when he abruptly ended an alliance between the CCP and Kuomintang which had been concluded with the cooperation of the Soviet Union, the Chinese Communist movement has been in a life-or-death struggle with the Kuomintang and its government. The final battle for the mainland began in 1946, after the Japanese surrender ending World War II. Three years later, in 1949, the Communist forces defeated the Kuomintang and expelled the Chiang Kai-shek government from the Chinese mainland. The United States gave very substantial material support to the Republic of China during 1946–49 but refrained from directly intervening with American military forces. In January 1950, the Truman administration indicated that the United States was withdrawing any further support from the remnants of the Republic of China government.

However, the outbreak of the Korean War on June 25, 1950, changed all that. Two days later, President Truman ordered the American Seventh Fleet into the Taiwan Straits, the 100-mile-wide body of water separating the Communist forces from the defeated Kuomintang. The Truman decision to intervene with American military forces to prevent the completion of the Communist victory placed the United States squarely in the middle of the Chinese civil war in a manner which continues today, a quarter century later.

The Truman intervention was apparently not expected in Peking. In the Chinese Communist view, the American action was totally unwarranted by events. China had not provoked the United States. The People's Republic was not a party to the Korean War and did not become involved in that conflict until after the American intervention on the side of the South Koreans had led to a "roll-back" effort which sought to overthrow the Communist government of North Korea.

In Peking's view, the only reason that there is a "Taiwan issue" today is that the United States intervened twenty-seven years ago. Had the United States not intervened to save the Republic of China (contrary to the Truman position of six months earlier), Communist forces would have launched their planned invasion of the island and the "Republic of China" would have disappeared into the history books. Taiwan would have been reunited with the Chinese mainland under Communist authority, and the long civil war would have finally come to an end. For the leaders of the People's Republic, the Kuomintang government in Taiwan is simply an appendage of American policy. The Republic of China's lifeline of support has been the United States. Moreover, Peking sees the entire Taiwan issue essentially as American-made. Thus, when Americans in negotiations ask the Chinese what they are prepared to give in return for an American withdrawal from Taiwan (that is, from their civil war), they are likely to find the Chinese responding with considerable irritation.

Since 1949, American support for the Republic of China has not been limited solely to its defense against the People's Republic. U.S. economic aid to the island up to 1965 has been estimated at $1.5 billion, enough to supply 34 percent of all capital investment in Taiwan during those years. In 1954, the American secretary of state, John Foster Dulles, negotiated a Mutual Defense Treaty with the Republic of China, thereby formalizing the American security commitment and building Taiwan into a military treaty system parallel to the SEATO pact, which was negotiated and concluded by Dulles during the same year. Substantial American military aid and technical assistance complemented the security treaty, and coordinated intelligence activities against the People's Republic were undertaken by the United States and the Republic of China. These activities in turn were a part of efforts by both governments to encourage and to support sabotage and insurrectionary movements against the Peking government. Hence, with American support, the Chinese civil war continued. In spite of having lost the mainland to the Communists, the Taipei government continued to claim to be the sole legitimate government of China, and the United States gave military, diplomatic, and material support to those claims.

Mustering its formidable diplomatic influence in the United
Nations year after year, Washington defended Taipei's hold
on China's seat, and the United States exerted great pressure
on other governments to withhold diplomatic recognition of
the People's Republic and to embargo trade relations with
China as well.

Finally after two decades, this pattern was broken in the
spring of 1971 with "ping-pong diplomacy"—to be followed
in turn by the secret Kissinger trip to meet the Chinese leaders
for the first time in Peking and the announcement on July 15
that President Nixon would visit the People's Republic. The
Shanghai Communiqué signed during that visit identifies the
objective of "normalization of relations between the two countries," but it is still unclear what notions of timing were discussed during the Sino-American negotiations in China. Two
important paragraphs in the Communiqué specifically address
the Taiwan issue:

The two sides reviewed the long-standing serious disputes between China and the United States. The Chinese side reaffirmed
its position: The Taiwan question is the crucial question ob-
structing the normalization of relations between China and the
United States; the Government of the People's Republic of China
is the sole legal government of China; Taiwan is a province of
China which has long been returned to the motherland; the
liberation of Taiwan is China's internal affair in which no other
country has the right to interfere; and all U.S. forces and military
installations must be withdrawn from Taiwan. The Chinese government firmly opposes any activities which aim at the creation
of "one China, one Taiwan," "one China, two governments,"
"two Chinas," an "independent Taiwan," or advocate that "the
status of Taiwan remains to be determined."

The U.S. side declared: The United States acknowledges that
all Chinese on either side of the Taiwan Strait maintain there is
but one China and that Taiwan is a part of China. The United
States Government does not challenge that position. It reaffirms
its interest in a peaceful settlement of the Taiwan question by the
Chinese themselves. With this prospect in mind, it affirms the

ultimate objective of the withdrawal of all U.S. forces and military installations from Taiwan. In the meantime, it will progressively reduce its forces and military installations on Taiwan as the tension in the area diminishes.

At a press conference convened to explain the meaning of the Shanghai Communiqué after its publication, Henry Kissinger interpreted the phrase "tension in the area" to refer to a geographical area including Southeast Asia as well as the Taiwan Straits and to tensions having to do with the Vietnam War. In January 1973, less than a year after Nixon's visit to China, the United States finally achieved the negotiated withdrawal from Vietnam which it had so persistently sought. Yet four years later, there were still some 1,400 American military men on the island of Taiwan.

Presumably, it was the firm intention of those leaders in both Peking and Washington who initiated détente that progress in the relationship, once begun, should move fairly quickly toward the establishment of formal diplomatic relations and an institutionalization of bilateral contacts before the inevitable process of choosing successors to Chairman Mao Tsetung and Premier Chou En-lai would begin. In 1972, Chinese as well as American supporters of détente had a common interest in advancing the relationship rapidly so as to avoid the possibility of its becoming an issue of controversy during the Chinese domestic process in which successors to Mao and Chou would be selected. As things turned out, however, it was the Watergate affair and the succession to Richard Nixon which halted the normalization process.

Nixon, apparently fearful that any improvement in relations with Peking at Taipei's expense would alienate those conservative senators who were his best hope of defeating a possible impeachment in the Senate, failed to press the relationship forward during his final months in office. After Nixon's resignation, Gerald Ford, wary of controversial political actions in his first weeks in power, especially after the hostile public reaction to his pardon of Nixon, later seemed prepared to continue the process of "normalization" with the People's Republic until confronted, first, by the Communist victories in Indochina during the spring of 1975 and, then, by Ronald Reagan's conservative challenge within the Republican Party to deprive him of the nomination for the presidency. Both events pressed the Ford administration to demonstrate its conservative credentials and, as a result, progress toward improved ties with Peking, particularly if it involved breaking formal relations with Taipei, was again postponed.

For the Chinese, who had every reason to expect that relations would continue to improve after helping the United States to achieve a negotiated conclusion to its military role in Vietnam in 1973 and following the exchange of Liaison Offices later that same year, American policy may have appeared designed actually to reverse the progress toward Sino-American détente, especially when Taipei was permitted by Washington to open five new consulates in the United States and a new American ambassador was appointed to the Taipei government.

Eventually, the delay in achieving full "normalization of relations" led to precisely the circumstances which both American and Chinese architects of détente had apparently been anxious to avoid: the deaths in 1976 of China's two principal leaders, Mao Tse-tung and Chou En-lai, before a foundation of formal, mutually beneficial Sino-American relations had been completed.

The Chinese conditions for establishment of formal diplomatic relations with the United States remained consistent during this period: (1) withdrawal of diplomatic recognition from Taipei and extension of recognition (with an embassy) in Peking; (2) termination of the Mutual Defense Treaty of 1954; (3) withdrawal of all American troops from Taiwan. Like Taipei, therefore, Peking demanded that the United

States would have to choose; it could not have formal diplomatic relations with both governments. For its part, the United States appeared to be attempting to gain a commitment from Peking not to use force against Taiwan as a precondition for U.S. recognition. China's response was that it did not intend at present to use force, but that a decision whether or not to seek a military resolution of its differences with Taipei would be made by the Chinese leadership alone, since the dispute with the Republic of China government was, in their view, a Chinese domestic matter in which no foreign government should attempt to interfere.

The People's Republic's actions, as well as words, during this period demonstrated a continuation of the moderate policy of seeking to resolve the Taiwan problem without the use of force. Taiwanese were invited to visit the mainland; three groups of former Kuomintang officials were released from confinement in China; and Chinese officials continued to remain flexible in their discussions of possible procedures for reunifying Taiwan with the mainland. American military forces on the island appeared perhaps to be less of a concern to Peking than they were in 1972 when the Shanghai Communiqué was being drafted, especially since China appeared anxious that an abrupt withdrawal of American military power from East Asia might provide enhanced opportunities in the region for Soviet expansion. Peking remained adamant, however, that the problem of Taiwan was a domestic issue, which the Chinese alone would resolve as they saw fit.

American visitors to Peking were advised to look to the Japanese precedent as an appropriate model for a change in the official American diplomatic status regarding China. In September 1972, the Japanese government, which formerly had established a trade mission in Peking and an embassy in Taipei, shifted its formal diplomatic recognition from Taipei to Peking, but was permitted by both Peking and Taipei to maintain a trade mission on the island of Taiwan in spite of the fact that Japan had broken formal diplomatic relations with the Taipei government. Since 1972, Japanese investment in Taiwan has increased, and Japanese commercial, cultural, and tourist activities on the island have continued very much as before.

Peking's intended message for the United States based on the "Japanese model" is that formal diplomatic relations could be achieved, in effect, by simply exchanging the name plates of the American embassy in Taipei and the Liaison Office in Peking. As in the case of Japan, trade, investment, and educational and cultural exchanges with Taiwan could continue in spite of the fact that the United States would no longer recognize the Taipei regime. However, one problem which Washington faces under such circumstances, which Japan did not, is what to do about the U.S.-Republic of China Mutual Defense Treaty of 1954. Presumably, the United States could not maintain a treaty commitment to a government which it did not recognize.

The Perspective from Taiwan: Government and People

The public position of the Taipei government has remained essentially the same from the 1950s to the present: the Republic of China claims to be the sole legitimate government of all of China; its leaders religiously proclaim their determination to regain control of the mainland and to defeat the Communists; and the Kuomintang-dominated regime refuses either in name or in fact to become a government which represents only Taiwan.

The Republic of China bases its legitimacy on national elections held on the mainland in 1947 when it was still at least nominally in power, and the Taipei government insists that new elections to national offices cannot be held until it has retaken control of all of China. The Taiwanese population is represented in local governmental institutions as well as through provincial Taiwan representatives to the national government, but the idea that the population of the island should have the right to choose all of those officials who actually govern them is denounced as treason.

At present, there is no indication of any significant support for the Taipei government among the population of the Chinese mainland, nor is it likely that the old Kuomintang regime would be considered by Chinese citizens as a viable alternative if the Peking government suffered a domestic crisis. Yet, the fiction of pretending to represent China and the farce of endless planning to regain control of the mainland perform vital political functions for the Taipei government. If the playacting ended, the Kuomintang government would be stripped bare of any justification for ruling the people of Taiwan and especially for continuing its repressive martial law. Many analysts have argued that time would resolve the major problems regarding Taiwan. In particular, they suggested that after the death of President Chiang Kai-shek, his son, Chiang Ching-kuo, would be prepared to deal pragmatically with the issues of Taiwan's future.

On April 5, 1975, Chiang Kai-shek died, and the sixty-six-year-old Chiang Ching-kuo, who had been in de facto political control for several years during the president's illness, succeeded his father. Although holding nominally different offices in both the Taipei government and the ruling Kuomintang (i.e., Chiang Ching-kuo is premier not president, and the post of "director general" of the Kuomintang, which his father held, has been retired in his honor), Chiang Ching-kuo has replaced Chiang Kai-shek as the principal leader of both the government and the Kuomintang. To date, however, what is most striking about the policies which Chiang Ching-kuo has articulated is the way they have forcefully continued, rather than departed from, those of his father.

In contrast to Chiang Kai-shek's aloof, imperial style, Chiang Ching-kuo makes many personal appearances, and he is described in government advertisements run in American magazines as a premier "in touch with the common man." Nevertheless, Premier Chiang has appeared to make a special effort in interviews with visiting American newsmen to emphasize both his personal commitment to retaking the mainland and a firm refusal to talk or to negotiate with the Chinese Communists about the future of Taiwan:

> The mainland is now in a state of widespread turmoil beyond Peiping's control.
>
> President Ford's recent visit only strengthened the Chinese Communists' dictatorial rule and exacerbates the agony of the Chinese people. It runs counter to their wishes.
>
> It is impossible to ease world tension by dealing with the Chinese Communists. Peace and stability in Asia and other parts of the world can be ensured only after freedom and democracy are restored to all of China. . . .
>
> It is absolutely impossible for the Republic of China to cooperate with the Chinese Communist Party in any field. The Communists rule the Chinese mainland with brute force, and it has never been accepted by the people there.
>
> To set our mainland compatriots free and restore their freedom is the unchangeable policy of the Republic of China.[1]

Although the premier's views are clear, there is no way of knowing under present circumstances what the preferences of the people of Taiwan are with regard to their future. Taipei has never been willing to permit the issue to be debated in public and, in fact, has often jailed those individuals who have questioned the wisdom of the return-to-the-mainland policy or suggested opening discussions with Peking. Nonetheless, Taiwan has been quite successful economically. For example, the annual increase in gross national product in the

[1] *Free China Weekly,* 4 January 1976.

period 1961–73 was an impressive 9.5 percent. Also, in spite of the fact that thirty-four foreign countries broke diplomatic relations with Taipei in the period from May 1971 (before the announcement of Nixon's trip to China and the Republic of China's subsequent expulsion from the United Nations) to the end of 1975, Taiwan's foreign trade and even investment from abroad have increased at an impressive rate. Many residents of the island seem apolitical and content to enjoy the substantial benefits of Taiwan's continuing economic growth. For his part, Premier Chiang Ching-kuo emphasizes the special relationship with the United States:

. . . between our two countries, the United States and the Republic of China, we share the same philosophy, the same ideology, the same institutions, as well as the same way of life. So it's much easier to communicate between our two peoples. We don't have to guess what the other side said, what's the real meaning behind what the other side said. We can communicate very freely without having to resort to any guesswork.[2]

Yet not everyone in Taiwan agrees with the premier. There are a number of different organizations, principally operating in exile in Japan or the United States, which constitute the so-called Taiwan independence movement. They share the common objective of majority rule for Taiwan. In their view, the American public has been continually misled by Republic of China propaganda and the activities of the "China Lobby" in the United States, which has been active since World War II in promoting American support for the Kuomintang regime. Republic of China officials, cooperating with sympathetic American congressmen and U.S. businessmen having important interests in Taiwan, have been tremendously influential in maintaining a positive American public opinion and official policy toward their government.

Contrary to the pronouncements of Premier Chiang,

[2] *Free China Weekly,* 28 December 1975.

Taiwanese activists maintain that the Taipei government does *not* share the same philosophy, same ideology, same institutions, and same way of life with the United States. The government is a single-party dictatorship which has ruled the island under martial law, occasionally behaving with the most shocking brutality, as in February and March 1947, when Taiwanese demonstrations against Republic of China repression and corruption were put down with a systematic execution of an estimated 10,000 to 20,000 Taiwanese. Moreover, members of the Taiwan independence movement go on to point out that in the months since the death of Chiang Kai-shek, several events have demonstrated that Chiang Ching-kuo has no intention of becoming any more tolerant of political opposition than his father was. For example, in August 1975, a new journal *Taiwan Chenglun* (Taiwan Political Review) established and operated by native Taiwanese seeking to promote democratic reform, was suppressed by the government before the end of the year, and subsequently two persons connected with the journal were arrested. More important, Pai Ya-ts'an, a Taiwanese candidate in an election for supplementary seats in the Legislative Yuan (the Parliament), was arrested in October after printing as a part of his electoral campaign a list of twenty-nine questions for Premier Chiang, which included queries regarding both martial law and negotiations with Peking. Mr. Pai was sentenced for these activities to life imprisonment! Amnesty International, the worldwide human rights organization, is actively seeking the release of Pai Ya-ts'an and other political prisoners held in Taiwan.

The argument in favor of independence for Taiwan is based on the principles of self-determination and majority rule in addition to the historical fact that the island of Taiwan in recent history has only briefly and irregularly been ruled by authorities in power on the mainland. As a result, the people of Taiwan have developed their own particular social identity.

In the seventeenth century, the Dutch and Spanish briefly ruled the island until they were defeated by Koxinga and his men, who used Taiwan as a base from which to attempt to restore the Ming dynasty on the mainland. The Ming had never controlled Taiwan, but finally in 1683 its successor, the Ch'ing dynasty, defeated the regime established on Taiwan by Koxinga and his offspring and placed Taiwan under mainland control for the next 200 years. There occurred a number of rebellions against Ch'ing control during that time, and the island did not formally become a province of the Ch'ing empire until 1887, eight years before Taiwan was ceded by the Ch'ing to Japan as a result of China's defeat in the Sino-Japanese War of 1894–95. Then, for fifty years, 1895–1945, Taiwan was ruled by Japan. The Republic of China first gained control of the island in 1945 from the defeated Japanese in concurrence with the Cairo and Potsdam conference agreements, which specified that Taiwan and other Japanese-held territories should be returned to China. Having held the island for only four years, the Republic of China government itself was forced to withdraw to Taiwan by the Communist victory on the mainland in 1949.

The people of Taiwan in 1945 received the Republic of China forces as liberators from Japanese colonialism, but they soon found themselves treated not as liberated countrymen but as a conquered people. Kuomintang carpetbaggers pillaged the island, and their offenses became so flagrant that the Taiwanese finally demonstrated in protest in February 1947, only to be attacked even more savagely through the systematic, official repression and the mass executions already described.

It seems to be the consensus among those people associated with the Taiwan independence movement that the regime is simply not capable of adequate reform. In fact, both Taiwanese and dissident mainlander residents of Taiwan note that since the legitimacy of the government is entirely dependent upon its claim to represent all of China, if it were to give up that claim it would theoretically have to give up power in Taiwan to the majority of the population. Thus, few people think that the Republic of China will forgo its return-to-the-mainland policy and implement the kinds of domestic reforms required to make it responsive to its only real constituency, the people of Taiwan. Moreover, the fact of the years of repression of Taiwanese activists no doubt makes Kuomintang leaders even more unwilling peaceably to give up power to a Taiwanese majority which might at some point seek revenge for past brutalities.

American Foreign Policy

Majority rule and self-determination, the future for Taiwan which presumably most Americans would prefer, probably has the least chance among the likely alternatives of ever taking place. Ideally, an internationally supervised plebiscite to determine the true preferences of the population, Taiwanese and mainlanders, would seem to be the best solution. However, the present Republic of China government will not permit such an election to be held.

Both the Nixon and Ford administrations have committed the United States to completing the "normalization of relations" with Peking, which in the vocabulary of Sino-American diplomacy means the establishment of formal diplomatic ties. As has been pointed out, both Taipei and Peking have required that any government which recognizes one cannot have formal governmental relations with the other. By early 1977, almost three-fourths of the world's countries (some 112 among 151 independent states) had chosen Peking, while aside from the United States, few governments remained accredited to Taipei—countries like El Salvador, Honduras, South Korea, and Paraguay. America's major allies had long since established relations with the People's Republic, including Britain, France, West Germany, Canada, Australia, Japan, Mexico, Brazil, Venezuela, the Philippines, and Thailand. Since the announcement in 1971 that Richard Nixon would travel to China signaled to the world that American Cold War policy toward the People's Republic was changing, much of the rest of the world had expected a formalization of relations between Washington and Peking. Many countries probably have been surprised at the long delay.

The hopes held by many observers that after the death of Chiang Kai-shek his son, Chiang Ching-kuo, would be prepared to enter into negotiations with Peking regarding the future of Taiwan and to undertake domestic political reforms simply have not been borne out. On the contrary, Taipei has remained adamant in defense of the status quo. Not surprisingly, the Chiang Ching-kuo government, in close cooperation with American business interests in Taiwan and traditional friends of the Kuomintang in the United States, has mounted a major campaign to stop U.S. recognition of the People's Republic. The American Chamber of Commerce in the Republic of China, representing a substantial proportion of the total U.S. investment in Taiwan (that investment total is almost $500 million) has been particularly active in attempting to demonstrate the costs of switching American recognition to Peking on the basis of the so-called "Japanese model." In spite of the success of the Japanese experience, the Chamber of Commerce group has argued that among other requirements, the U.S.-Republic of China Mutual Defense Treaty is indispensable to the success of American business activities on the island.

Taiwan independence activists, the World United Formosans for Independence, for example, acknowledge that the People's Republic is clearly in control on the Chinese mainland and that it deserves full international recognition, by the United States and other countries. They realize that U.S. recognition of Peking would require breaking relations with Taipei and that, as a result, almost inevitably the Defense Treaty would lapse.

However, observers note that the Defense Treaty itself is not of critical importance, because, first, the language of the agreement is quite vague with regard to concrete American commitments in the event of an attack on Taiwan, and more important, the likelihood of an attack on the island will probably be determined by factors other than the treaty per se. Among the more significant deterrents to a possible use of force against Taiwan is the political relationship between Washington and Peking, especially with regard to the Chinese perception of a Soviet military threat. Also the People's Republic is eager to maintain the good will of those non-Communist countries of Asia with which it has been successful in establishing relations (particularly Japan, which has substantial commerce with Taiwan). At present, it seems most probable that China's principal enemy, the Soviet Union, would be the main beneficiary from events involving a Chinese threat or use of force against Taiwan. The Soviet Union has long charged that China is an expansionist power, threatening the security of Asian states, and Moscow is fully prepared to welcome fearful non-Communist nations into anti-Chinese defense arrangements under the rubric of their notion of Collective Security in Asia.

The Ford administration in the months before leaving office had seemed intent on preparing the way for a shift in diplomatic relations to Peking. On the one hand, Washington had gradually cut the number of American military personnel stationed on Taiwan, as Nixon had pledged in the Shanghai Communiqué. On the other hand, the administration endorsed major new sales of military hardware to Taipei (including a $34 million radar air defense system, Hawk ground-to-air missiles at $85 million, and sixty new F-5E jet interceptors said to total $95 million) in order to enhance its capacity to defend itself—the apparent logic being that the stronger Taipei was militarily, the easier it would be politically in the United States to abrogate the Mutual Defense Treaty. Although during 1976 there were reports from the CIA that Taiwan had begun to reprocess spent nuclear reactor fuel to create stockpiles of plutonium usable for the development of nuclear weapons, official Taipei statements denied both that such reprocessing was taking place and that the Republic of China, a signatory of the Nuclear Nonproliferation Treaty, had any intention of building nuclear weapons.

With regard to comparative military capabilities on the two sides of the Taiwan Straits, the People's Republic has been a nuclear power since 1964, and the People's Liberation Army is armed with both missiles and aircraft delivery systems. However, short of a nuclear attack, which is thought to be highly unlikely under present circumstances, the People's Republic apparently lacks the conventional capability (especially in attack aircraft and amphibious assault ships) to win a quick, decisive battle with Republic of China forces for the island—particularly when preoccupied at the same time by a Soviet military threat on the Chinese northern border.

Ultimately for the United States, the central question is, What is to be gained by shifting recognition to Peking? Doesn't the United States enjoy the best of all possible worlds at present, what with a Liaison Office in Peking and an embassy in Taipei? Moreover, some American travelers to China have returned reporting that Peking's leaders are patient; they are willing to wait even decades to resolve the Taiwan question. In addition, many Soviet specialists in this country, both academics and government officials, have continually argued that if the United States is eager to make progress in negotiations with the Soviet Union (for example, on sensitive arms control questions), Washington must not make initiatives to

Peking at the same time or Moscow will not cooperate. In short, the price of Soviet willingness to negotiate must be American restraint in improving relations with Moscow's enemy, the People's Republic of China.

The Kissinger experience in negotiations with China and the Soviet Union seems to suggest just the opposite. Indeed, the Soviets will not be happy when the United States takes new initiatives to improve relations with Peking—and they may even break off temporarily an important negotiation—but over the long run, one of the best available means to bring pressure to bear on Moscow is through closer cooperation with Peking. The record since 1971, for instance in the strategic arms negotiations, would seem to be quite clear on this point.

Further, since 1971, the People's Republic has demonstrated parallel interests with the United States on a variety of important questions around the world (NATO in Europe, the U.S. security treaty with Japan), and the potential for further cooperation on the basis of common opposition to Soviet expansion is significant. Moreover, understandings with China could facilitate a number of American initiatives in Asia (for example, withdrawal of American troops from South Korea), and they are clearly indispensable over the long run regarding such vital issues as arms control and disarmament.

China's leaders have indeed told American visitors that they can wait for an ultimate resolution of the Taiwan question, because they feel that inevitably Taiwan will be rejoined with the mainland. But American delay in establishing formal diplomatic relations with Peking is not the same thing. Not surprisingly, the Chinese have indicated that further Sino-American cooperation on points of substance requires American recognition. After all, diplomatic recognition does not imply endorsement of a regime, and such recognition according to the norms of international diplomacy is generally viewed as a prerequisite to any meaningful government-to-government co-operation. Moreover, for the United States to maintain relations with the Taipei regime, claiming as it does to be the rightful government of China, constitutes a continuing American affront to Peking. Of central importance in all of this is the fact that there is, in the evolution of Chinese foreign policy, always the option of rapproachement with the Soviet Union rather than improving relations with the United States —a possibility with potentially dire consequences for the United States.

American advocates of reform in the Republic of China or self-determination for the Taiwanese majority on the island are faced with an adamant Chiang Ching-kuo defense of the status quo. The best hope for domestic change in Taiwan seems to be an American break in relations with Taipei, which would virtually complete the Republic of China's diplomatic isolation and hopefully prompt meaningful reform. As for Taiwan independence movement activists, they do not oppose American recognition of Peking; they simply request that in the statement establishing formal relations, the United States not go further than it has in the Shanghai Communiqué to preclude the possibility of a separate future for Taiwan.

Ultimately, it is not America's right or responsibility to determine which government or what political future is the best one for the people of Taiwan. Perhaps what is most appropriate for the United States at this point is, first, to recognize that twenty-seven years ago we intervened in the Chinese civil war and, then, to extricate ourselves without prejudicing the outcome any more than our formidable presence over the past several decades already has done.

12

MICHAEL H. HUNT

Northeast Asia in Sino-American Relations

MANCHURIA and Korea have
been unflatteringly yet accurately described as the "cockpit of
Asia." For the last hundred years three powers have fought to
preserve their interests on the Northeast Asian mainland. Russia has regarded the region as a strategic flank to defend or as
a gateway to a warm water port. Japan has sought to exploit
the economic resources of the region and prevent any threatening power from gaining a foothold there. And finally China
has, as a result of Russian and Japanese pressures, come to
regard the region as strategically vital to China's security. With
the loss of Korea as a buffer zone along the northeastern frontier, Manchuria became and has remained China's last line of
defense on the road to Peking.

For the United States, with no obvious tangible stake, the

region would seem an unlikely area of involvement. Its remoteness requires the projection of power over long distances. And the immediate and often intense concerns of the regional powers confront any intruder with the risks of setting off new local tensions or becoming entangled in preexisting ones. Even so, the United States has become involved; the Manchurian crisis of 1931–32 and the Korean War come immediately to mind.

The roots of this recent American involvement extend back nearly a century. Over that time it has undergone some major changes. At the outset, in the 1870s and early 1880s, Americans concentrated on "opening" Korea. By the turn of the century interest had shifted to Manchuria, where in 1909–10, Washington directly challenged Russian and Japanese preponderance. Through this early period, policy goals were largely commercial. Thereafter a generalized concern for a stable international order in East Asia tended to eclipse the earlier, essentially commercial considerations. That concern, applied to Manchuria in the 1930s, set the United States on a collision course with Japan and then two decades later led to a commitment to Korea that persists down to today. The pursuit of stability has entailed a marked expansion of American power in the region. Late in the nineteenth century the handful of aging American gunboats in East Asia were not even equal to their task of protecting American life and property against restless "natives." But by the end of World War II the American fleet dominated the western Pacific from newly acquired advance bases. Strategic and tactical air forces (armed with atomic weaponry) and more than 100,000 troops provided an additional guarantee of regional stability.

Yet through these changes one continuity persisted. Policy makers time and again advanced into the region with little sense of the opportunities and perils before them. Once there they sought to promote the abstract goal of commercial expansion or international stability with scant attention to the local

obstacles to the success of those policies, the complex and over-
lapping power relationships in the area, and the perspective of
the regional powers. American policy might best be described
as ethnocentric. Those who made it regarded regional leaders
with condescension and sometimes contempt, and in general
failed to grasp the importance of Northeast Asia in Chinese
(and, incidentally, Japanese) foreign policy. The costly result
of this ethnocentric policy in Northeast Asia has been to
estrange potential allies, antagonize potential enemies, and
intensify regional tensions. The four case studies that follow
demonstrate these points.

The Open Door in Korea: 1880–82

Americans went to Northeast Asia in the mid-nineteenth century with markets in Korea in mind; but they found that
Korea's 200-year-old policy of seclusion fenced those markets
off. The ensuing American effort to penetrate that trade
barrier had made no headway when Commodore Robert
Shufeldt reached East Asia in 1880 with instructions to open
talks with the reclusive Koreans. He immediately turned for
assistance to the Japanese, who in 1876 had already coerced
Korea into her first treaty. Japan seemed to Shufeldt and other
Americans the most progressive nation in East Asia, and thus
likely to sympathize with American commercial goals. But
Japanese assistance and even a personal visit to Korea failed to
draw out the Koreans. Shufeldt then turned to the Chinese as
intermediaries. In the spring of 1880, he dropped a hint to the
Chinese consul in Nagasaki of his difficulties and in August received an invitation from Li Hung-chang, the Chinese official
responsible for Korean affairs, to come to Tientsin for talks.
After an auspicious first meeting, the talks suffered a series of

delays that consumed nearly a year and a half and soured Shufeldt on the Chinese. Li, who had initially struck the American as a man of "intelligence and judgment," had by early 1882 evolved into a ruthless and powerful yet backward-looking figure with "a clear, cold, cruel eye and an imperious manner. He is a thorough Oriental and an intense Chinaman. These imply contempt for western nations and hatred for all foreigners." [1] Nevertheless, Shufeldt persevered and finally in May 1882 got his commercial treaty with Korea.

Persistence alone, however, does not account for Shufeldt's success. Equally important was China's imperiled security in Korea. Russian and Japanese encroachments threatened not only China's preponderant position in Korea but also her adjoining Manchurian territory. The Korean policy that Li Hung-chang devised was to open Korea to all the powers but under Chinese supervision. He hoped thus to forestall a conflict between Korea and the West over seclusion, to offset Japan's growing influence, and to maintain China's oversight of Korea's foreign affairs. But Li needed the assistance of one of the powers in carrying out his policy. He invited Shufeldt to Tientsin because he saw the United States as the ideal power to involve in China's behalf. Its commercial interests were far less threatening than the territorial ambitions of the other powers. Even as far back as the Opium War, Chinese officials had turned over in their minds the possibility of pitting the Americans against other barbarians, particularly the English. Through the 1840s and 1850s they had intermittently sought to put this policy into practice although without success. Even so, the prospect of using the Americans, who "have always been sincerely loyal to China," continued to appeal to some Chinese policy makers.

Li himself had already in 1879 applied the strategy when

[1] Oscar Paullin, *Diplomatic Negotiations of American Naval Officers, 1778–1883* (Baltimore, Md.: Johns Hopkins Press, 1912), pp. 301, 303.

he involved former president Ulysses S. Grant in a dispute with Japan over the Liuchius. Now Li tried again. While Shufeldt waited, Li devoted himself to maneuvering the Koreans toward accepting a treaty. Letters and emissaries moved back and forth between Seoul and Tientsin from mid-1879 to late 1881 before he gained the assent of a divided Korean court. In March 1882, Li's lieutenants drew up a commercial treaty and presented it to Shufeldt as a Korean draft. The Koreans appeared only to sign the treaty that China had negotiated.

As it turned out, both Shufeldt's and Li's expectations proved exaggerated. The treaty aroused no enthusiasm in the United States, and the Korean market never materialized. On the other side, Li's reliance on the United States undercut rather than augmented China's influence in Korea. Li had wanted the United States to formally recognize Korea's dependency on China and to promise to "aid and protect" Korea, but Shufeldt would make no more than vague promises of American "good offices" in case Korea got into difficulties. He refused to recognize China's claim to a special relationship with Korea. For the next decade and a half, the State Department and Americans in Korea did their best— sometimes in league with the "progressive" Japanese—to undermine what they saw as the reactionary Chinese influence there. They puzzled over the Chinese mind which could square Korea's subordination to China with Korea's status as an independent sovereign state. They saw only the shadow of the past and pretentious claims to cultural superiority in a Chinese policy which for Li was grounded on current and substantial strategic concerns.

As Japan drove first China and later Russia from the peninsula, the United States stood clear. In 1894 the administration of Grover Cleveland refused to become diplomatically embroiled in China's war with Japan over Korea. A decade later, in the wake of Japanese successes against Russia, Theodore Roosevelt conceded Japan's preponderance in Korea, underlining the point by withdrawing the American legation in Seoul. More concerned with interests in China and the Philippines, Washington accepted Korea's new form of dependency with the happy thought that the Koreans were better off under the modern-minded Japanese than if left to themselves.

The Open Door in Manchuria: 1909–10

Manchuria captured the American imagination at the outset of the twentieth century just as Korea faded from view. Businessmen and diplomats were excited by the economic potential of this rugged frontier region but also worried by the advance of Russia and Japan which threatened to shut them out along with the Chinese. Russian designs prompted Secretary of State John Hay first to formalize the long-extant Open Door idea in 1899 and then, during the subsequent Russian military occupation of Manchuria (1900–1903), to take an increasingly tough stance in defense of the Open Door there. However, Roosevelt was convinced that his naval power and public support were insufficient for a resort to arms and hence restrained Hay. Instead he looked to Japan to play the American game and drive Russia from southern Manchuria. Japan succeeded in 1904–05, and Roosevelt held to his hands-off policy in Northeast Asia despite persistent warnings from some of the foreign service that Japan would succeed Russia as a threat to American commercial opportunity in Manchuria.

William Howard Taft, Roosevelt's hand-picked successor, switched from a policy of strategic realism in Northeast Asia to one of commercial expansion. Taft selected Philander C. Knox as his secretary of state and gave him broad latitude to defend the American commercial stake against Japan. Knox, with his belief that "today diplomacy works for trade," set the State Department in pursuit of what he thought were long-term American commercial interests. The new administration listened carefully to the junior diplomats who had earlier been frustrated by Roosevelt's caution. It ignored those who questioned the economic value of Manchuria, and even removed the American minister in Peking, the most accomplished American China expert of that day, because he was out of sympathy with the developing commercial crusade.

Knox's plan was to stimulate American trade by making major investments in China, particularly in railways. Such investments would also enhance the political influence Washington could exercise in behalf of the open door. Knox put together a group of powerful Wall Street firms to function as his financial instrument in Manchuria. He sought to apply his financial power in two different ways—indirectly through investments undertaken in cooperation with local Chinese authorities and directly through a proposal to internationalize Japan's and Russia's Manchurian railways. However, those two countries, supported by their European allies, intimidated the Chinese and forced the embarrassed Knox to retreat from Manchuria in the latter part of 1910. Thereafter, he confined his attention to China proper, cooperating with the other powers against the Chinese government.

Knox maneuvered in Manchuria with an insensitivity to the opportunities and dangers confronting him. Rather than driving either Russia or Japan from the region, he drove them together to the detriment of both China and the Open Door. The Chinese were well aware that their goals in defending their Manchurian frontier substantially coincided with those of the Americans and had sought in effect to revive Li Hung-chang's strategy of involving the United States in Northeast Asia. They had failed to interest the Roosevelt administration, but when they gained the Taft administration's support for a strategically important railway, they assumed that they had laid the basis for a coordinated Manchurian policy. Soon disillusioneed by Knox's sudden retreat from Manchuria, the

Chinese were left to cope as best they could with their old antagonists, now aroused by the Chinese-American challenge.

These failures of policy flowed logically from a contempt for Asians. Taft and Knox, as well as Roosevelt, looked down on the Chinese as a backward people, unpatriotic, weak, and indecisive. In the case of Japan, Roosevelt at least recognized the rise of a "civilized" power and accorded Japan the cultural role of tutor to China and the strategic role of dominant power in Northeast Asia. But where Roosevelt felt respect Taft felt contempt and suspicion: "A Jap is first of all a Jap and would be glad to aggrandize himself at the expense of anybody." When the Japanese sought to explain their position, Taft and Knox listened uncomprehending.

The Taft administration's commercial goals and the means employed to attain them both proved defective. Taft and Knox began by exaggerating the commercial potential of the Manchurian frontier and the dangers posed by Japanese control. They then failed to recognize the limits of American investment strength, especially the heavy dependence of Wall Street on the financial markets of Japan's European allies. And finally, in its pursuit of a piece of the China market, Washington succeeded in antagonizing Japan, a major trading partner, in addition to disillusioning China. In the end, an inept dollar diplomacy not only diminished American prestige and influence but harmed more than it helped American commerce in East Asia.

Stopping Aggression in Manchuria: 1931–32

By the time of the second Manchurian crisis American policy makers had abandoned a narrow policy of commercial expansion and had come to look on events in Northeast Asia in relation to their hopes for world peace and progress. Their vision of a liberal world order did embrace a free and flourishing international economy, but its emphasis was on orderly international change and the encouragement of democratic and westernized regimes in backward areas of the globe. The enlightened and powerful Western nations, which had inspired this new international order, had the duty to lead and defend it.

When the Japanese Kwantung army began eating away at China's Manchurian territory in September 1931, it challenged this liberal vision and revived latent tensions between the United States and Japan. China's future development and her security as a member of the new international order were at stake. Washington was equally concerned with the structure of world peace. The Covenant of the League of Nations and the Kellogg-Briand Pact of 1928 had stigmatized international aggression, and the Nine Power Treaty of 1922 had guaranteed Chinese sovereignty and integrity. Japan had signed those agreements. Now that she violated them, the United States had the obligation as an advanced nation to speak out and rally the international community. Secretary of State Henry L. Stimson had already risen to the occasion—albeit ineffectually—during the 1929 Russo-Chinese railway dispute in Manchuria. Now, when Tokyo failed to bring her Manchurian army under control, Stimson again took a stand. He applied direct pressure on Japan and looked to the League to formulate sanctions.

President Herbert Hoover shared Stimson's impulse to "uphold the moral foundations of international life," but he felt that sanctions might lead to a long Asian war, unwanted by a public preoccupied with economic crisis at home. Stimson was himself unsure how far and how forcefully to proceed against Japan. In early January 1932, Hoover and Stimson settled on a simple public statement that the United States would not recognize the fruits of aggression. They intended their statement as a standard to which law-abiding nations could—but in fact did not—rally. When later in the month

Japanese troops attacked Shanghai, Stimson publicly warned the Japanese that they risked provoking the United States into a Pacific naval rivalry. As a policy maker, Stimson left a potent legacy. The Roosevelt administration maintained Stimson's nonrecognition policy right down to Pearl Harbor, and an entire generation accepted his views that peace was indivisible and that the appetite of aggressors only grew with the eating.

Through this second Manchurian crisis American policy makers continued to misinterpret regional developments. Stimson and his advisers within the State Department saw Japan as a country developing toward the Western model but encountering tremendous strains as modern, Western-looking civilians struggled against the forces of reactionary militarism. Consequently, they framed their policy to encourage those moderate civilians to exert their control. However, Stimson magnified into a basic rupture over strategy what was, in fact, only a division within the Japanese elite over the tactics of foreign policy. Although Japanese leaders disagreed over the best way to handle the Manchurian crisis, they did at the same time share an overriding concern about the danger posed to Japanese security by a newly aroused Chinese nationalism, revived Soviet power in Asia, and apparent Anglo-American cooperation in the Pacific. The widely accepted solution to this fearsome strategic insecurity was to establish economic and strategic dominance in East Asia in a sort of Japanese Monroe Doctrine. Where Stimson with his lack of historical perspective could only see a fresh and barbaric act of aggression, the Japanese saw the Manchurian crisis as but the latest episode in sixty years of struggle in that region. And where Stimson and the generation that followed believed that a resolute stand by right-minded men would suffice to stop any aggressor, the Japanese regarded Western opposition to their new order as justification for a more intense search for security, thus increasing the prospects of collision.

Just as insensitivity to Japanese security needs led to deepening Japanese-American tensions, so condescension toward China created a gulf between the United States and a natural ally. Policy makers in this period viewed the Chinese with the same mistrust evinced by their predecessors. Although the United States and China once again faced the same enemy, Washington saw no reason to take into its confidence Chinese leaders whom it regarded as lacking in patriotism and politically inept. Stimson's China experts, Stanley Hornbeck and Nelson T. Johnson, had begun their careers in the teens under the shadow of the faltering Chinese Republic. They had deplored the political chaos of the 1920s and the irresponsible disrespect for treaties and foreign interests in China displayed by Chiang Kai-shek's Nationalist government after it established itself in power in the latter part of the decade. Finally, the new government proved to them its bankruptcy by failing to marshal the nation in a resolute stand against Japan. They concluded that a paternalistic American policy would serve China far better than its own leaders could.

Chiang's perspective was different. The Japanese attack threatened to disrupt his campaign to extend his control over the nation and consolidate his authority within the Nationalist party. Despite the strong public reaction against the Japanese invasion of Manchuria, Chiang refused to take up the challenge at the expense of his domestic program. He calculated that any attempt by a politically divided and militarily weak China to expel Japan would fail disastrously and compound the nation's already severe problems. The achievement of national unity on the other hand, would fulfill the preconditions for effective national resistance. In the meantime, he would have to temporize in his dealings with Japan, maintaining China's claim to Manchuria without provoking war. The Western nations in the League and the United States were important accessories in his strategy. He would ask them to stand up against Japan, thus bolstering China's position at no cost or risk to himself. In the short term Chiang's strategy failed and Japan tightened her grip on the Northeast. The League of Nations could only manage a report which even-handedly apportioned blame between China and Japan. And Washington, although it agreed with China that the principle of peaceful change was at issue, behaved cautiously. Whatever bitterness Chiang felt over the emptiness of Western pretensions to international leadership, he maintained his course and patiently waited for the Japanese to overstep themselves. By eventually imperiling American security in the Pacific, they would force the United States into a war that would redeem China's claim to Manchuria.

Stopping Aggression in Korea: 1950

Northeast Asia became an important testing ground in the early Cold War. World War II had brought on the collapse of the Japanese empire, but the United States remained involved in the region as it moved to meet new threats to stability and peace. Manchuria was the subject of some early sparring between the United States and the Soviet Union. In the last days of the Pacific war, Soviet troops had moved rapidly across Manchuria, taking control from the Japanese. Wartime military calculations had inclined the Roosevelt administration to encourage the commitment of Soviet forces in Asia. But in the atmosphere of growing distrust in the immediate post-war period, the Truman administration began to worry about long-term Soviet ambitions in Manchuria and in early 1946 successfully pressed for a prompt Russian withdrawal. Thereafter Moscow and Washington each limited its involvement, thus leaving the issue of control to the Nationalist and Communist forces to fight out. When the Communists triumphed in the region in the fall of 1948, Washington decided not to react because it saw no evidence of a clear-cut Soviet challenge. Thereafter, Manchuria faded as an area of American concern.

After the war it was Korea that again became the main focus of American concern in Northeast Asia. In 1945 a hastily contrived American military occupation had excluded Soviet troops from Korea south of the Thirty-Eighth Parallel and guaranteed the United States a voice in determining Korea's future. When negotiations with the Soviet Union over a unified and independent Korea failed, policy makers in Washington decided to continue to shoulder their responsibility in the south. Harry Truman had in 1946 already accepted the view that Korea was "an ideological battleground upon which our entire success in Asia may depend." An American retreat would invite a Communist takeover, while American protection and guidance would enable Korea to shake off the "many decades . . . of international rivalries" and avoid "again becoming the source of future conflict." In 1947 the United States gave up on Korean unification, settling instead on an independent and "democratic" government under Syngman Rhee. However, democracy never took root. American proconsuls, acting from a mix of anti-Communist zeal and ignorance of Korean affairs, compromised the democratic experiment from the start. As much concerned with building an anti-Communist bastion in the south as with implanting democracy, they excluded the Korean left from the political process and favored foreign-trained, English-speaking politicians. The American experiment in good government also ran up against the bias of Korea's traditional political culture toward centralized power, autocratic rule, and extreme factionalism. The United States had sought to create in Korea national unity and democracy but ended up instead with national division and strongman rule.

The Truman administration took an ambiguous position on support for the newly independent South Korean government. It wished to keep communism out but it also accepted the contention of the military planners that the United States simply lacked the forces to defend South Korea during the initial stages of a general war. Realism required setting

Korea outside the American defense perimeter in the Pacific. But when a Communist invasion did come in June 1950, Truman resolved to meet the challenge head on. An area of minor strategic significance suddenly took on major importance as an imperiled portion of the free world. Truman feared that any display of weakness or hesitation would dispirit European allies, embolden the U.S.S.R., and ultimately precipitate a catastrophic third world war. Truman recalled the lesson of the 1930s: "how each time that the democracies failed to act it had encouraged the aggressors to keep going ahead." A State Department aide, Dean Rusk, observed that the decision to intervene in Korea "was in the process of being made for an entire generation since Manchuria." Truman first committed American air and naval forces to the war and then American combat troops. Their initial mission was to repel the attack and restore the status quo, but in August, as the tide of battle turned, Truman raised the ante by his decision to try for the unification of Korea. He allowed MacArthur to march his army north past the Thirty-Eighth Parallel and on toward the Yalu River boundary between China and Korea. When Peking began expressing alarm over the advance, Washington offered assurances that it meant no harm. When in late October and early November Chinese forces briefly entered combat and then broke off contact, Washington wrote off the incident as an empty threat. Finally, late in November the Chinese decisively intervened, routing MacArthur's army. Acheson denounced this "fresh and unprovoked aggressive act" and spurned proposals for peace talks. What began as an American parry to an apparent Soviet Cold War thrust turned into a Chinese-American slugging match. "Limited war" in Korea inflicted roughly 4 million casualties and devastated the entire peninsula.

American policy makers, governed by the abstract goal of containment, had made few allowances for conditions within Korea and the differing perspectives of the regional powers. At the outset of the war, Truman and Acheson acted on the assumption that everywhere along the Cold War perimeter they faced the same dangerous Communist monolith guided by the Kremlin. Hence Kim Il-sung's invasion became Stalin's as well. Equating Kim with Stalin had the virtue of reducing policy making to manageable terms when Washington had little time, less information, and a fear of seeming to hesitate. But Washington may have as a result of its easy assumptions exaggerated Moscow's role in initiating and supporting the invasion and overlooked the strains within the Communist monolith—both between Moscow and Pyongyang and within North Korea's highly factionalized leadership—over the issue of Korean unification.

Once war began, Washington blundered by failing first to anticipate the possibility of a Chinese intervention and later to take seriously Peking's warning signals. American policy makers sized up the Chinese Communists as another set of China's misguided leaders. Washington imagined that the Communists had descended from the hills after World War II like so many bandits and had by default won the ensuing civil war against the corrupt and ineffectual Nationalists. Washington knew that real Communists could not be nationalists, an assumption confirmed by Peking's seeming acquiescence in Soviet control of north China and acceptance of an unequal alliance with Moscow. But policy makers were still sanguine that the Chinese Communists would stand back from the Korean conflict. Those with an understanding of "oriental psychology" offered the reassuring view that the Communists could not have strong roots in China. Their fanatical zeal, their ruthless methods, and their totalitarian goals were all opposed to "the basic Chinese way of life" and especially the "democratic individualism" of the people. The Communists' foreign policy, especially their hostility toward the United States, had already cost them popular support. Intervention in the Korean War after Washington had openly offered reassurances would further undermine their own position at home and possibly even precipitate a split within their own ranks between pragmatic nationalists and Moscow-oriented ideologues. Washington also took comfort in the belief that Peking would not throw its weight around until it had overcome the destruction and disorganization left in the wake of more than a decade of warfare within China.

Washington made its assessments of China either in the dark or under the shadow of its own misperceptions. It failed to see how the Chinese could regard MacArthur's advance as a threat because it was oblivious to China's traditional concerns with Korea's strategic role as a buffer. It stressed past friendship between the United States and China and current benign intentions while overlooking the reasons the United States had recently given Chinese leaders to fear for the safety of their revolution. The United States had aided the Nationalists through the civil war, refused recognition to the People's Republic, and perpetuated China's political division by sending the Seventh Fleet into the Taiwan Straits on the outbreak of the Korean War. Washington's conviction that the Chinese Communists were estranged from the people reflected a profound misunderstanding of China's domestic situation and especially the revolution. The Communist rise to power depended in large measure on popular support gained through a sophisticated process of social mobilization. It was a kind of politics foreign to the experience of American policy makers, and the China experts who might have shed some light on it were either no longer around or under a cloud because they had "lost" China.

Present Policy in Historical Perspective

Today the United States remains deeply involved in Northeast Asia. While American policy elsewhere around the globe has begun to move out from under the shadow of the Cold War,

Korean policy remains as rigidly committed to the status quo and the containment of communism as it was in June 1950. Washington avows that it seeks regional stability to preserve peace and keep the confidence of Japan, the major American ally in the Pacific. To that end it maintains the 1953 South Korean security treaty, backed by about 40,000 American troops including a division guarding the northern approach to Seoul, a nuclear armed tactical missile force, and about fifty advanced fighter aircraft operating from bases on the peninsula. To ensure that this containment policy rests on a stable foundation, Washington has funneled economic and military aid to South Korea for nearly three decades.

The essentials of Korean policy seem widely accepted today. The most often heard criticism, expressed by prominent congressmen, journalists, and academics, concerns the political repressiveness of our South Korean ally. A military junta took charge in 1961 following bloody student riots which drove Rhee into exile. Park Chung Hee, who emerged as leader of the junta, has since 1972 strengthened his control by rewriting the constitution, limiting civil liberties, and intimidating the political opposition. American critics fear that authoritarian Korean military leaders may be repeating the mistakes of their counterparts in China in the 1940s and Vietnam in the 1960s by breeding popular disaffection—with disastrous consequences for domestic stability and American interests. These liberal critics urge Washington to use its influence to promote freedom and democracy in Korea and thus not only fulfill American political ideals and obligations to the people of South Korea but also avert political upheaval.

Viewed in historical perspective, American involvement in Northeast Asia seems more potentially troublesome than Washington or even its liberal critics suspect. Current discussions of Korean policy tend to set tensions in the region in the foreshortened perspective of the recent Cold War and to ignore the fundamental sources of conflict which are likely to persist, Cold War or no. Americans overlook the degree to which regional conflict has arisen from the geographic proximity of major powers and the political instability within the region.

Sino-Soviet hostilities are the most striking example of the old rivalries which continue to affect the peninsula. Disagreements between Peking and Moscow broke out into the open in the late 1950s and climaxed violently in the 1969 Manchurian border clashes. Since then China, anxious to have a friendly neighbor on the eastern flank of the long, tense Soviet frontier, has carefully cultivated Pyongyang and eclipsed the once ascendent Soviet influence. China would almost certainly oppose any reassertion of that influence. But China's Korean policy must respect minimum Soviet interests or risk provoking the Soviets to counteraction. China also has to recognize the unprecedented strength of Korean nationalism, which has led the North since the early 1960s toward self-reliance in its international relations. Any Chinese attempt to impose her own policy would antagonize Pyongyang and perhaps send it on a search for outside support.

But China and the U.S.S.R. are not the only powers concerned with developments on the Korean peninsula. While North Korea looks to the Soviet Union for advanced weaponry and to China for diplomatic support, South Korea is tied politically and militarily to the United States and economically to Japan. The presence of American troops and nuclear weapons in the middle of the peninsula further complicates the situation. The region can already boast three nuclear powers— the United States, the Soviet Union, and China; Japan could become the fourth. Thus, Korea's continuing political division and dependence on outside powers poses the potential danger that a local crisis might rapidly develop into a serious international confrontation.

But whatever the United States does to reduce tensions, it still must count the possibly high costs of its Korean commitment. As long as the behavior of regional powers in this culturally unfamiliar and politically complex part of the world remains difficult to predict, the United States will continue to run the real risk of involvement in an unwanted and perhaps ultimately unjustifiable Korean conflict. The United States might in some circumstances come to regret its fixed commitments to stability in a region that has a high potential for instability and to the cause of containment when it may have difficulty deciding whom to contain. Rather than attempting to shore up a Cold War status quo, the United States might better serve its own interests by promoting an equilibrium of regional power in Northeast Asia, and by moving toward a flexible and detached relationship with South Korea.

The United States could reduce its exposed position on the Korean peninsula by shifting a larger share of responsibility for managing regional affairs to regional powers. An obvious first step would be to acknowledge China's major stake, thus settling a long-standing point of dispute in Chinese-American relations. Chou En-lai and Li Hung-chang have both invoked the same standard expression—that China is related to Korea as lips are to teeth—to emphasize a vital strategic link. Recognition of this fixed Chinese claim would serve American interests by strengthening the balance of power between China and the U.S.S.R. in the region. But Washington must be wary of China's tendency to play balance of power politics in the region, and must avoid needless entanglement in the Sino-Soviet rivalry. Washington must also be alert to China's tendency to exaggerate American power and intentions—as evident in the 1950 Korean confrontation as in earlier, more amicable contacts over Northeast Asia. The United States must make clear to China the limits of its policy toward the region.

The United States might also encourage Japan to play a greater role in regional affairs. Japan is already a primary economic power with a stake in South Korean trade and investment far larger than that of the United States. Japan is also a potential military power in the region with an acute concern over military and political developments on the peninsula, and with a capacity to mobilize rapidly against any strategic threat not adequately met by her American ally. In gradually shifting to the Japanese the responsibility for defining and defending their own interests, the United States would further extricate itself from its leading role in an area of secondary importance to American security. But in doing so, it must act with prudence and finesse to minimize disruptions in the regional power balance. It must also assume along with the Soviet Union an important, albeit secondary, restraining role in this new regional order dominated by China and Japan. The weight of Soviet and American power and influence should serve as a safeguard against a repetition of the sharp Sino-Japanese rivalry which convulsed East Asia earlier in this century.

Finally, if the United States wishes to become more the master and less the prisoner of events on the Korean peninsula, it must gradually withdraw American forces and substitute some less binding agreement for the current South Korean security treaty. Only thus can Washington gain the time and flexibility it needs in responding to any Korean crisis. In an age of Soviet-American nuclear parity and general nuclear proliferation the United States cannot afford to act with haste, and in a multipolar world of shifting power relationships the United States should not depend on any fixed definition of Korea's importance to American security. Korean commitments made when the world was starkly bipolar and American nuclear superiority unquestioned no longer make sense in a new international environment. It is time to adjust Korean policy to the limits of American power, interest, and understanding. "Our commitments in Asia too often dictate our interests." Henry Kissinger, who spoke these words, began to bring American commitments in line with American interests in relations with China and Vietnam. It remains for the Carter administration to take up the task in Korea.

13

ALEXANDER WOODSIDE

The Rise and Fall of the Southeast Asia Obsession in Sino-American Relations

---

IN a foreign policy address to the United Nations on September 26, 1975, the head of the Chinese delegation, Ch'iao Kuan-hua, stated that he wished to express the Chinese government's opinions on five crucial problems. One was the problem of anticolonialism, particularly in southern Africa. The second was the problem of Korea, where the United States wished to "legalize" a permanent military presence for itself, beyond the control of the United Nations, and where it claimed it would not scruple to use nuclear weapons against a North Korean attack. The third was the question of the Middle East, where the two super-

powers, the United States and the Soviet Union, tacitly con-
nived at preserving a situation, neither of peace nor of war,
which facilitated their continued sales of weaponry as a means
of "palliating their own economic difficulties." The fourth was
the problem of disarmament, which was being exacerbated by
the "bogus disarmament" of the two superpowers, and by
their notorious refusal publicly to pledge that they would not
use nuclear arms against those countries and regions which did
not have nuclear weapons of their own. The fifth was the
problem of economic development, whose central difficulty,
the perpetuation of an inequitable world economic order by
which rich countries could exploit the Third World, the superpowers attempted to dissemble, through a sophistical cosmo-
politanism characterized by talk of "economic interdepen-
dence" and of an "international division of labor."

There is little doubt that as far as the Chinese government is
concerned, the immediate future of Sino-American relations
will be heavily governed by these five problems, their Asian
offshoots and embodiments, and the Taiwan issue. (I leave
aside any consideration of Chinese efforts to play the United
States off against the Soviet Union, the mirror-image of current American hopes for China.) From the historical point of
view, what is so remarkable about this 1975 Chinese summa-
tion of the threats to world civilization is that Southeast
Asians—300 million of them—are cast in so insignificant and
so general a part, and treated, at first sight, almost as if they
belonged to a kind of international backwater. The Chinese
government, very obviously, does not believe that Southeast
Asia is a backwater. Yet it is clear that the period when
Southeast Asia was the luckless forcing house of most of the
major tensions and confrontations, symbolic and substantive,
in Chinese-American relations, has now come to an end.

This change has been ensured by the American defeat in
the second Indochina War and, almost equally significantly,
by China's apparently greater theoretical fondness for its role

as a global arbiter than for a more modest mission as the prophet and the catalyst of a regional "pan-Asian" coalition of any sort. There is no reason not to applaud the relative decline of Southeast Asia's function as the great supplier of the frameworks and myths which conditioned Chinese and American perceptions of each other and which gave these perceptions, especially on the American side between 1954 and 1969, a bleak ingenuity and dynamism indeed. The sharp-edged, somewhat Manchurian vocabulary of politics and of political hypotheses upon which so many American politicians and bureaucrats once impaled themselves—the falling dominoes, Laos as another Lebanon, neutralization agreements as Munichs, the unquestioned inevitability of gross Chinese expansionism—have now receded almost into a kind of prehistoric twilight. This vocabulary could, of course, enjoy a revival some day. But at the moment our greatest need may not be to deflate the old calculus of the "falling dominoes" era of international relations so much as to recollect and understand its indiscreet, ruinous inflation in the first place—as it was applied to the countries of Southeast Asia between 1950 and 1972.

The formidable position which Southeast Asia occupied in American policy making before 1975 was far more than just a reflection of the economic and strategic importance of the Southeast Asian societies themselves. Stanley Hoffman, who has written eloquently about American foreign policy habits, has suggested that a characteristic weakness in the formation of American foreign policy has been the tendency to reason by analogy, to look for common features in very complex situations, however culturally diversified they may be, and then to conclude that if one of these common features was decisive in one of the situations, it must be decisive in the others as well. Hoffman believes that the unusually large influence and participation of lawyers in American government has only reinforced such a dangerous love of analogy, because of the hallowed lawyers' custom of reasoning in terms of precedents. It is certainly true that an astonishing ignorance of Southeast Asian history led, by default, to facile, perilous analogy building where Vietnam was concerned, as did a more astute sense that the success of any one Communist revolution in any one Southeast Asian country might have a "demonstration effect" throughout Latin America, Africa, and the rest of Asia, endangering American economic investments as well as American security.

But the main point is that Southeast Asia—and Vietnam in particular—were not always seen purely in terms of themselves by Washington foreign policy architects. To my knowledge, no formal, comprehensive analysis of Vietnam's importance to the United States, purely within its own context, was ever carried out by the members of any American government. As for the lawyers who searched for talismanic precedents for a Vietnam policy, they could find none within Southeast Asia. President Franklin Roosevelt did propose the neutralization of Indochina in 1941. But he did so as part of an effort to prevent a future collision between Japanese expansionism and the Southeast Asian colonies of America's European allies (notably Great Britain and Holland). Southeast Asia itself had a far lesser significance for him; China's relationship to Southeast Asia had no significance at all; and, with the obvious exception of the Philippines, Southeast Asia attracted little American attention in the years right after Pearl Harbor.

A worsening disequilibrium between abstract fears and real knowledge shaped American involvement in Southeast Asia after World War II. Out of the mists an unprecedented if artificial consensus was rapidly generated—spanning liberals, centrists, and conservatives alike—which held that because of Southeast Asia's proximity and presumed vulnerability to a revolutionary, renegade China, the defense of the region was now of critical importance to the survival of Western security and prestige. After the consensus had been created,

mainly on the basis of Cold War political instincts which had
been born not in Asia but in Europe, its leaders, conscious of its
thinness and fearful of its dissolution by a revived isolationism,
struggled to find popularly comprehensible economic reasons
for justifying their concerted vision. Claude Julien, the French
author of a recent, dogmatically pessimistic book about the
growth and exercise of American world power, has argued that
the "real strength" of this power lies in the amazing solidarity
of the American domestic opinion which supports it, and
which rarely if ever criticizes its fundamental principles.[1] It
would be hard not to concede the validity of Julien's assertion
for the early 1950s at least, provided we recognize that this
domestic opinion was carefully organized by a bipartisan political effort. One has only to look at a list of the official American visitors to the Thailand of the military dictator Phibun
Songkhram in the years 1950–52, immediately after a U.S.
military advisory assistance group had been established there
to train the Thai armed forces and to expound the evils of
Communist aggression, to appreciate the somewhat contrived
breadth of the postwar consensus. Harold Stassen, Henry Luce,
Mrs. Eleanor Roosevelt, General Joseph Collins, Admiral
Arthur Radford, Justice William O. Douglas, Senator Burke
Hickenlooper, and Chester Bowles all suddenly came to observe, and in most instances to flatter, a Thai ruler who had
declared war on the United States, with Japanese approval,
less than ten years earlier. In our more antinomian and skeptical age, the problem of explaining this consensus—what
caused it, how it could develop so quickly, and so on—is surely
one of the great problems in the study of Sino-American re-
tions in their Southeast Asian context.

Then there was the American search for economic reasons
which would vanquish isolationism by making even more clear
the importance of protecting Southeast Asia against China.

[1] Claude Julien, *America's Empire* (New York: Vintage Books,
1973), p. 401.

The search itself was slovenly. No one, ironically, worked harder publicly to confirm the specious persuasiveness of Marxist economic explanations of American foreign policy than the chief foreign policy makers themselves. Thus President Eisenhower, in the first volume of his memoirs published in 1963, recalled that rescuing Indochina from communism had been a vital enterprise to him because, on "the material side," the loss of Vietnam, Cambodia, and Laos "would have spelled the loss of valuable deposits of tin and prodigious supplies of rubber and rice." [2] The facts were that Malaya, not Indochina, was the great treasure house of the world's tin supplies and that synthetic rubber production had long since diminished the Western need for access to Malayan, Indonesian, and Vietnamese natural rubber.

By the 1960s, more left-wing framers of the postwar American consensus about Southeast Asia and China were finding it more genteel to detect a great mythic hunger for Southeast Asian food and raw materials behind the impenetrable facade of Chinese foreign policy in the region, rather than continue to make it a Western motive, as in the 1950s. Chester Bowles, a liberal Democratic congressman from Connecticut and former U.S. ambassador to India, in an April 1960 attempt to "reconsider" the China "problem" for *Foreign Affairs,* called bravely for an improvement in Chinese-American relations. But he conceded that it was imperative to warn China about the "total commitment" of the United States "to defend Southeast Asia against Chinese attack." There was the "possibility," Bowles declared, of Chinese "expansion into Southeast Asia, with its wealth of underpopulated, food-rich countryside, as well as the great reserves of oil, tin, rubber, and other resources which China badly needs. Our objective must be to create a military, political, and economic barrier sufficient to discourage any such attempt." Such Chinese expan-

[2] Dwight D. Eisenhower, *The White House Years: Mandate for Change 1953–1956* (New York: Doubleday, 1963), p. 333.

sionism would be the result of Chinese Communism's "experiment" in industrializing "its 650 million people on a resource base which is woefully inadequate." [3]

No doubt these hypotheses all have an archaic ring today, at least in polite liberal discourse. The very superficiality of American knowledge about Southeast Asia, combined with the absence of long-descended American government involvement in the region outside the Philippines before the late 1940s (the numbers of American government officials in Thailand surpassed the numbers of American missionaries there for the first time only in 1952) created fluctuations in the practice and the exposition of American statecraft that were as surprising, if not as entertaining, as the changing productions of the wheel of incarnation in medieval Chinese popular novels. Yet it is probably necessary, even today, to dissect some of the great American fears of the 1950s and 1960s—about China's role in Southeast Asia, and desires for an aggressive preponderance there—as the first step toward clearing the ground for the construction of a more fruitful Sino-American relationship in the future. It is, after all, unlikely that the final resolution of the Indochina struggle in 1975 actually exorcised all these demons. It is more likely that it simply benumbed them temporarily.

If it is unlikely that China would ever invade Southeast Asia in order to seize its mineral resources and its "food-rich countryside," why is it so unlikely? To this question there are economic answers, which are likely to endure, and ideological answers, which of course can change. The economic answers are simply stated. While Southeast Asian societies are not, on the whole, as densely populated as South Asian ones, and once, indeed, did export "prodigious supplies" of rice as far away as Uruguay, the margin between population growth and available food supplies has been narrowing dangerously in all

[3] Chester Bowles, "The 'China Problem' Reconsidered," *Foreign Affairs* 38:3 (April 1960), p. 483.

the Southeast Asian countries since 1950. In fact northern Vietnam, which occupies a crucial part of Southeast Asia's border with China, has not been self-sufficient in food since the nineteenth century. Thailand, another presumed target of Chinese expansion, did export several million tons of rice a year in the 1960s but had to impose a temporary ban on rice exports in 1973; in whole regions of Thailand like the land-locked Khorat Plateau in the northeast, the water-poor agricultural system cannot now support the swelling, and restless, local population. One American scholar cautioned his readers in 1965, the year Washington disastrously raised the stakes in the second Indochina War, that the total annual rice surplus of Thailand, Burma, and Vietnam combined could feed the existing population of China for no more than a single week. A decade later, this once shrewd calculation has probably become a prodigal overestimation.

Yet in some American minds the existence of relatively tolerable population densities in much of Southeast Asia, combined with the existence of relatively unexploited Southeast Asian forest and river systems like the Mekong, seem to have excited ancestral memories of the gambling farmer-entrepreneurs who once tamed the great American sea of grass in the middle of the 1800s. In 1965 a high-ranking University of Texas delegation to South Vietnam scandalized the Saigon agricultural specialists they met by advising their Vietnamese hosts to experiment casually with crop diversification, at the height of the war, despite the facts that no established markets existed in which to sell the new crops and that the diversification itself would leave South Vietnam short of rice. Southeast Asian agriculture, with all its historic social inflexibilities, has never been capable of stimulating the internal optimism or the external envy or the political freedoms with which American and Canadian and Australian agriculture have been associated. Even technological breakthroughs, like "miracle rice," cannot bring Kansas or Texas to Vietnam or

Thailand. The opportunities for foreign invaders to plunder such an economic environment, in which the results of applying new irrigation systems can barely satisfy the requirements of rapidly rising populations, are very small indeed.

Ideologically, there are two cardinal reasons for assuming Chinese lack of interest in any invasion of Southeast Asia as a means of augmenting China's "inadequate resource base." For one thing, the Japanese occupation of Southeast Asia between 1942 and 1945 had a revolutionary significance that, almost certainly, has been better appreciated in Peking than in the West. The Japanese deliberately encouraged the beginnings of a revival of national Southeast Asian military traditions which the Western colonial powers had comprehensively suppressed. As early as 1945, Southeast Asian nationalists had profited enough from this revival to go beyond it and to become the apostles of a most formidable anticolonial guerrilla warfare.

In Indonesia, the Japanese-trained "Volunteer Army of Defenders of the Fatherland" (Peta), first organized in 1943, became the nucleus of the army of Sukarno's Indonesian Republic; by 1949 this army and its guerrilla supporters had made it impossible for the Dutch to hold on to more than a few Indonesian cities and towns and thus had doomed the oldest European colony in Southeast Asia. In Burma, the "Burma Independence Army"—officered by young Burman student nationalists like Aung San and Ne Win, sponsored by the Japanese, and introduced by them into Burma in December 1941—turned upon the Japanese in March 1945; General Aung San then made it clear to the British, when they returned to Burma, that if they did not agree to decolonization he would confront them with a crippling renewal of the guerrilla wars of Burma's thirteenth-century Pagan dynasty, which had defeated an invading army of Mongols by a "scorched earth policy" and by "mass evacuations" of civilians. In Vietnam, the young Communist schoolteacher Vo Nguyen Giap participated in this general Southeast Asian enterprise (but without Japanese encouragement) by creating a Vietnamese army in 1944, with its statutes and plans often lovingly based upon the military traditions of Le Loi and Nguyen Hue, Vietnamese generals who had triumphantly routed Chinese invaders of Vietnam in A.D. 1427 and A.D. 1789 respectively. Ten years later Giap's army conquered the French at Dien Bien Phu. By the late 1940s, in sum, new and rediscovered powers of self-protective nationalism and of military populism had made many Southeast Asian revolutionary anticolonial movements most difficult to defeat on their home terrains and quite unwilling to tolerate supinely new forms of colonial intrusion by outsiders. China must contend with this extraordinary transformation of Southeast Asian nationalism, which the Japanese first helped to make possible, as much as any other power. Wisely enough, the Chinese have generally chosen to celebrate the transformation, and even, sometimes falsely, to take much credit for it, rather than to try to undermine it.

A second ideological factor of importance which seems to make nonsense of the recent fears of Chester Bowles and so many others is that Chinese Communist leaders have habitually been less pessimistic about population problems—their own, and others—than American policy makers have been. Nor have they ever deviated significantly from their optimism about the successful management of population growth or ever ceased disdaining what they regard as the subjective anxieties of a cold-blooded, valetudinarian capitalism. Hence, in 1950 the People's Republic of China conducted a campaign against old, still-circulating Kuomintang middle school geography textbooks in China, partly on the grounds that such textbooks treated a "population surplus" as if it were a "natural" phenomenon, rather than as the "artificial" creation of stagnant economies which were the prisoners of feudalism and imperialism. In August 1974, in a speech to the UN world population conference, the Chinese delegation head, Huang Shutse, observed that it was suspicious that the two superpowers were more concerned about rising world populations than were the "have-not" countries, that world poverty was caused not so much by excessive populations as by unjust international economic relations and their domestic ramifications, that the Chinese population had increased from 500 million in 1949 to 800 million in the 1970s while escaping any purgatorial return to the notorious famines and unemployment of the early 1940s, and that this fact proved that the overthrow of feudalism and imperialism were even more important than "planned child rearing" (which China also practices) in solving crises of material scarcities in the Third World. Ultimately, American policy makers will have to take account of this radically different Chinese perspective on world development problems, rather than diplomatically circumventing it as they have since 1972. What is important here is that it is hardly a platform for invading Southeast Asia in pursuit of compensatory economic resources.

It is safe to assert that Peking has not misunderstood Southeast Asia in the past three decades as fundamentally as Washington has, at least in the crude sense that, unlike the United States, China has not lavished $150 billion upon a history-defying policy of trying to reverse the progress of a well-entrenched Southeast Asian nationalist movement like that of the Vietnamese Communists. But it is far less safe to assert that Peking's understanding of Southeast Asia has a predestined subtlety, or even that it rests upon a foundation of ancient diplomatic arts and expertise. As recently as a century ago, China was a majestic but fragile multiethnic empire, governed by a Manchu dynasty, whose official foreign policy interests were much more sharply focused upon Central Asia than upon Indochina. In fact the Chinese and Manchu upper-class civil service of this empire was barely capable of grasping the needs of the substantial minority populations which lived within western and southwestern China itself, let alone the behavior of Southeast Asians. For example, Ti-

betan copyists had to be assigned to the provincial bureaucracy of the gigantic, seething, multiethnic province of Szechwan; frontier specialists who worked for the Superintendency
of Dependencies in Peking, the agency which managed relations with Tibet, Mongolia, and Russia, also had to staff local
government positions in Szechwan, because only they could
appreciate the "barbarian languages" spoken in western China
as well as those spoken by the Russians; central and southwestern China were devastated in the 1700s and 1800s by land
wars between the Chinese and the Miao (Hmong) people.
The Miao people, who set parts of Hunan, Kweichow, and
Kwangsi aflame in 1795 and even later with their anti-Chinese
slogan of "expel the guest people and recover the old lands,"
are today, ironically, alleged to be the carriers of subversive
Chinese influences to Southeast Asia by way of their ethnic
brethren living in Vietnam, Laos, and northern Thailand.
(This is almost on a par with assuming that the Indians of
the southwest United States would be eager and capable trans-
mitters of Americanizing influences into Mexico.)

The Ch'ing empire sought to encompass Southeast Asian
states themselves within the framework of its hierarchical
tributary system. This system required these states to present
tribute on a periodic basis in Peking and to request investiture
for their rulers from the Ch'ing government; the last emperor
of Vietnam to be legitimized in his position by China in this
way received his Chinese seal of investiture in Hanoi in 1848.
But tributary relations between China and Southeast Asia,
the only diplomatic relations which existed, were never very
intimate and were not given a very high priority by Chinese
governments. In 1743, loftily declaring that Laos was a "rus-
tic place" at "the end of the sky," the emperor of China
requested the Lao royal family at Luang Prabang to send
tribute only once every ten years, instead of every seven. There
were no tribute relations at all between China and Burma
between the 1500s and 1751.

Moreover, because the tributary system was not intimate or

flexible or knowledgeably sympathetic to Southeast Asian political predispositions, it could not prevent wars between China
and Southeast Asia, every one of which China lost. One of
China's great eighteenth century historians, Chao I, even
served on an unsuccessful Ch'ing expedition into Burma in
the 1760s in order to enforce the loyalty of certain Shan states
to Peking rather than to the Burmese court; he did not hesitate to give his fellow mandarins an unforgettable eyewitness
account of the failure. During the Ch'ing retreat from Burma,
he wrote, the firecracker-like gunfire of the pursuing Burman
army was so loud and so close that "one could not hear human speech even when one was face-to-face." It has commonly been argued that China's traditional hierarchy of external relations, in which China was cast as the central suzerain
of a host of inferior foreign vassal states, was merely a complacent reflection of the Confucian social and political hierarchies within China itself. But much of the time China's
hierarchy of external relations was of a wholly different nature from the internal hierarchies, being much less the plau-
sible distillation of any powerful moral consciousness. When a
rebellious Vietnamese emperor, Nguyen Hue, humbled the
Chinese forces which had been sent to chastise him in 1789,
the emperor of China, remarking that Vietnam was a "petty
state" with a "degenerate climate" which could not support a
long-term Chinese occupation, violently reprobated the Vietnamese ruler himself as a bestially mischievous, unstable
"praying mantis"; the greater China's frustration, the more
omnifariously zoological the Chinese language of contempt
for Southeast Asian politicians became. At no time was there
ever much of a meeting of minds.

To put the matter simply, there are no grounds whatsoever
for assuming that geographical proximity and history have
given China a superior capacity for dealing with Southeast
Asia, a capacity that Western states cannot match. Recent
American failures in Southeast Asia have not been caused by

the operations of an unimpeachable richer wisdom on the Chinese side. There is no question, of course, that the modern Chinese Communist revolution has had vital reverberations in Southeast Asia. Post-1949 Chinese government policy toward Southeast Asia has, as is so well known, alternated between the exaltation of peaceful coexistence with established Southeast Asian regimes, and the promotion of Asian revolutions, sometimes against such regimes. The Maoist vision of these revolutions themselves, as requiring broad nationalist united front leaderships, heavily politicized popular armies, a maximum appeal to the discontented peasantry, and a cult of self-reliance, circulated in Southeast Asia even before 1949.

Hence, for instance, in the American colony of the Philippines, the "Anti-Japanese People's Army" or Huk guerrilla movement, which flourished in parts of central and southern Luzon after March 1942, used Edgar Snow's *Red Star over China* as one of its first training manuals, American descriptions of "Maoism" being easier to obtain at that time than Chinese ones. The Filipino intellectuals who lead the Communist "New People's Army" created in 1969—which offers a serious challenge to the current Ferdinand Marcos dictatorship in the Philippines—have continued this early Huk interest in Chinese revolutionary theory. José Maria Sison, a university lecturer who fled to the hills in 1969, even published a remarkable encomium to the Chinese Red Guards in the Manila press before he disappeared. At the height of the second Indochina War, needless to say, Indochina Communist delegations to China, like the Pathet Lao labor union group which made a famous pilgrimage to Chingkangshan in 1966, publicly pronounced their adherence to the "total correctness" of Mao Tse-tung's general theories of armed struggle. Broadly speaking, Maoist theories of revolution have proven to be most popular in those Southeast Asian countries which have had the most serious imbalances in their rural social structures (Vietnam, Java, the Philippines), or the most oppressive penetration of American military and commercial influences (Cambodia, Laos, the Philippines). They have been least broadly contagious in Southeast Asian societies which are not afflicted by really serious maldistributions of rural wealth (Thailand, and Burma in the 1960s and 1970s), whose governments have managed to avoid too much destructive American interference, and whose cardinal schisms are more ethnic than social or ideological (Thailand, Burma, Malaysia).

The truth is that the West has habitually overestimated the unimpeded facility with which outside ideologies and religions could permeate Southeast Asia. It has also seriously underestimated the leading role of Southeast Asia in its own right as a maker, rather than as an importer, of general Asian historical patterns. It should be remembered more often than it is that the Indonesian Communist Party, not the Chinese one, is the oldest Communist party in Asia, and that Indonesia, not China, was the first great nursery of Comintern strategies in Asia. (The "bloc within" strategy which the Comintern agent Maring [H. Sneevliet] proposed to the Chinese Communists in the 1920s was inspired by his own experience as a Dutch radical in the Netherlands Indies after 1912, developing a socialist movement there within the very body of the great Indonesian Islamic revival movement known as the Sarekat Islam.) China has never been a one-way exporter of revolutionary doctrines. Even if it were, few Southeast Asian nationalists wish to enter an exhibitionistic ideological servitude to a foreign power. The strength of Southeast Asian "boundary-maintaining devices" against this fate appears only to be the greater, the more closely has a given Southeast Asian country been culturally aligned with China in the past. Hence the Vietnamese Communists, the masters of the only Southeast Asian country whose higher culture was ever systematically if incompletely Sinicized, have taken pains to state that the specific Maoist gospel of building a revolution exclusively from rural bases has never been their theoretical line. They have also, more privately, taken pains to restrict and to monitor the flow of Chinese political terminology into Vietnam.

It would be tempting to suspect that the real foundation of any effective Chinese political appeal to Southeast Asians would not be a precise revolutionary doctrine of any kind but would be, rather, a purposive celebration of the mere facts of China's Asianness and an effort to satisfy a certain Southeast Asian hunger for pan-Asian associations and concerted action against white-skinned Western economic (and political) dominance. In November 1943 the Japanese empire convened an assembly of "greater East Asiatic nations" in Tokyo, and encouraged Burmese nationalists (Ba Maw) and Thai political leaders (Prince Wan Waithayakon) and Philippine presidents (José Laurel) and Chinese puppets (Wang Ching-wei) to mingle with each other as "members of a single historical family," as Ba Maw proudly put it. In convening such an assembly, the Japanese were unlocking basic political and psychological reflexes which, however tawdry the circumstances of their first activity in 1943, were nonetheless more important than most Westerners supposed. These reflexes in fact have reappeared during such later moments of history as the Bandung Conference of 1955 (whose host, President Sukarno of Indonesia, grandly described it as "the first intercontinental conference of colored peoples in the history of mankind") and the formation of ASEAN, the Association of Southeast Asian Nations (Thailand, Malaysia, Indonesia, the Philippines, and Singapore), in 1967.

Yet the Chinese Communists, in fascinating contrast to their Kuomintang and T'ung-meng-hui predecessors, have never shown any great sustaining interest in the evocation of the pan-Asian spirit as a bedrock principle of their foreign policy. Their ambitions and their interests have usually been far more universal. The most cogent recent example of their evident unwillingness to cultivate assiduously what pan-Asian sentiments exist in Southeast Asia was provided by the visit of Philippine president Ferdinand Marcos to China in June 1975. Marcos' main speech in Peking exhaled the spirit of an almost mystical (if platitudinous) historicism. About one-quarter of the speech was filled with complex, sentimental references to such things as the visit of the ruler of Sulu to Peking in A.D. 1417, and the early descriptions of Chinese-Philippine trade which the medieval Chinese geographers Chao Ju-kua and Wang Ta-yuan had written in A.D. 1225 and A.D. 1349 respectively. The remainder of his speech declared that China was the "natural leader" of the Third World, that his government intended to reappraise its old alliances and revise its assessments of the world, that Filipinos were an indisputably "Asian people," that, as an "Easterner," he was proud of the Chinese revolution's accomplishments, and that the inadequacies of Filipino society could be redeemed by the "spiritual forces" which are "the strongest weapons in the arsenal of weapons of our Asia." In his reply to Marcos, Teng Hsiao-p'ing, with unflinching Marxist rationalism, avoided all contemplation of Asia's "spiritual forces." He proposed that Southeast Asian states create a peaceful, neutral zone for themselves devoid of superpower influence, said it was necessary for Asian countries to ally themselves with "other Third World countries," and described China modestly as a "developing socialist state which belongs to the Third World," rather than being its "Eastern" beacon and "natural leader."

Why is the People's Republic of China relatively uninterested in the pan-Asian option, such as it is? No doubt Peking correctly regards Southeast Asian political leaders like Marcos as being ephemeral and unreliable, as men who appeal to the pan-Asian idea out of weakness, or, more precisely, out of a desperate need for some sort of crystallizing ideology for their governments. But there are two more important reasons. One, I think, is that China takes very seriously its role as a world power, not merely as an Asian power, and also takes very seriously its role as a Communist state in a global Communist commonwealth, albeit a commonwealth presently divided against itself. These other two roles distract the attention of Communist China, as the attention of Kuomintang China was not distracted, from the more emotional, regionally idiomatic pan-Asian possibilities. The second reason is that any effort by China to lead a pan-Asian political awakening in Southeast Asia runs some risk of magnifying the controversial nature of China's greatest single liability there: the overseas Chinese communities.

There are at least 12.5 million overseas Chinese living in Southeast Asia. Outside the city-state of Singapore, the most important concentrations of overseas Chinese are in Malaysia (where they represent 35–40 percent of the total population), and Thailand (where they represent perhaps 10 percent of the population). The Malayan Communist Party—which launched a guerrilla rebellion in the Malay Peninsula in 1948 that has never been perfectly quelled—is almost entirely composed of ethnic Chinese. It has never been able to build any significant bridges to the Malay peasantry, or to Malay city workers, despite the fact that even in 1948 almost 18 percent of the Malaysian proletariat was Malay. For that matter, no Southeast Asian state takes the loyalty of its overseas Chinese for granted. Even Hanoi must publicly struggle to persuade its overseas Chinese to think of Vietnam as their "second ancestral land," not as their first. When the Thai National Assembly passed an act forbidding Communist activities in 1952, General Phao Sriyanond, the architect of its passage, estimated that there were 2,000 ethnic Thai Communists in Thailand and 10,000 ethnic Chinese ones. Most observers regarded even these estimates as tendentious inflations of the facts. For the real root of so many anti-Communist fears in Thailand was and is an impacted anxiety about the patriotic political gullibility of Thailand's overseas Chinese. To some extent, talk about the dangers of communism in Thailand is an indirect and therefore less publicly provocative way of raising the question of the continuing dangers of ethnic pluralism.

The overseas Chinese communities are a liability to China because the very fragility of Southeast Asian political systems predisposes insecure Southeast Asian leaders to the belief that Peking, whatever its protestations and its proclaimed policies, will inevitably seek to use the overseas Chinese as fifth columnists against governments that it dislikes. There is little evidence that China has ever systematically resorted to such a difficult and unpromising enterprise. But the point is that Peking is forever deprived of any final means of proving its innocence. Many of the overseas Chinese cannot in fact speak Chinese; many of them are conservative businessmen with a horror of communism; all of them fear being used, not as fifth columnists, but as pawns in Southeast Asian domestic political convulsions. This fear is hardly groundless. When the pro-Chinese ruler of Indonesia, Sukarno, was compromised in 1965 by an unsuccessful Indonesian Communist coup against the more conservative senior Indonesian army officers, one of the levers which these officers then used to pry Sukarno out of the presidency was an emotional (and cathartic) campaign against both Peking and Indonesia's overseas Chinese. Violent anti-Chinese riots erupted, thousands of Indonesian Chinese were forcibly repatriated to China, and in 1967 the Indonesian government declared that its official designation for China would no longer be Tionghoa, but Tjina, an ancient and derogatory word. The very existence of such possibilities of linguistic insult in Southeast Asian vocabularies has its own significance.

China, therefore, has a double image in Southeast Asia, that of the pan-Asian redeemer and revolutionary pacesetter, and that of the massive, seemingly ethnocentric state with its own ready-made spy system ineradicably diffused among its neighbors. This is very much a world of ironic symmetries; for the

United States also has a double image in Southeast Asia, although neither its assets nor its liabilities (at least before 1965) have been quite as formidable as China's.

On the other hand, there is the image (and the substance) of American colonialism in Southeast Asia, which takes its formal beginnings in 1899–1901, with General Arthur MacArthur's military repression of the independent Philippine Republic of Emilio Aguinaldo. During the brief episode of American rule in the Philippines (1901–46), American governments did practice the limited heresy of repeatedly offering the Filipinos a rapid transition to political independence. Southeast Asian nationalists could note the instructive contrast between the 1935 American guarantee of such independence to the Philippines within a decade or so and the Olympian pronouncement of the Dutch governor-general of Indonesia, B. C. DeJonge, in 1936, that Indonesians required another 300 years of Dutch rule before they would be ready for "some kind of autonomy."

In the economic sphere, however, American policies toward the Philippines were quite often everything that a Communist revolutionary hungry for an issue might have wanted them to be. From the point of view of Filipino nationalists, the definitive climax of these colonial policies came, ironically, at the time Philippines independence was granted, on July 4, 1946. As the price of independence and of war rehabilitation aid, the U.S. Congress required the Philippine people to write into their constitution a "parity clause" giving Americans equal rights with Filipinos in the exploitation of Philippine natural resources; the Congress also required the newly independent Philippines to agree not to alter the value of its national currency without the permission of the U.S. president. In the realm of more indirect frictions, involving even the most Americanized segments of the Philippine elite, in recent years a Filipino business class has emerged which is anxious to "slay the American father image" by using "the

techniques of the Harvard Business School," as Raul Mang-
lapus has put it; this business class, confronted by large, heavily subsidized American business firms operating unrestrict-
edly within Philippine society, has tended to regard American
free enterprise doctrines as being somewhat hypocritical. In
1976, with its American military bases, its festering social and
economic discontents in central and southern Luzon and
elsewhere, its Muslim rebellion, and its mercurial Marcos
family dictatorship, the Philippines must be regarded as the
single greatest American foreign policy problem in Southeast
Asia.

The other American image in Southeast Asia was that of
the apparently exceptionalist white-skinned power which had
its own anticolonial instincts. Even Sukarno, who was more
anti-American than any other Southeast Asian nationalist
leader, including Ho Chi Minh, quoted Longfellow at Bandung in 1955, and warmly described the American War of
Independence as "the first successful anti-colonial war in
history." Side by side with their interest in the American
revolution, Southeast Asians, especially before the 1930s, regarded the United States as the home of advanced and eminently imitable political and judicial and educational practices and institutions. Thus, in the 1920s, the last absolute
king of Thailand, Prajadhipok, eagerly solicited the advice of
Francis B. Sayre, the Harvard Law School professor who
served as his foreign policy counselor (much of Thailand's
foreign policy, before 1932, was helpfully suggested by members of the Harvard Law School) on such problems as the
proper construction of a parliamentary legislature or how to
choose a successor to his throne. The Chinese took an active
interest in both aspects of this contradictory American role
in Southeast Asia. Reacting to American imperialism, Sun
Yat-sen, at the beginning of the century, helped diplomats of
the struggling Philippine Republic purchase arms in Japan
during their vain effort to resist American colonization. Reacting to the American revolution and its legacies, Chinese

educators like Chiang Wei-ch'iao made special visits to the Philippines during World War I to study the "pragmatism" of American trade and industrial schools there; Chinese reformers' wide knowledge of American progressive education, during the May Fourth movement and later, came in part from the Philippines.

The contradictions which inhere within this double image have never paralyzed American policy making where Southeast Asia was concerned, but they have not provided it with stable guidelines either. Thus, President Eisenhower could compare the ill-fated French colonial garrison at Dien Bien Phu in 1954 both to the Greeks at Thermopylae and to the Americans at the Alamo (contrary to popular belief, Lyndon Johnson was not the American president who first talked of Vietnam in terms of the Alamo); the American experience in Southeast Asia had never been profound enough, or coherent enough, to make these comparisons seem as spectacularly absurd to an American audience as they would to a Southeast Asian one. To block a Communist "take-over" of Southeast Asia comparable to the Communist "take-over" of eastern Europe in the late 1940s, the Eisenhower administration sought to Europeanize the whole Southeast Asian contest of resistance to such a prospect by creating a Southeast Asian replica of NATO, the Southeast Asia Treaty Organization. Eisenhower, to be fair, was not the only Europeanizer of Southeast Asia, although he did give the myths which supported U.S. policy there between 1950 and 1975 a kind of grandiose, episcopal enlargement. Churchill, it seems, also specifically proposed a Southeast Asian NATO. And Ramón Magsaysay, the president of the Philippines, gave this heavily analogical foreign policy architecture an even greater complexity by successfully urging in 1954 (possibly upon request) that the United States enter into a "Pacific Charter," inspired by the 1941 Atlantic Charter, which would affirm assistance for threatened Asian nations.

For years nothing disrupted this deadly, mutilating foreign-

policy parallelism between Europe and Southeast Asia—
neither the damning fact that SEATO amounted to little
more than a disguised white man's club in Asia (its two
Southeast Asian members, Thailand and the Philippines,
were overmatched by the Western memberships of Britain,
the United States, France, Australia, and New Zealand),
nor the almost equally discordant fact that SEATO was almost as much a new version of the Council of Trent as of
NATO (its Asian members suppressed their domestic Communists, unlike the NATO countries). The British did wish
both to found SEATO and to negotiate with China over
Southeast Asia's ultimate fate. Eisenhower rejected a policy
of negotiations with China as "unrealistic." He attributed
the British desire for negotiations to the long British historical
experience of shifting alliances and conditional enmities on
the European continent. Unfortunately, he did not pay equal
attention to the effects upon himself of the even less common
American historical experience of isolationism alternating with
"a succession of unlimited enmities."

By the 1960s, it is true, even the promoters of American
intervention in Vietnam were well aware that their actions
seemed, to much of the rest of the world as well as to much
of their own citizenry, to be a final consummation of the imperialist side of the American image in Southeast Asia rather
than a consummation of the idealistic, anticolonial side. Officials as important as Secretary of Defense Robert McNamara
and Major General Edward Lansdale sought to breathe life
into the primordial American role as the custodian of the
modern world's first revolution, either by comparing American soldiers in South Vietnam to the Europeans like
Kosciusko, von Steuben, and Pulaski who had come to assist
the United States in its own fight for liberty (McNamara),
or by claiming that it was not "improper" for the United
States to supply Saigon with "the motivation for conducting
a successful counter-insurgency effort" and to share "the best

possible American political thinking" with anti-Communist Southeast Asians (Lansdale).

Yet I think it is fair to conclude that, overall, the bloody, destructive American struggle to "contain" China in Southeast Asia in the 1960s only accelerated the emergence of the United States, both in its own eyes and in those of others, as the preeminent external counterrevolutionary symbol and actor in Southeast Asian affairs. This acceleration (I think) went far beyond what was either necessary or historically inevitable. In the last analysis, the United States does not have to fear revolutions, even Communist ones, in the relatively small, export-dependent countries of Southeast Asia. The United States nonetheless remains in this unbecoming—and, in my view, wholly unnecessary—counterrevolutionary position in Southeast Asia in 1976 and seems to have lost the will to extricate itself even from the intellectual atmosphere which such a position breeds.

It occupies this counterrevolutionary position with a more sophisticated patience, of course, and with that fashionable, temperature-lowering skepticism about its earlier anti-Communist crusades which McGeorge Bundy may have first begun to enunciate, in January 1967, when the prospect of failure in Vietnam became more real: "Vietnam is indeed a test of Communist revolutionary doctrine, and what happens there will affect what happens elsewhere; but victory for Ho would not mean automatic communization of all Asia, and the defeat of aggression would not mean an end to the pervasive—if sometimes exaggerated—threat of China." But the point is that the United States does still occupy such a position. One has, therefore, no right to interpret Bundy's skepticism, and that of his successors, as reflecting anything more than the beginning of that transition from fanatical sainthood to ambiguous, temporizing scholarship which is so characteristic of a declining religion or a declining world view. No positive new policies or orientations—or world views—

have yet been discovered which can adequately and sensibly replace the old. The need for such discoveries is very great indeed.

In the immediate future, the Southeast Asian countries themselves will no doubt try to write a new chapter in their long postcolonial struggle to avoid what Aung San of Burma fearfully referred to in August 1945 as their "camouflaged balkanization." They may even seek, fitfully, to convert their Association of Southeast Asian Nations, which was originally created in 1967 to promote greater regional economic coop-eration against outside exploitation, into a partial realization of Aung San's greatest postwar dream of all, a "United States of Indochina," comprehending Burma, Vietnam, Laos, and Cambodia as well as the five existing ASEAN states. United or divided, as relatively weak countries their foreign policies will necessarily be flexible: this will be true not merely of Thailand, which is famous in the West for "bending with the wind," but also of a ruling group like the Vietnamese Communists, who have an intense interest in American sci-ence and technology and whose foreign policy tradition, after all, includes a 1941 Party Central decision to offer the British and the Americans special economic privileges in Indochina if they agreed to "help the Indochina revolution."

China, for its part, appears now to approve of the neutral-ized Southeast Asia to which the ASEAN countries aspire, since such a uniform regional neutralization would make it more difficult for the U.S.S.R. to follow its alleged strategy of "scooping out hollows" (wa-k'ung) in Southeast Asia, that is, of looking for weaknesses to exploit in what is now a relatively unpromising part of the world from the Russian point of view. At the same time, China must continue to live with the fact that Southeast Asian suspicions of China can be muted but never dissolved.

About the ultimate policies of the United States, as well as Russia, the Chinese will no doubt continue to nourish a deep residual pessimism. This pessimism is historic and it transcends Communist theory. In 1922, for example, the Chinese Confucian modernist philosopher Liang Shu-ming, in a famous book comparing Eastern and Western cultures, described the West as the natural home of "hegemonial" politics, filled with rapacious competition and struggle devoid of all moral principle, as contrasted with China, the home of ethically superior "kingly way" politics, moral and well-ordered; the Chinese Communists, who presumably have little else in common with Liang Shu-ming, share his classical perspective and even his classical language when they denounce the international schemes of the "two hegemons," the United States and the U.S.S.R., fifty-four years later. On the purely tactical level, the Chinese Communists will also continue to debate the issue of how far peaceful coexistence between dissimilar nation-states can be "extended" (*yin-shen*), a foreign policy controversy whose chronic uncertainties have already claimed numerous illustrious victims, like Li Ch'i in 1966. But China is on the defensive in Southeast Asia, as the United States is (for similar and different reasons) in Latin America; there is no need for an expensive Sino-American rivalry in this region. The United States would be wise to begin putting its house in order in Southeast Asia; a new, intelligent sympathy for all species of Southeast Asian revolutionary nationalisms, beginning with the initiation of diplomatic relations with Hanoi and Phnom Penh, is still the first general prerequisite.

Part VI

THE LEGAL
CONTEXT

14

JEROME A. COHEN

Sino-American Relations and International Law

IN 1784 the first American ship ever to venture into a Chinese port became embroiled in a legal dispute concerning China's claim to exercise judicial jurisdiction over a British seaman charged with homicide. Throughout the almost two centuries that have followed, China and the United States—whether in cooperation or contention—have continued to resort to public international law as a principal vehicle of communication.

The Nineteenth Century Legal Context

In the nineteenth century the newly founded United States, like the more experienced European trading nations, became increasingly concerned about several kinds of international

legal questions that arose in its contacts with China. During
the period prior to the Sino-British "Opium War" of 1839–
42, considerable attention was devoted to the problems of
protecting Westerners from the arbitrary exercise of Chinese
criminal jurisdiction, which the Westerners branded as "bar-
barous" even though Chinese officials sought to win their good
will by asserting jurisdiction only when a Chinese had been
killed and by swiftly and sternly punishing Chinese who committed offenses against Westerners. Although China's substantive law recognized such basic concepts as self-defense
and unavoidable accident, the Westerners believed that in
practice the magistrates of Canton ignored such provisions in
their zeal to convict foreign defendants. The Western sense of
injustice was compounded by the felt lack of due process in
China's procedural system. Even in treating Chinese defendants that system seemed to presume that anyone unsavory
enough to be accused of crime must be guilty. It denied an
accused the aid of counsel, a fair opportunity to rebut the
charges and a privilege against self-incrimination; indeed, it
generally insisted upon a confession as a prerequisite to conviction and authorized the infliction of torture to assure that
confession would be forthcoming. Moreover, truncated procedures devised for the prosecution of foreigners made the
system appear especially unfair to them. Occasionally Chinese
officials did not even seem to care whether the person punished was in fact the one who had committed the offense, so
long as someone was punished for it.

Problems of commercial law also began to develop with the
growth of trade between China and the Western nations. Although the law codes of the Manchu dynasty were complex
and impressive products of a sophisticated bureaucratic tradition, because of their preoccupation with what we term
criminal law, they provided virtually no legal framework for
the conduct of trade. China had no civil or commercial code
upon which the foreigners could rely. It did not adhere to the

familiar law merchant that had evolved in Europe. Nor was there ready access to Chinese courts for the settlement of contract disputes. China even made it an offense for foreigners to acquire copies of its law codes. As time went on, the Westerners became dissatisfied with the vagaries of the so-called "Canton system," by which a small number of Chinese "hong merchants," who were designated by the government, served as exclusive intermediaries for the conduct of foreign trade. Prominent among their distinctive customary practices was the "squeeze"—the exaction of large arbitrary payoffs as the price of doing business.

A third set of international legal issues also plagued Sino-Western relations from the outset. China consistently rejected the demands of the Western powers that they be allowed to establish diplomatic missions in the capital at Peking and to have their envoys received by the emperor as the representatives of foreign sovereigns whose status was equal to his own. Rather than accept the diplomatic system that had evolved among the European Christian states, China—the "Middle Kingdom"—insisted that official Western emissaries conform to the rules of the "tribute system" that it had long maintained in the Sinocentric world of East Asia. Those rules permitted only widely spaced visits to Peking by foreign envoys, who were required to pay tribute to the Son of Heaven and to perform what in Western eyes was the humiliating series of prostrations and head-knockings known as the *"k'o-t'ou,"* from which our own word "kowtow" derives.

The series of bilateral treaties that the major Western powers imposed upon China during the two decades following the Opium War provided a radical "solution" to the problem of judicial jurisdiction—the "extraterritoriality" that gradually came to symbolize China's humiliation. These first "unequal treaties" exempted nationals of the treaty powers who were suspected of crime from the administration of Chinese justice and subjected them instead to the jurisdiction of their own nation's consular officials. Moreover, these consular officials were authorized to judge the conduct of the accused not according to the law of China but according to the law of their own land.

As part of the Western program for "opening up" China to trade, the new "treaty system" also began to construct a legal environment that granted Western merchants greater advantages and a higher degree of predictability than had the Canton system. For example, in Shanghai, which became the principal center for Sino-Western transactions, if a Chinese wanted to file a legal claim against an American trader, he had to bring suit before the American consul. Although an American with a civil claim against a Chinese had to sue before a Chinese tribunal, that tribunal developed into a "mixed court" in which an American consular official played an influential role sitting as an "assessor" beside the Chinese judge in cases involving Americans.

In addition, the treaties provided for the establishment of permanent diplomatic missions in Peking that were guaranteed access to China's officialdom according to Western usages, based upon the sovereign equality of all states, rather than upon the principles of the hierarchical East Asian tribute system. So reluctant was China to accept this institutional framework of Western-style international relations that even after it had been prescribed by the treaty of 1858 with Britain, the British literally had to shoot their way into Peking to implement it. Furthermore, another generation passed before China succumbed to foreign pressures to overcome its millennial policy against maintaining its own resident diplomatic missions abroad.

The advent of the treaty system made inevitable China's sustained exposure to, and gradual assimilation of, Western international law. Americans, whose country had not actually participated in the forcible imposition of the treaty system but had been quick to benefit from it, played an important role in facilitating this process. As early as 1839, on the eve of the Opium War, an American medical missionary, Dr. Peter Parker, had helped to translate into Chinese certain passages of Emmerich de Vattel's *Le Droit des gens,* which Commissioner Lin Tse-hsü invoked in a vain effort to put an end to the importation of opium by British traders in Canton. In the early 1860s another American missionary, W. A. P. Martin, translated Henry Wheaton's *Elements of International Law,* then the leading text on the subject, and persuaded Chinese officials to publish it and use it in their international dealings. Martin believed that knowledge of the legal principles of Christian civilization not only would lead the heathens to Christ but would also help them cope with overzealous Western diplomats and traders whose demands were often couched in terms of international law. Precisely for the latter reason, some of the foreign diplomats residing in Peking opposed his project. They were convinced that, once the Chinese learned international law, they would appreciate the extent to which the system of extraterritorial privileges recently imposed by the West varied from the treatment accorded the "civilized" states of Christendom. As a French diplomat correctly predicted, Martin's translation "will make us endless trouble." The Western trading community was also apprehensive about supplying an instrument that might curb newly acquired commercial privileges and prevent the exaction of further concessions. Other diplomats, including Americans, endorsed Martin's effort in the belief that it would show the Chinese that force was not the West's only law and would help them understand and deal with the outside world, to the benefit of both China and the West.

After some initial hesitancy and suspicion, the Chinese authorities increasingly invoked the principles set forth by Wheaton. To their surprise they discovered that, within the narrow limits imposed by their deteriorating power, this new technique was quite useful in defending the nation's in-

terests. They therefore added international law to the subjects
to be taught at the new educational institutions that had been
founded, with the aid of missionary Martin and other foreigners, to dispense the Western learning with which China
hoped to strengthen itself to fend off the West. China also began to send students to Europe and America to study a
number of topics, including international law. Just as Chinese
modernizers sought to acquire the secrets of Western shipbuilding and military technology, so too did they seek to
master the law of nations as another weapon to be used in
China's defense.

Mastery of this discipline took some time, and China's incomplete grasp of it occasionally produced difficulty. For example, because the leading reformer, Prince Kung, did not
understand that the customary principle of nonextradition of
political criminals remained unaffected by the provisions of
the Sino-American Treaty of 1844, China in 1874 unsuccessfully persisted in requesting extradition of an alleged political
offender who had fled to the United States. Nevertheless, with
the help of some experienced foreign scholars and diplomats,
including the former American minister to Peking, Anson
Burlingame, who headed China's first ad hoc diplomatic mission to the West, by the end of the nineteenth century the
mandarins of imperial China seem not only to have accepted
international law in lieu of their traditional pattern of foreign
relations but also to have acquired enough experience to feel
comfortable in applying it.

Their eventual mastery of the Western doctrines and practices, however, made Chinese officials increasingly aware of
the limited value of this legal learning to a China that lacked
the military, political, and economic power to defend itself by
other than verbal means. Indeed, China's weakness prevented
it from fully exercising its rights under international law, even
in relation to relatively friendly countries such as the United
States. For example, the enactment by the United States of the
so-called Chinese Exclusion Act in 1888 violated all four of the

Sino-American treaties that had been concluded between 1844 and 1880. The Chinese minister to Washington pointed out that this "abrogation . . . of an important treaty stipulation, releases China from the observance of all its treaties with the United States," and the United States recognized that China was entitled to denounce the treaties. Yet political considerations prevented China from seizing upon what in theory was a golden opportunity to rid itself of unequal obligations perceived to be contrary to its interests.

This unhappy situation bred a certain cynicism about international law among the Chinese elite. As one of China's early diplomats commented in 1891: "International law is just like Chinese statutory law—reasonable but unreliable. If there is right without might, the right will not prevail." This view is strikingly like that of Fukuzawa Yukichi, Meiji Japan's leading interpreter of the West, who wrote: "A hundred volumes of international law and numerous treaties of amity are weaker than one barrel of cannon." Thus, Mao Tse-tung was not the first East Asian leader whose experience with the West confirmed the belief, for which Mao was castigated so often in the West, that "political power grows out of the barrel of a gun." Communist Chinese scholars, like their predecessors, have pointed out how fruitless it would have been at the end of the Manchu era for China's enfeebled government to demand that the increasingly rapacious imperialists respect international legal principles such as the integrity of a country's internal waters.

Perhaps the feeling of powerlessness and futility accounts for the fact that, once having recognized the unavoidability of participation in the Western state system, the Manchu government appeared to accept all of its rules. Little effort was made to subject them to critical scrutiny with a view to adapting, modifying, or even rejecting those that did not suit China's national interest. Certainly officials in Peking might justifiably have believed that any effort to change the rules could place China in an even more disadvantageous position and that the best they could hope for would be to restrain the foreigners by persuading them to adhere to the existing system and to admit China to its benefits on the basis of equality.

Not only were the Chinese cynical about the tendency of Western states to prefer force to law in foreign relations, but they were also profoundly skeptical about the manner in which the Western powers resorted to law. Because of race, culture, geographic propinquity, common political circumstances, and other factors, they especially doubted whether Western nations would apply international law in an even-handed manner in dealing with East Asia. This distrust of the West led the Manchus to prefer as modes of conflict resolution either direct negotiations between the parties to a dispute or mediation, conciliation, or other forms of nonbinding third-party assistance that did not require China to surrender control to outsiders. For example, in 1909, China rejected Portugal's suggestion that their bilateral dispute be referred to an international arbitration tribunal organized under the 1907 Hague Convention for the Pacific Settlement of International Disputes; in addition to other reasons, China claimed that "European and American countries have a bias against East Asian people" and that such a tribunal would therefore favor Portugal.

Some Chinese also came to resent the fact that their country felt forced to imitate the domestic law as well as the international law of the West. The first Western legal concepts to be adopted by China were those of international law. For decades after the translation of Wheaton's text the Chinese had resisted significant changes in their domestic law. By the turn of the century, however, especially after Japan succeeded in throwing off the yoke of extraterritoriality by complying with Western demands that it "modernize" its legal system, China's leaders realized that the price of ending the increasingly detested system of extraterritorial jurisdiction that symbolized foreign domination was the adoption of Western internal legal institutions. These demands became official when, beginning in 1902, the major powers including the United States, in a series of bilateral treaties, promised that if China managed "to reform its judicial system and to bring it into accord with that of the western nations" they will "be prepared to relinquish extraterritorial rights when satisfied that the state of the Chinese laws, the arrangements for their administration and other considerations warrant it."

Law and U.S.-China Relations under the Chinese Republic: 1912–49

Despite Chinese distrust and resentment of the West, by the time the Manchu dynasty collapsed in 1911 the country had become a participant in the Western state system and was conversant with its institutions, processes, and norms. Although China had not attained the sovereign equality that had become its goal, it had learned to make use of the resources of international law in a modest way to defend against future foreign incursions and to press for the elimination of existing ones. With the exception of the so-called Boxer Rebellion in 1900, when both Chinese and foreign forces committed outrages, the late Manchu officials gradually brought China's state practice into conformity with international standards, if only to avoid giving the imperialists pretexts for further hostile acts. Through its participation in multilateral conferences and organizations China was also beginning to play a role in the legislative development of international law.

In his declaration inaugurating the Republic of China on January 1, 1912, Dr. Sun Yat-sen, its founder, stated that its goal was "to obtain the rights of a civilized state" and "to place China in a respectable place in international society." This objective has also guided subsequent leaders of the Republic and even, one may say, the revolutionary leaders of the People's Republic, who have shared with other Chinese patriots the intense desire to attain national self-respect.

In this quest Republican statesmen, like their predecessors during the last half century of the Ch'ing dynasty, regarded international law as a principal asset. They suffered grievous disappointments at the inability of legal arguments to protect enfeebled China against the harsh realities of power politics, such as Japan's "Twenty-one Demands" of 1915, refusal of the Paris Peace Conference of 1919 to restore to China former German rights in the Shantung Peninsula, and failure of the League of Nations to provide an effective response to Japanese aggression in Manchuria in 1931. Nevertheless, their patient diplomacy, effective mobilization of the resources of international law, and persistent political pressure did gradually succeed in dismantling the elaborate structure of extraterritorial rights; inequitable tariff restrictions; leased territories; concessions; settlements; armed forces; railway, postal, and wireless networks; and other privileges by which the foreign powers had dominated China.

Both before and after World War II the Republic of China contributed to the progressive development of international law, considerably enlarged the number of China's official and academic specialists in the subject, and participated in many international governmental and nongovernmental organizations. It consistently advocated not only that states settle all disputes by pacific means but also that they accept the compulsory jurisdiction of the International Court of Justice in all legal controversies. Although at the 1945 San Francisco Conference, which launched the United Nations, the United States and the Soviet Union successfully opposed a Chinese proposal that would have required all states to accept the court's compulsory jurisdiction, the Chinese Nationalist government itself accepted the court's compulsory jurisdiction vis-à-vis those states making a reciprocal acceptance. Thus, Republican statesmen proved even more receptive to international law than did their Ch'ing predecessors.

The Republican government's defeat in the Chinese civil war, which required its removal to Taiwan in 1949, has obviously diminished its political influence in the world community. Yet the Republic of China's attitude toward international law has remained essentially unchanged. Indeed, it has used international law to the best of its ability to shore up its shaky status. Although the long record of the Republic's theory and practice, like that of the late Ch'ing, deserves far more study than it has received from legal scholars, it seems fair to state that its efforts have contributed to the evolutionary process by which international law is being transformed from an exclusively Western product to one that more truly reflects the composition of the world.

In the Republican era, as during the last half century of imperial rule, the United States played a special role with respect to China's development of international law. The United States had been the first country with which imperial China had concluded a treaty to arbitrate certain bilateral disputes, and the empire had also obligated the United States to mediate disputes between China and other powers if China so requested. During the stormy Republican period China looked to the United States to vindicate its hope that international law would eventually prevail over raw power politics. If the Paris Peace Conference of 1919 proved a bitter pill, at least Chinese patriots knew that President Woodrow Wilson had opposed awarding Japan the former German rights in the Shantung Peninsula. If the League of Nations failed to meet the challenge of Japan's assault upon Manchuria in 1931, at least the American Secretary of State, Henry L. Stimson, had espoused a doctrine calling for nonrecognition of Japan's unlawful gains. And it was President Franklin D. Roosevelt who in the closing days of World War II insisted that China be treated as a great power and installed as a veto-wielding permanent member of the United Nations Security Council.

Yet the American record toward the Republic of China has proved to be as mixed as it had been toward the Manchus.

The United States and the United Kingdom were the very last countries to agree to end their extraterritorial privileges in China, and did so only in 1943 under the pressures of wartime political exigencies. Moreover, since the Republican government's flight from the mainland to Taiwan in 1949, patriotic Chinese on the island, as well as those in the People's Republic, have criticized the United States for continuing to devise ways to exempt American military personnel from the Republic's criminal jurisdiction, both before and under the 1965 Status of Forces Agreement. And the Republic of China, like the People's Republic, became furious when, after the outbreak of the Korean conflict in 1950, the United States suddenly switched its legal position from considering Taiwan restored to China in accordance with the 1943 Cairo Declaration and the 1945 Potsdam Proclamation to one that regarded the status of the island as undetermined. Thus, under the Republic, some distrust and resentment have continued to mark China's attitude toward international law even as practiced by the United States, not to mention the more obviously imperialistic powers. Nevertheless, like their imperial predecessors, Republican officials have realized, particularly in view of their nation's weakness, that international law would continue to be an important, if imperfect, instrument for defending the national interest and preserving whatever improvements might be made in China's situation.

The Legal Context of U.S. Relations with the People's Republic

A survey of the historical background that is the heritage of the leaders of the People's Republic should help us to understand their perceptions of international law and its role in Sino-American relations.

That the Chinese Communists' attitude toward international law would be distinctive and have an important impact upon their relations with the United States became apparent even before the founding of the People's Republic on October 1, 1949. As early as 1947, upon the renewal of civil war between the Communists and the Nationalists, the Central Committee of the Chinese Communist Party had declared that it would not recognize many types of military, political, and economic agreements concluded by the Republican government since the previous year and in the future. This action implicitly suggested that, if the Communist revolution proved successful, the new regime would regard itself as the successor government of the continuing state of China but would, to some extent, reject or modify the principle espoused by the United States and other bourgeois powers that a successor government is required by international law to perform all obligations assumed on behalf of the state by its predecessor. As the Communist forces took over the mainland, abuses committed against American consuls and consular premises also indicated that the revolutionary government intended to challenge other principles long endorsed by the dominant forces of the world community. Shortly thereafter, Secretary of State Dean Acheson invoked these Chinese Communist actions as justification for the American refusal to recognize the newly established People's Republic as the legitimate government of China, despite its evident control of the overwhelming bulk of the country's population and territory.

Nonrecognition, like the related decision to block Peking's replacement of Taipei as the representative of China in the United Nations, was only one of a series of American efforts to use international law to legitimize conduct toward Mao's China that was plainly inspired by political expediency. Mentioned earlier was the startling change of position, made just two days after the Korean conflict began, in which the United States announced that the legal status of Taiwan, which the United States had previously treated as Chinese territory, was actually undetermined. This dramatic shift enabled Washington to rationalize stationing the Seventh Fleet in Taiwanese waters, an action which it had earlier rejected as constituting intervention in the Chinese civil war. The United States then masterminded the erection of a postwar peace treaty structure that formalized Japan's renunciation of all claim to Taiwan without confirming China's reincorporation of the island.

Also noteworthy was the American engrafting of an exception upon Article 118 of the Geneva Convention for the Protection of Prisoners of War. Unlike Article 109, which authorized repatriation during hostilities of sick and wounded prisoners who did not object, on its face Article 118 seemed to call for the return of all prisoners of war at the conclusion of hostilities without regard to their consent. Contrary to the position adopted by the United States during the drafting of the convention, and contrary to the views of the American military command in Korea, Washington insisted that prisoners who did not wish to return to their army were not to be repatriated. This newly minted principle of "nonforcible repatriation"—endorsed by an American-dominated UN General Assembly—delayed agreement upon an armistice for eighteen months.

Similar "creative lawyering" led the United States to invent the "Uniting for Peace Resolution," a device that, contrary to the expectations of those who framed the UN Charter, conferred upon the UN General Assembly powers to mobilize military support against the Communist attack in Korea after the Soviet veto power had frustrated action by the Security Council, the organ endowed with responsibility for enforcement action under the Charter. Other American maneuvering in the United Nations was also legalistic in form but opportunistic in substance. For example, in 1950, at a time when the United States controlled a voting majority in the Security Council, Washington claimed that the veto power of the permanent members did not apply to China's representation because under the Charter that question was "procedural" rather than "substantive." In 1954, however, when its voting control had begun to slip, the United States argued that the question was indeed "substantive" and therefore subject to its veto. The People's Republic also resented being branded an aggressor by the United Nations for entering the Korean conflict after the American armies advancing through North Korea toward the Chinese border ignored repeated warnings to halt.

Of course, legal legerdemain was not the only technique in the American bag of tricks. Outright violations of international law, accompanied by lying about the facts, alternated with manipulation of the law. Not only did U.S. airplanes systematically invade China's territorial airspace on both reconnaissance and sabotage missions but American spies and saboteurs were also posted on the ground inside China in cooperation with the Nationalist regime on Taiwan. The detention and punishment of CIA agents by the People's Republic, as in the Downey-Fecteau case, elicited Washington's feigned outrage and hypocritical castigation of Peking for having "trumped up" charges against supposedly innocent Americans. The cynicism of China's leaders was further enhanced when the United States undermined the implementation of the 1954 Geneva Agreement relating to Indochina and when it covertly supported a Tibetan rebellion against Chinese rule in 1958–59.

In the light of this background one can well understand why in 1972 the late Premier Chou En-lai, Vice Foreign Minister Ch'iao Kuan-hua (since promoted and then sacked), and other high Chinese diplomats could not resist derisory smiles as I brought up the topic of international law. And, at an earlier meeting with middle-level officials of the Ministry of Foreign Affairs, open laughter greeted my suggestion that China might soon wish to put forth a candidate for a seat on the International Court of Justice. This response was not surprising given Peking's strong preference for settling international disputes through negotiation rather than through mediation, not to mention adjudication, and given its disdain for bourgeois legal technicalities, its reluctance to be in a minority position in any international institution, its cynicism about some of the court's decisions, and its scorn for the prominent participation of the Chiang Kai-shek regime in the court's work. Contemporary Chinese diplomats, even more than their predecessors, seem to regard international law as a bag of tricks manipulated by the imperialists to the disadvantage of China and other unfortunates. The Chinese Communists have been profoundly shaped by their perception of China's "century of humiliation" that began with the Opium War and of the role that international law played in forging their country's semicolonial chains. Nothing that has occurred in Sino-American relations during the past generation has caused them to alter their outlook.

Yet, also like their predecessors, they have not labored under the illusion that China can do without international law. Although the late Chou En-lai was amused at its mention, when I asked him why the People's Republic had been slow to take part in the range of international organizations that became accessible to it upon entry into the United Nations in October 1971, he did not say that Peking would not participate in those organizations. Rather, he said that he had not anticipated that Peking would be seated as early as 1971, that the government had therefore not prepared adequate numbers of specialists to represent China in the various organizations, and that the situation would gradually improve.

Similarly, although Chou censured the United States for having undermined the Geneva Agreement of 1954, he explained that, at Geneva, China's diplomats had been inexperienced and unprepared for what had been their first major international conference and had thus believed that the

United States would not interfere with the agreement to hold free elections in Vietnam. Significantly, he went on to say that China would not act so naively again. Pointing to the able Ch'iao Kuan-hua, he said that China was now well prepared for such conferences and would negotiate more wisely. The moral that the premier had evidently extracted from his disappointment over Geneva was not that Peking should not make agreements with the imperialists but that it must be shrewder in doing so. And when asked why China did not establish a New China News Agency office in Washington prior to the normalization of diplomatic relations and why in the absence of normalization Peking did not send students to study at American universities, Chou mentioned his concern about whether, in view of international law, such actions might not create a "two China" situation. That is, he was worried about acting in ways that might tacitly imply Peking's acceptance of the legitimacy of its rival in Taipei (a worry that did not preclude the People's Republic and the United States from establishing diplomatic "liaison offices" in 1973). Thus, the mastermind of the first quarter century of the People's Republic's foreign policy seemed to believe that, despite the distrust and even scorn that he evidently felt for international law, China had no choice but to make the most of it. This attitude brings to mind the old male cliché about women—you can't live with them but you can't live without them.

Of course, as we have seen, the Chinese Communists had become involved with international law even before the founding of the People's Republic. Like the late imperial modernizers, from the very outset they used it as a weapon in defense of their interests. Beginning in 1949, as a new government that sought recognition, diplomatic relations, representation in the United Nations, and the other symbols of legitimacy, the People's Republic had to argue its case in the most persuasive light, especially because of the continuing existence on Taiwan of the preceding regime. It therefore mustered the intellectual resources that all new governments have drawn upon to demonstrate that these legitimating symbols are their "rights." Having come to power on a platform that promised to restore China's territorial integrity, the Communists also sought to convince the world community that Tibet had traditionally been part of China, that Hong Kong and Macao continue to be Chinese territory despite temporary imperialist occupations, that the status of Taiwan was not undetermined because the island had been reincorporated by China after World War II without waiting for a merely confirmatory peace treaty, that new China's boundaries should be established not on the basis of the "unequal treaties" but after uncoerced negotiations between the People's Republic and each of its neighbors on the basis of equality and mutual benefit, and that the broad territorial sea (twelve nautical miles from straight baselines) sought for military, political, and economic reasons conforms to international standards. Confronted by American espionage and sabotage within its borders, Peking had to win world sympathy by exposing these acts as blatant violations of its sovereignty. When its diplomats and nationals suffered outrages abroad, it invoked the customary norms of international law in an effort to assure their protection. And when it sent military forces to fight in Korea in 1950, it sought to forestall charges of intervention and aggression by claiming that these were "volunteers" rather than official army units.

Moreover, the People's Republic resorted not only to the international law of claims and protests but also to that of agreement and cooperation, making thousands of bilateral and multilateral treaties and other pacts for military, political, economic, cultural, and other purposes. Between 1949 and the initiation of Sino-American détente in 1971 there were many more Chinese claims and protests against the United States than instances of agreements with it. Yet there were isolated examples of the latter, particularly the 1955 bilateral "agreed announcement" concerning the return of civilians to their respective countries and the 1953 Korean armistice agreement, which was actually signed by North Korea in behalf of the "Chinese People's Volunteers" and by the United States in behalf of the UN command.

More than previous Chinese elites the Communists have sought to reshape aspects of existing international law that do not conform to their perception of the national interest. We have already seen that the People's Republic has rejected traditional doctrine by claiming a right to choose which of China's pre-1949 treaty commitments it would acknowledge as binding upon it, a claim that the United States characterized as a refusal by Peking to "honor its international obligations." The People's Republic rejected the three-mile limit and became an early supporter of the principle that each country is entitled to determine the breadth of its territorial sea in light of its economic, security, and transportation interests and other relevant historical and geographical factors. Although Peking claimed only a twelve-mile breadth for its own sea, in 1970 it began to voice strong support for the intensifying effort of Latin American countries to win acceptance of a 200-mile limit, an effort that to some observers seemed laughable at first but that is now reaching fruition in the form of a 200-mile "economic zone" for all coastal states.

Yet in the past decade Peking has not been as innovative as it was during the previous one, especially during the Cultural Revolution. Then, for example, its treatment of foreign diplomats in China curtailed accepted protections at the same time that the People's Republic not only continued to claim protection for its diplomats abroad but also appeared to be claiming the equivalent of diplomatic immunity for a variety of nondiplomatic Chinese emissaries traveling overseas. Although prior to entering the United Nations, Peking made many proposals to reorganize the United Nations and even to establish a new revolutionary world organization, little has subsequently been heard from it on this score. Despite the fact that Peking had castigated the United Nations for devising the "Uniting for Peace Resolution" during the Korean War, when conflict broke out between India and Pakistan over Bangladesh in 1971, Peking voted to invoke that resolution's procedures. To be sure, because of its desire to support "Third World" political demands, China has endorsed a pending reconsideration of the UN Charter, but in a very vague and cautious way that conveys little enthusiasm for revision. It is unlikely that Peking will take the lead in advocating reforms such as abolition of the great power veto that it now enjoys in the Security Council, even though the opposition of the other permanent members of the council is sure to preclude such an action regardless of Peking's stand. By and large, despite its rejection of certain aspects of traditional international law, the People's Republic has not sought many revolutionary changes in the rules of the game. Indeed, some Western commentators have criticized Peking not for radicalism but for conservatism, arguing that it is today's arch exponent of classical nineteenth century notions of sovereignty. China, they claim, still uses international law as a weapon at a time when the world needs to go beyond the nation-state toward some form of supranational government.

Revolutionary China has also demonstrated the ability to manipulate international law as cynically as other major powers including the United States. It has endorsed the principle of nonintervention in the internal affairs of other countries as an essential feature of peaceful coexistence. At the same time it has preached and practiced the doctrine of giving, as Mao put it, "active support to the national independence and liberation movement in countries in Asia, Africa, and Latin America, as well as to the peace movement and to just struggles in all countries throughout the world." It has condemned the UN General Assembly for adopting resolutions that charge

China with violations of human rights and fundamental freedoms in Tibet, arguing that such resolutions contravene the UN Charter by interfering in matters that are essentially within China's domestic jurisdiction. Nevertheless, it has chastised "colonial countries" for making the same argument against UN resolutions concerning their acts of suppressing "national liberation movements," and since entering the United Nations the People's Republic has joined in such resolutions and even in those censuring South Africa for the repression of human rights within its own territory. The People's Republic has demanded that countries that jail its nationals grant Chinese consuls the right promptly to visit the detained persons in accordance with international standards. Yet when the People's Republic detains an alien it claims that it is under no obligation to grant his government consular access until all judicial proceedings, including appeal, have run their course, and in practice it has often denied foreign officials even that opportunity. As scrutiny of Peking's positions on protecting prisoners of war and diplomats reveals, there are many other inconsistencies in its record. Indeed, there are so many that one acerbic critic with diplomatic experience in Peking has written that China "puts into practice the duality of attitude toward liberty espoused by Louis Veuillot: 'I demand liberty from you in the name of your principles, but I refuse it to you in the name of mine.' " [1]

The Chinese Communists' success in manipulating the rules of the game as adeptly and hypocritically as the countries that invented them is testimony to the lack of correlation between a country's domestic legal system and its ability to participate in the global legal process. To say that the public order of China is distinctive, even for Communist countries, is

[1] Philippe Ardent, "Chinese Diplomatic Practice During the Cultural Revolution," in Jerome Alan Cohen, ed., *China's Practice of International Law: Some Case Studies* (Cambridge, Mass.: Harvard University Press, 1972), p. 88.

an understatement. Contemporary China has rejected not only the impressive bureaucratic legal structures of its "feudal" imperial past and the "bourgeois" European-style codes that the Republican government sought to adapt to China's very different circumstances but also the "revisionist" Soviet legal model with which the People's Republic had experimented during the first decade of its existence. Searching for an autochthonous legal system that will suit its revolutionary political, social, and economic goals and Chinese conditions, the People's Republic has thus far developed one that lacks many of the conventional indicia of a legal system, whether bourgeois or Communist. It has dispensed with codes, lawyers, prosecutors, professionally trained judges, publication of judicial opinions, virtually all legal scholarship, and most legal education. Instead it has developed an administrative apparatus that, under the close control of the Communist Party, integrates the courts and public security organs with urban and rural residential and work units. Although an inquisitorial criminal process metes out stern punishments to serious offenders, in most cases the participants in this network seek to settle disputes and impose sanctions through ideological indoctrination and social pressure, preferably applied informally through the "persuasion-education" of popular groups rather than through official procedures. Informal negotiation and conciliation through the application of Maoist principles to daily life are also widely employed to resolve disputes between state enterprises, communes, and other organizations of China's socialized economy; where persuasion is unsuccessful, administrative rather than judicial decision making prevails. Deformalization, decentralization, and politicization are the hallmarks of a system that has gone much further than has the U.S.S.R. toward achieving the vision of those Bolsheviks who believed that their 1917 revolution would put an end to complex laws and legal institutions and establish a system of proletarian simplicity.

The public order of the United States, of course, is at the

opposite end of the spectrum from that of the People's Republic in theory and to a large extent in practice. Almost a century and a half ago Alexis de Tocqueville noted that in America virtually every political controversy becomes a legal matter. Today hundreds of thousands of lawyers continue to make the United States the most legalistic and litigious of societies, the price that we pay to vindicate our belief in the rule of law. Yet, despite this tradition and the contemporary vitality of law reform at home, the American record abroad does not always reflect out professed belief in the autonomy of law. We have already seen this vis-à-vis China, and the U.S. government's conduct toward third countries has not been lost upon China's leaders, whether it has been covert action such as at the Bay of Pigs; overt intervention that we try to rationalize as "another creative chapter in the development of international law," as we did in the case of our 1965 intervention in the Dominican Republic; or acts that we simply label vital to our security, as in the recent case of Chile.

International Law and the Future of U.S.-China Relations

Interestingly, some of the issues that now confront us are reminiscent of those that plagued America's first experiences with China prior to the Opium War. Although no Americans are known to be in Chinese prisons since the release of John Downey in 1973, increasing contacts will inevitably produce problems between some visiting Americans and China's law-enforcement agencies, even if the ordinary administration of justice should not be interrupted by mass movements such as the periodic cultural revolutions which Chairman Mao predicted.

If the experience of Americans detained by Chinese public

security authorities since 1949 is any guide, we can expect friction to arise over both the substantive and procedural norms of contemporary Chinese law. The substantive law will be subject to challenge because of its inaccessibility and imprecision. It is difficult for foreigners to avoid violating norms if they have been given no clear warning of them. Thus, the plight of Americans in China today resembles that of their ancestors under the "Canton system" when they were required to obey Manchu law but were forbidden to acquire copies of it. Moreover, those norms about which foreigners have been warned are often so broad and vague as to keep the promise of fair warning to the ear but break it to the hope. The contemporary Chinese definition of espionage, for example, as some aliens have discovered to their sorrow, embraces many activities which other countries regard as legitimate.

The application to Americans of Chinese criminal procedures is also likely to create problems. In criminal cases of any seriousness it is not the masses who deal with a foreign accused but the public security apparatus, and its procedures, more than those of any other foreign system with which Americans are likely to come in contact, perpetuate the Inquisition. A suspect is simply detained, held indefinitely, cut off from all communication with the outside world including family, friends, and his diplomatic mission and subjected to repeated intense interrogations in circumstances which generally exclude torture but which are nevertheless calculated to elicit a confession. Once the dossier has been filled out, for foreigners there is usually, but not always, a "trial," which is little more than a pro forma recitation of the charges, facts, and confession. Only for purposes of this "trial" can the foreign defendant, if he desires, have the assistance of an advocate. Because China has done away with professional lawyers, the advocate summoned to assist the foreign accused is usually a law professor, whose services are limited to a brief plea for lenient punishment. Thus, although for Americans today the result of the Chinese criminal process is likely to be less arbitrary than in the early nineteenth century and the punishment less severe than the death penalty that was then occasionally imposed on hapless seamen, according to contemporary Western standards the opportunity to make a meaningful defense is still lacking.

By the same token, American businessmen again confront an unusual legal environment, one that offers little civil or commercial legislation, that prevents ready access to the courts, and that features institutions for dispute resolution which are of uncertain reliability. And the United States is again eager to regularize the position of its diplomatic representation in Peking and obtain China's adherence to a set of rules that will guarantee our diplomats there the privileges and immunities which ordinarily accompany their status.

The long-awaited normalization of relations between Washington and Peking is unlikely to resolve all of these problems, but it will at least eliminate our formal diplomatic handicap. It should remove an obstacle to negotiation of agreements such as those designed to guarantee prompt consular access to detained nationals and to erect an infrastructure to facilitate trade. Yet the prospects for normalization itself will turn upon how China and the United States deal with some difficult international legal questions. The People's Republic insists that the United States recognize it as the only legitimate government of China, as have all other countries which have established formal diplomatic relations with Peking. This would require withdrawal of Washington's recognition from the Republican government on Taiwan, an act that Washington, which would prefer a "two China" or "one China, two governments" solution along the lines of the "two Germanies" model, has been reluctant to contemplate. This reluctance derives in part from the fact that derecognition would end the 1954 U.S.–Republic of China defense treaty guaranteeing the security of Taiwan. Peking, of course, has always maintained that the treaty is a nullity, and therefore it cannot be expected to accede to the commitment, particularly when the purpose of the treaty is to protect Taiwan against an attack by the People's Republic. Moreover, because the Peking government insists that Taiwan is Chinese territory, it cannot be expected to offer any assurances that it will not use force to take over the island once the defense treaty lapses. Nor will it be easy to persuade Peking to tolerate any American effort to develop an informal U.S. substitute for the lapsed treaty in order to prevent prosperity on the island from turning into panic.

Peking and Washington may turn out to have differing interpretations of the crucial portion of the 1972 Shanghai Communiqué relating to the status of Taiwan in which the United States stated:

The United States acknowledges that all Chinese on either side of the Taiwan Strait maintain there is but one China and that Taiwan is a part of China. The United States government does not challenge that position. It reaffirms its interest in a peaceful settlement of the Taiwan question by the Chinese themselves. With this prospect in mind, it affirms the ultimate objective of the withdrawal of all U.S. forces and military installations from Taiwan. In the meantime, it will progressively reduce its forces and military installations on Taiwan as the tension in the area diminishes.

The meaning and significance of this declaration have been debated by commentators. American officials denied that it represented any change in the position held by the United States since mid-1950, the position that the status of Taiwan is undetermined. The People's Republic, interestingly, remained silent for a year on this question before claiming, in only a semiofficial way, that in the Shanghai Communiqué the United States recognizes Taiwan as China's territory. There is the further question whether the Shanghai Communiqué should be regarded as a binding international agreement, an issue that neither side has directly addressed. What position the United States adopts concerning the status of Taiwan will plainly have important implications for the legitimacy of any effort to continue to protect Taiwan following normalization, for if Washington confirms that Taiwan is Chinese territory and couples this with recognition of Peking as the only legitimate government of China, it will no longer have any legal basis for protecting the island.

Thus, international law is importantly involved in the major problem confronting Sino-American relations and, as in the past, differences in legal views may obstruct reconciliation. Yet we should not overlook the extent to which Peking and Washington already share assumptions about international law and the resulting contribution that this makes to an improved relationship. The "liaison offices" that each government has established in the capital of the other could not function if there were not at least minimal agreement on the privileges and immunities due their diplomatic staff even in the absence of normalization. Trade could not be conducted if there were not some common understanding about contracts, corporations, and the rules of transnational transactions. Cultural exchange could not exist if each government were not confident that its nationals were unlikely to be arbitrarily victimized by the other government's law enforcement agencies in the present political climate. In sending an airplane to call for former President Richard Nixon in Los Angeles in February 1976, the People's Republic was relying on American courts to honor its claim to sovereign immunity from litigation if a private claimant sought to attach the plane and initiate a lawsuit.

Despite many departures from the rules of the game by both sides since 1949, even politico-military relations between the People's Republic and the United States have benefited from observance of international law. During the Taiwan Strait crisis of 1958, for example, American warships convoyed Nationalist ships from Taiwan to points only three miles from the mainland's offshore island of Quemoy, which is held by the Nationalists; Peking, despite its claim to a twelve-mile coastal sea and its "serious warning" against U.S. failure to respect that claim, confined its bombardment to the three-mile coastal sea that both sides recognized as Chinese waters. Since ping-pong diplomacy captured the world's imagination in 1971, Washington's newly acquired respect for Peking's territorial jurisdiction, leading it to cease illegal overflights and subversion, has contributed to better relations.

We should also not ignore the increasing importance of Sino-American interaction in the many multilateral forums that are developing new international institutions, rules, and procedures to meet the varied challenges facing the world community. The People's Republic is gradually becoming more active in international efforts to cope with problems of trade, industrialization, population, the environment, food, ocean and undersea resources, and other matters. On many subjects Peking is moving, if only reluctantly and gradually, from generalized political posturing to positions of a more detailed, useful nature.

Peking has shown especial interest in reshaping the law of the sea. Although not as active at the working level as many other countries, it nevertheless seizes the occasional opportunities that the seemingly interminable conference sessions present for mustering Third World support against both the superpowers. The particularly difficult negotiations to devise arrangements for mining undersea resources in areas beyond national jurisdiction have witnessed one significant development in Peking's attitude toward international law. For purposes of mining the seabed Peking has favored formation of a strong supranational authority despite China's usual distrust of proposals for supranational agencies of any kind. Ironically the United States, so often suspected by China of foisting such schemes on the world as neo-imperialist strategems, in this case has only grudgingly begun to acquiesce in establishment of a strong supranational enterprise.

However one evaluates Peking's record of cooperation with international programs during the six years since it entered the United Nations—and opinions do differ—it is safe to say that those commentators who prior to 1971 issued Cassandra-like warnings that Peking's advent would wreck the United Nations and other world institutions have proved quite wrong. Peking may seem extreme to some in its efforts to obliterate UN references to the Republic of China and even to the entity of Taiwan, but it has not stymied the Security Council, undermined the Secretariat, blocked the selection of a new secretary-general or done any of the mischief that had been predicted. We have yet to see a Peking representative thump the table with his shoe à la Khrushchev or act beyond the pale in any other way. Indeed, it is far healthier for all concerned for China to be fully engaged in international life than for it to continue its sniping on the sidelines as a pariah.

Perhaps the most important thing for the United States to remember in contemplating the role of international law in future relations with China is that international law is a dynamic process that is grounded in reciprocity. Just as one bad deed begot another in the dark night of 1949–71, in subsequent years good deeds by each side have elicited positive responses from the other. It is essential that the United States continue along these more hopeful lines, making clear by what it does as well as by what it says that it will no longer manipulate the rules of the game according to the expediency of the moment but will act in farsighted and even generous ways that set a standard for all, including China, to emulate. It will take a long time to persuade the Chinese to abandon the cynicism and distrust of international law that the past century and a half have taught them. Yet we have to make the effort, for soon China is expected to have intercontinental missiles capable of destroying our cities. As in the case of the U.S.S.R., arms control will be the ultimate challenge, and mutual confidence in international law will be essential to meet it.

BIBLIOGRAPHY

American-East Asian and Sino-American relations have stimulated much research in the last generation, and the essays in this volume draw extensively on that work. The following bibliography, intended to guide the reader in pursuing topics at greater depth, begins with a list of general works, and is followed by short bibliographic essays that correspond to each chapter. Evaluations of many of the volumes can be found in Ernest R. May and James C. Thomson, Jr., eds., *American-East Asian Relations: A Survey* (Cambridge, Mass.: Harvard University Press, 1972). The journals, *China Quarterly, Asian Survey,* and *Journal of Asian Studies* may be consulted for recent research. Official pronouncements of the People's Republic of China are printed in the weekly, *Peking Review.*

General Works

Borg, Dorothy. *American Policy and the Chinese Revolution, 1925–1928.* Rev. ed. New York: Columbia University Press, 1967.

Clyde, Paul H. and Burton F. Beers. *The Far East: A History of Western Impacts and Eastern Responses.* 6th ed. Englewood Cliffs, N.J.: Prentice-Hall, 1975.

Dulles, Foster Rhea. *China and America: The History of Their Relations Since 1784.* Port Washington, N.Y.: Kennikat Press, 1967.

———. *American Policy Toward Communist China: The Historical Record, 1949–1969.* New York: Crowell, 1972.

Fairbank, John King, ed. *The Chinese World Order: Traditional China's Foreign Relations.* Cambridge, Mass.: Harvard University Press, 1968.

————. *The United States and China.* 3rd ed. Cambridge, Mass.: Harvard University Press, 1972.

Friedman, Edward and Mark Selden, eds. *America's Asia: Dissenting Essays on Asian-American Relations.* New York: Pantheon Books, 1969.

Griswold, A. Whitney. *The Far Eastern Policy of the United States.* New Haven, Conn.: Yale University Press, 1962.

Johnson, Cecil. *Communist China and Latin America, 1959–1967.* New York: Columbia University Press, 1970.

Larkin, Bruce. *China and Africa, 1949–1970.* Berkeley: University of California Press, 1971.

MacFarquhar, Roderick, ed. *Sino-American Relations, 1949–1971.* New York: Praeger, 1972.

Ojha, Ishwer. *Chinese Foreign Policy in an Age of Transition: The Diplomacy of Cultural Despair.* Boston: Beacon Press, 1969.

U.S. Department of State. *United States Relations with China: With Special Reference to the Period 1944–1949.* Washington, D.C., 1949. Also cited as *The China White Paper, August 1949.* Stanford, Calif.: Stanford University Press, 1967.

Varg, Paul A. *The Closing of the Door: Sino-American Relations, 1936–1946.* Lansing: Michigan State University Press, 1973.

————. *The Making of a Myth: The United States and China, 1897–1912.* Lansing: Michigan State University Press, 1968.

American Perceptions of China

Harold R. Isaacs, *Images of Asia: American Views of China and India* (Cambridge: M.I.T. Press, 1958), also published under the title *Scratches on Our Minds,* is the classic work on the subject. It has since been supplemented by Warren I. Cohen, *America's Response to China: An Interpretative History of Sino-American Relations* (New York: Wiley, 1971); Akira Iriye, *Across the Pacific: An Inner History of American East-Asian Relations* (New York: Harcourt, Brace and World, 1967); and A. T. Steele, *The American People and China* (New York: McGraw Hill, 1966).

Many books detail the China experience of specific groups. Marilyn B. Young's *The Rhetoric of Empire: American China Policy, 1895–1901* (Cambridge, Mass.: Harvard University Press, 1968) relates the role of businessmen in the formation of William McKinley's policy towards China, while Arthur N. Young's *China and the Helping Hand, 1937–1945* (Cambridge, Mass.: Harvard University Press, 1963) is a participant observer's account of wartime economic relations. Paul Varg's *Missionaries, Chinese, and Diplomats: The American Protestant Missionary Movement in China, 1890–1952* (Princeton, N.J.: Princeton University Press, 1958) and John King Fairbank, ed., *The Missionary Enterprise in China and America* (Cambridge, Mass.: Harvard University Press, 1974) examine the missionary effort, Shirley Garrett treats the Y.M.C.A. in her *Social Reformers in Urban China: The Chinese Y.M.C.A., 1895–1926* (Cambridge, Mass.: Harvard University Press, 1970), and James C. Thomson, Jr., *While China Faced West: American Reformers in Nationalist China, 1928–1937* (Cambridge, Mass.: Harvard University Press, 1969) details the problems of those Americans who tried to bring about social reform by working through the Chinese political authorities. Kenneth Shewmaker discusses the positive wartime reaction of Americans in China to the Chinese Communists in his *Americans and Chinese Communists, 1927–1945: A Persuading Encounter* (Ithaca, N.Y.: Cornell University Press, 1971). Edgar Snow, *Red Star Over China* (New York: Random House, 1938) and Theodore H. White and Annalee Jacoby, *Thunder Out of China* (New York: William Sloane Associates, 1946) are classics of éngage reporting. Ross Y. Koen, *The China Lobby in American Politics* (New York: Harper and Row, 1974) and Stanley D. Bachrack, *The Committee of One Million: "China Lobby" Politics, 1953–1971* (New York: Columbia University Press, 1976) traces the development of China as an issue in U.S. domestic politics. George H. Gallup, ed., *The Gallup Poll: Public Opinion, 1935–1971*, 3 vols. (New York: Random House, 1972) is a basic source for gauging the movement of public opinion.

Chinese Perceptions of America

A perceptive general treatment of this subject is Francois Geoffroy-Dechaume, *China Looks at the World,* translated from the French by Jean Steward (New York: Pantheon Books, 1967). Akira Iriye's *Mutual Images: Essays in American-Japanese Relations* (Cambridge, Mass.: Harvard University Press, 1975) is very helpful in suggesting a comparative Asian perspective.

There are a number of discussions of individual Chinese intellectuals' views of the West in general and the United States in particular. *China Charts the World: Hsü Chi-yü and his Geography of 1848,* translated by Frederick W. Drake (Cambridge, Mass.: Harvard University Press, 1975), is noteworthy because it is one of the earliest Chinese analyses of the Western world. Y. C. Wang's *Chinese In-*

tellectuals and the West, 1872–1949 (Chapel Hill: University of North Carolina Press, 1966) examines the foreign education of a large group of Chinese intellectuals and their later impact on Chinese politics and economic development. Chow Tse-tsung's classic, *The May Fourth Movement: Intellectual Revolution in Modern China* (Cambridge, Mass.: Harvard University Press, 1964) describes the formative intellectual event of the generation of Chinese leaders only now leaving the political stage. Individual Chinese perceptions of Western and American solutions to China's crisis are examined in Kung-chuan Hsiao, *A Modern China and a New World: K'ang Yu-wei, Reformer and Utopian, 1858–1927* (Seattle: University of Washington Press, 1975); Jerome Greider, *Hu Shih and the Chinese Renaissance: Liberalism in the Chinese Revolution, 1917–1937* (Cambridge, Mass.: Harvard University Press, 1970); Charlotte Furth, *Ting Wen-chiang: Science and China's New Culture* (Cambridge, Mass.: Harvard University Press, 1970); and David T. Roy, *Kuo Mo-jo: The Early Years* (Cambridge, Mass.: Harvard University Press, 1971), among others.

The Structure of Sino-American Relations

Of the many books that deal with the history of Chinese foreign policy, Immanuel Hsu's *China's Entry into the Family of Nations: The Diplomatic Phase, 1858–1880* (Cambridge, Mass.: Harvard University Press, 1968) most explicitly examines China's adaptation to the Western system of diplomatic practice. The development of the PRC foreign affairs establishment is explored in Donald W. Klein's "The Management of Foreign Affairs in Communist China," in *China: Management of a Revolutionary Society,* John H. Lindbeck, ed. (Seattle: University of Washington Press, 1971) and "The Men and Institutions Behind China's Foreign Policy," in *Sino-American Relations, 1949–71,* Roderick MacFarquhar, ed. (New York: Praeger, 1972). Chinese negotiating practice is treated in Arthur Lall, *How Communist China Negotiates* (New York: Columbia University Press, 1968) and Kenneth Young, *Negotiating with the Chinese Communists: The United States Experience, 1953–1967* (New York: McGraw-Hill, 1968).

Young's volume is also useful for charting U.S. government decision making on China during the Eisenhower years. For the 1960s, it should be supplemented with Roger Hilsman, *To Move a Nation* (Garden City, N.Y.: Doubleday, 1967) and James C. Thomson, Jr., "On the Making of U.S. China Policy, 1961–9: A Study in

Bureaucratic Politics," *China Quarterly* 50 (April–June 1972): 220–243. Both Thomson's essay and Richard Moorsteen and Morton Abramowitz, *Remaking China Policy: U.S.-China Relations and Governmental Decisionmaking* (Cambridge, Mass.: Harvard University Press, 1971) usefully explore the effect of bureaucratic structure on the making of policy.

Culture, Society, and Technology in Sino-American Relations

Joseph Needham is the premier specialist on science and technology in pre-modern China, and has produced several volumes in a multi-volume series on science and civilization in China. Perhaps the most accessible of Needham's works is his *Clerks and Craftsmen in China and the West: Lectures and Addresses on the History of Science and Technology* (New York: Cambridge University Press, 1970). An insightful comparative perspective on the subject can be found in Nathan Rosenberg, *Technology and American Economic Growth* (New York: Harper & Row, 1972). Dwight Perkins, ed., *China's Modern Economy in Historical Perspective* (Stanford, Calif.: Stanford University Press, 1975) contains a number of essays that explore the relative role of domestic and foreign factors affecting Chinese economic development.

The subject of past Sino-American cultural cooperation has been examined from both long-term and short-term perspectives in the following volumes: Jonathan Spence, *To Change China: Western Advisers in China, 1620–1960* (Boston: Little, Brown and Co., 1969); John King Fairbank, ed., *The Missionary Experience in China and America* (Cambridge, Mass.: Harvard University Press, 1974); James C. Thomson, Jr., *While China Faced West: American Reformers in Nationalist China, 1928–1937* (Cambridge, Mass.: Harvard University Press, 1969); and Wilma Fairbank, *America's Cultural Experiment in China, 1942–49* (Washington, D.C.: U.S. Department of State, 1976).

For the contemporary period, Michel Oksenberg, ed., *China's Developmental Experience* (New York: Praeger, 1973) explores the Chinese government's approaches to the issues on its agenda in a number of short essays. Richard P. Suttmeier, *Research and Revolution: Science Policy and Societal Change in China* (Lexington, Mass.: D.C. Heath, 1974) is a detailed treatment of one of those issues, while Genevieve C. Dean, *Science and Technology in the Development of Modern China: An Annotated Bibliography* (London: Mansel, 1974) provides extensive suggestions for further study on the subject.

Dwight Perkins, ed., *Rural Small-scale Industry in the People's Republic of China* (Berkeley: University of California Press, forthcoming) is the report of an American delegation which visited China in 1975. There is much information on science and technology in Sino-American relations in U.S. Congress, House Special Subcommittee on Investigations of the Committee on International Relations, *United States-China Relations: The Process of Normalization of Relations* (Washington, D.C.: Government Printing Office, 1976). And the Committee on Scholarly Communication with the People's Republic of China publishes the trip reports of American delegations to China which it sponsors; the Committee's *China Exchange Newsletter* should be consulted for the reports available.

The Use and Threat of Force in Sino-American Relations

The general history and theory of American military policy is reviewed in the following: James A. Field, Jr., *America and the Mediterranean World, 1776–1882* (Princeton, N.J.: Princeton University Press, 1969); Alexander L. George and Richard Smoke, *Deterrence in American Foreign Policy: Theory and Practice* (New York: Columbia University Press, 1974); and Russell F. Weigley, *The American Way of War: A History of United States Military Strategy and Policy* (New York: Macmillan, 1973). Surveys of U.S. military involvement in China and East Asia are presented in Akira Iriye, *Across the Pacific: An Inner History of American-East Asian Relations* (New York: Harcourt, Brace and World, 1967), and in A. Doak Barnett, *Uncertain Passage: China's Transition to the Post-Mao Era* (Washington, D.C.: The Brookings Institution, 1974).

Charles F. Romanus and Riley Sutherland detail the problems of the wartime alliance in their *Stilwell's Mission to China* and *Stilwell's Command Problems* (Washington, D.C.: Department of the Army, Historical Division, 1953 and 1956). Tang Tsou's *America's Failure in China, 1941–50*, 2 vols. (Chicago: University of Chicago Press, 1963) carries the story through the Civil War period. Representative treatments of the post-1949 military relationship include Allen S. Whiting, *China Crosses the Yalu: The Decision to Enter the Korean War* (New York: Macmillan, 1960); J. H. Kalicki, *The Pattern of Sino-American Crises: Political-Military Interactions in the 1950s* (New York: Cambridge University Press, 1975); Allen S. Whiting, *The Chinese Calculus of Deterrence: India and Indochina* (Ann Arbor: University of Michigan Press, 1975); and Frank E.

Rogers, "Sino-American Relations and the Vietnam War," *China Quarterly* 66 (June 1976): 293–314.

For basic information on the Chinese military, the reader should consult John Gittings, *The Role of the Chinese Army* (London: Oxford University Press, 1967); Angus M. Fraser, *The People's Liberation Army* (New York: Crane Russak and Co., 1973); Samuel B. Griffith, II, *The Chinese People's Liberation Army* (New York: McGraw-Hill, 1967); and Alexander L. George, *The Chinese Communist Army in Action* (New York: Columbia University Press, 1967). Chinese military strategy is the specific subject of Mao Tse-tung, *Selected Military Writings* (Peking: Foreign Language Press, 1966); and Scott A. Boorman, *The Protracted Game: A Wei-ch'i Interpretation of Maoist Revolutionary Strategy* (New York: Oxford University Press, 1969). William W. Whitson (with Chen-hsia Huang), *The Chinese High Command: A History of Communist Military Politics, 1927–71* (New York: Praeger, 1971) offers a revisionist interpretation of the development of military institutions and strategy, besides providing a wealth of factual material. On the issue of nuclear weapons, Morton H. Halperin and Dwight H. Perkins, *Communist China and Arms Control* (Cambridge, Mass.: Harvard University East Asian Research Center/Center for International Affairs, 1965) and Alice Langley Hsieh, *Communist China's Strategy in the Nuclear Era* (Englewood Cliffs, N.J.: Prentice-Hall, 1962) are among the better early works. They have since been supplemented by Ralph N. Clough, A. Doak Barnett, Morton H. Halperin, and Jerome H. Kahan, *The United States, China, and Arms Control* (Washington, D.C.: The Brookings Institution, 1975) and Jonathan D. Pollack, "Chinese Attitudes toward Nuclear Weapons, 1964–9," *China Quarterly* 50 (April–June 1972): 244–271.

Trade and Sino-American Relations

The nineteenth century opening of trade with China is ably recounted in Michael Greenburg, *British Trade and the Opening of China, 1800–1842* (Cambridge, England: Cambridge University Press, 1951) and in John King Fairbank, *Trade and Diplomacy on the China Coast, 1842–1854* (Cambridge, Mass.: Harvard University Press, 1953). The institution of the compradore is described in Yen-p'ing Hao's *Compradore in Nineteenth Century China* (Cambridge, Mass.: Harvard University Press, 1970). Albert Feuerwerker has summarized the restricted place of foreign trade in China's economic system in his two essays *The Chinese Economy, ca. 1870–1911* and *The Chinese Economy, 1912–1949* (Ann Arbor, Michigan: Center for Chinese Studies, 1969 and 1968). The limited role of businessmen in making U.S.-China policy at the turn of the century is documented in Marilyn B. Young, *The Rhetoric of Empire: American China Policy, 1895–1901* (Cambridge, Mass.: Harvard University Press, 1968).

For the contemporary period, Alexander Eckstein's *China's Economic Revolution* (New York: Cambridge University Press, 1977) examines Chinese economic development strategy and the implications for foreign trade. Eckstein's *Communist China's Economic Growth and Foreign Trade* (New York: McGraw-Hill, 1966) and his edited volume, *China Trade Prospects and U.S. Policy* (New York: Praeger, 1971) review developments of the first two decades of the People's Republic. Victor H. Li, ed., *Law and Politics in China's Foreign Trade* (Seattle: University of Washington Press, 1977) presents a contemporary perspective. The recent state of the Chinese economy in a number of sectors—foreign trade included—is reviewed in *China: A Reassessment of the Economy, A Compendium of Papers submitted to the Joint Economic Committee, Congress of the United States* (Washington, D.C.: Government Printing Office, 1975). The *U.S.-China Business Review*, published by the National Council for U.S.-China Trade in Washington, D.C., is an excellent source of up-to-date information. The National Council also publishes reports on specific sectors of the Chinese economy. On the specific question of petroleum, Chu-yuan Cheng, *China's Petroleum Industry: Output Growth and Export Potential* (New York: Praeger, 1976) and Selig S. Harrison, *China, Oil, and Asia: Conflict Ahead?* (New York: Columbia University Press, 1977) are among the recent treatments.

Japan and Sino-American Relations

Three volumes provide excellent reviews of the broad history of Japan's place in American-East Asian relations: Charles Neu, in *Troubled Encounter* (New York: Wiley, 1975) concentrates on American-Japanese relations, Marius Jansen's recent *Japan and China from War to Peace, 1894–1972* (New York: Rand McNally, 1975) exhaustively summarizes Western scholarship, and Akira Iriye, *Across the Pacific: An Inner History of American-East Asian Relations* (New York: Harcourt, Brace and World, 1967) studies the interplay between China, Japan, and the United States.

A number of volumes examine events of the nineteenth and early twentieth century. Foster Rhea Dulles' *Yankees and Samurai: America's Role in the Emergence of Modern Japan, 1791–1900* (New

York: Harper and Row, 1965) is a useful synthesis on the first period. Those books that directly deal with Sino-Japanese-American relations after the turn of the century include Howard K. Beale, *Theodore Roosevelt and the Rise of America to World Power* (Baltimore, Md.: Johns Hopkins Press, 1956); Akira Iriye, *Pacific Estrangement: Japanese and American Expansion, 1897–1911* (Cambridge, Mass.: Harvard University Press, 1972); and Michael Hunt, *Frontier Defense and the Open Door: Manchuria in Chinese-American Relations, 1895–1911* (New Haven, Conn.: Yale University Press, 1973).

Japan's effort to expand its influence in China after the fall of the Empire and during the First World War and the American response is described in several perceptive works. Roy W. Curry's *Woodrow Wilson and Far Eastern Policy, 1913–1921* (New York: Bookman Associates, 1957) provides a general context, while Tien-yi Li, *Woodrow Wilson's China Policy, 1913–1917* (New York: Twayne Publishers, 1952) and Russell H. Fifield, *Woodrow Wilson and the Far East: The Diplomacy of the Shantung Question* (New York: Crowell, 1952) have a narrower focus. Madeleine Chi, in her *China Diplomacy, 1914–1918* (Cambridge, Mass.: Harvard University Press, 1970), examines this critical period from the perspective of the Chinese government, and Marius Jansen, *The Japanese and Sun Yat-sen* (Cambridge, Mass.: Harvard University Press, 1954) recounts the reaction of Japanese to one revolutionary Chinese group.

The contours of the triangular relationship shifted once again as the Nationalist Party halted the slide toward disintegration and as Japan sought to solve its foreign policy problems by military occupation of parts of the China mainland. Akira Iriye surveys the diplomacy of the great powers from the Washington Conference to the Manchurian Incident in *After Imperialism: The Search for a New Order in the Far East, 1921–1931* (Cambridge, Mass.: Harvard University Press, 1965). The terminal point of Iriye's study is treated in detail in Sadako N. Ogata, *Defiance in Manchuria: The Making of Japanese Foreign Policy, 1931–1932* (Berkeley: University of California Press, 1964). Japanese foreign and defense policy in the 1930s is the subject of James B. Crowley's revisionist *Japan's Quest for Autonomy: National Security and Foreign Policy, 1930–1938* (Princeton, N.J.: Princeton University Press, 1966). The unwillingness of the Roosevelt Administration to respond to Japanese expansion is documented in Dorothy Borg's excellent *The United States and the Far Eastern Crisis of 1933–1938* (Cambridge, Mass.: Harvard University Press, 1964).

The Pacific War is the subject of a number of recent books, building on the work of Herbert Feis, *The Road to Pearl Harbor* (Princeton, N.J.: Princeton University Press, 1950) and *The China Tangle* (Princeton, N.J.: Princeton University Press, 1953). Waldo H. Heinrichs, Jr., *American Ambassador: Joseph C. Grew and the Development of the United States Diplomatic Tradition* (Boston: Little, Brown and Co., 1966) and Dorothy Borg and Shumpei Okamoto, eds., *Pearl Harbor as History: Japanese American Relations, 1931–1941* (New York: Columbia University Press, 1973) both map aspects of the road to war. Barbara Tuchman's *Stilwell and the American Experience in China* (New York: Macmillan, 1971) recounts the difficulties of the wartime alliance. John Boyle's *China and Japan at War, 1937–1945: The Politics of Collaboration* (Stanford, Calif.: Stanford University Press, 1972) is a fascinating account of complexities of Sino-Japanese wartime relations.

Chae-jin Lee's *Japan Faces China: Political and Economic Relations in the Postwar Era* (Baltimore, Md.: Johns Hopkins Press, 1976) is an excellent review of contemporary developments. It joins a number of more specialized treatments. In the latter category, those that take the perspective of American-East Asian relations include Frederick S. Dunn, *Peace-Making and the Settlement with Japan* (Princeton, N.J.: Princeton University Press, 1963) on the 1952 peace treaty, George R. Packard III, *Protest in Tokyo: The Security Treaty Crisis of 1960* (Princeton, N.J.: Princeton University Press, 1966); Martin E. Weinstein, *Japan's Postwar Defense Policy, 1947–1968* (New York: Columbia University Press, 1971); and Ralph Clough, *East Asia and U.S. Security* (Washington, D.C.: The Brookings Institution, 1975). Among volumes that focus on Japan's role in the world are John K. Emmerson, *Arms, Yen and Power, The Japanese Dilemma* (New York, Dunellen, 1971); James William Morley, ed., *Forecast for Japan: Security in the 1970's* (Princeton, N.J.: Princeton University Press, 1972); and Donald C. Hellman, ed., *China and Japan: A New Balance of Power* (Lexington, Mass.: D.C. Heath, 1976).

The Soviet Factor in Sino-American Relations

Broad overviews of Sino-Soviet relations are supplied in O. Edmund Clubb, *China and Russia, The Great Game* (New York: Columbia University Press, 1971) and John Gittings, *The World and China, 1922–72* (New York: Harper and Row, 1975), the former spanning centuries, the latter decades.

On a more specific level, Michael Hunt examines Russian policy toward China at the turn of the century in *Frontier Defense and the Open Door: Manchuria in Chinese-American Relations, 1895–1911* (New Haven, Conn.: Yale University Press, 1973). Allen Whiting's *Soviet Policies in China, 1917–1924* (Stanford, Calif.: Stanford University Press, 1953) describes the evolution of Russian-China policy under Lenin. The complexities of the relationship of the Comintern and the Chinese Communist Party are debated in a number of books: among them are Benjamin Schwartz, *Chinese Communism and the Rise of Mao* (Cambridge, Mass.: Harvard University Press, 1951); Richard C. Thornton, *The Comintern and the Chinese Communists, 1928–1931* (Seattle: University of Washington Press, 1969) and Thornton's *China: The Struggle for Power, 1921–1972* (Bloomington: Indiana University Press, 1973).

Akira Iriye's *The Cold War in Asia: A Historical Introduction* (Englewood Cliffs, N.J.: Prentice-Hall, 1974) is a brief and useful treatment of the early postwar period. Three books detail the emergence and development of the Sino-Soviet split: Donald S. Zagoria, *The Sino-Soviet Conflict, 1956–1961* (Princeton, N.J.: Princeton University Press, 1962); William E. Griffith, *The Sino-Soviet Rift* (Cambridge, Mass.: M. I. T. Press, 1964); and William E. Griffith, *Sino-Soviet Relations, 1964–1965* (Cambridge: M. I. T. Press, 1967). More recent aspects of the relationship are explored in Kenneth Lieberthal, *The Foreign Policy Debate in Peking, 1973–1976* (Santa Monica, Calif.: Rand Corporation, 1977) and Morris Rothenberg, *Soviet Perceptions of the Chinese Succession,* Occasional Papers in International Studies (Miami, Fla.: University of Miami, 1976).

Taiwan and Sino-American Relations

Not unexpectedly, much of the literature on Taiwan is written with either an implicit or explicit point of view, and should thus be regarded with care. This applies even to studies of the history of Taiwan. For example, George Kerr, in his *Formosa Betrayed* (Boston: Houghton Mifflin, 1965) and *Formosa: Licensed Revolution and the Home Rule Movement, 1895–1945* (Honolulu: University Press of Hawaii, 1974) is partial to the Taiwanese natives of the island. Douglas Mendel's *Politics of Formosan Nationalism* (Berkeley: University of California Press, 1970) brings that point of view more up-to-date. Hungdah Chiu, ed., *China and the Question of Taiwan: Documents and Analysis* (New York: Praeger, 1973) has essays that examine both Taiwan's past and present from a perspective more favorable to the Nationalist government.

The future of Taiwan is the subject of a continuing lively debate in newspapers and journals. Also, Jo Yung-hwan, ed., *Taiwan's Future?* (Tempe, Arizona: Union Research Institute for Arizona State University, 1974) is one collection of a broad spectrum of views. Jerome A. Cohen, Edward Friedman, Harold Hinton, and Allen S. Whiting, *Taiwan and American Policy* (New York: Praeger, 1971) is dated but useful. Recent individuals' opinions can be found in A. Doak Barnett, *China Policy: Old Problems and New Challenges* (Washington, D.C.: The Brookings Institution, 1977); Ralph Clough, *East Asia and U.S. Security* (Washington, D.C.: The Brookings Institution, 1975); Donald C. Hellman, ed., *China and Japan: A New Balance of Power* (Lexington, Mass.: D.C. Heath, 1976); Victor Li, *De-recognizing Taiwan: The Legal Problems* (New York: Carnegie Endowment for International Peace, 1977); Michel Oksenberg and Robert B. Oxnam, *China and America: Past and Future* (New York: Foreign Policy Association, 1977); Robert Scalapino, *Asia and the Road Ahead: Issues for the Major Powers* (Berkeley: University of California Press, 1975); U.S. Congress, House Special Subcommittee on Investigations of the Committee on International Relations, *United States-China Relations: The Process of Normalization of Relations* (Washington, D.C.: Government Printing Office, 1976); and Allen S. Whiting, *China and the U.S.: What Next?* (New York: Foreign Policy Association, 1976).

Northeast Asia in Sino-American Relations

Two provocative general works help define the broad framework of American policy toward the Northeast Asian mainland. Walter LaFeber's *The New Empire* (Ithaca, N.Y.: Cornell University Press, 1963) deals with commercial expansionism in the late nineteenth century. N. Gordon Levin, Jr.'s *Woodrow Wilson and World Politics* (Oxford, England: Oxford University Press, 1968) covers the shift to a liberal, internationalist outlook. John K. Fairbank, ed., *The Chinese World Order* (Cambridge, Mass.: Harvard University Press, 1968) and John Gittings, *The World and China, 1922–1972* (Pantheon Books, 1974) establish a comparable sense of context for Chinese foreign policy.

Tyler Dennett's dated classic *Americans in Eastern Asia* (New York: Macmillan, 1922), chaps. 24–26, describes early American involvement in Korea from the American side while C.I. Eugene Kim and Han-Kyo Kim, *Korea and the Politics of Imperialism, 1876–1910* (Berkeley: University of California Press, 1967), suggests the Korean and Chinese perspectives. Michael Hunt, *Frontier Defense and the*

Open Door (New Haven, Conn.: Yale University Press, 1973); Christopher Thorne, *The Limits of Foreign Policy* (New York: Putnam, 1973); and Dorothy Borg and Shumpei Okamoto, eds., *Pearl Harbor as History* (New York: Columbia University Press, 1973) are recent reappraisals of the two Manchurian crises. David Rees, *Korea: The Limited War* (New York: St. Martin, 1964); Allen Whiting, *China Crosses the Yalu* (New York: Macmillan, 1960); and Gregory Henderson, *Korea: The Politics of Vortex* (Cambridge, Mass.: Harvard University Press, 1968) are established works on the post-World War II entanglement in Korea. Controversial new entries include Frank Baldwin, ed., *Without Parallel* (New York: Columbia University Press, 1974), and Robert Simmons, *The Strained Alliance* (New York: The Free Press, 1975). Selig Harrison's "One Korea?" *Foreign Policy*, no. 17 (Winter 1974–75): 35–62, is a stimulating examination of contemporary policy alternatives.

The Rise and Fall of the Southeast Asia Obsession in Sino-American Relations

One of the consequences of the war in Indochina was the generation of a mass of scholarly work on the United States and Chinese involvement in Southeast Asia, especially Vietnam. Consequently, only a small fraction can be mentioned here. Two books provide an introduction to Chinese involvement in Southeast Asia: Jay Taylor, ed., *China and Southeast Asia: Peking's Relations with Revolutionary Movements,* 2nd ed. (New York: Praeger, 1976) and Peter Van Ness, *Revolution and Chinese Foreign Policy: Peking's Support for Wars of National Liberation* (Berkeley: University of California Press, 1970). David Mozingo, *Chinese Policy toward Indonesia, 1949–1967* (Ithaca, N.Y.: Cornell University Press, 1976) is a thorough treatment.

On Vietnam, Alexander B. Woodside describes the historical background of Sino-Vietnamese relations in his *Vietnam and the Chinese Model: A Comparative Study of Nguyen and Ch'ing Civil Government in the First Half of the Nineteenth Century* (Cambridge, Mass.: Harvard University Press, 1971) and of the Vietnamese revolution in *Community and Revolution in Modern Vietnam* (Boston: Houghton Mifflin, 1976). American and Chinese policies toward Indochina in the early 1950s are documented in Melvin Gurtov, *The First Vietnam Crisis* (New York: Columbia University Press, 1967). The intellectual roots of American involvement in the Vietnam War are examined in David Halberstam, *The Best and the Brightest* (New York: Random House, 1971) and in *Pentagon Papers: The Senator*

Gravel Edition, 4 vols. (Boston: Beacon Press, 1971), among others. Sino-American interaction over Vietnam is the subject of Allen S. Whiting, *The Chinese Calculus of Deterrence: India and Indochina* (Ann Arbor: University of Michigan Press, 1975), and Frank E. Rogers, "Sino-American Relations and the Vietnam War," *China Quarterly* 66 (June 1976): 293–314.

Sino-American Relations and International Law

Victor Li provides an excellent summary of the Chinese legal system in his recent *Law Without Lawyers: A Comparative View of Law in China and the United States* (Stanford, Calif.: Stanford Alumni Association, 1977). The historical background is explored in Sybille Van Der Sprinkel, *Legal Institutions in Manchu China* (London: Athlone Press, 1962). John King Fairbank, *Trade and Diplomacy on the China Coast, 1842–1854* (Cambridge, Mass.: Harvard University Press, 1953) recounts the application of traditional law to cases involving western traders.

For the contemporary period, the basic volumes on domestic Chinese law are Jerome A. Cohen, *The Criminal Process in the People's Republic of China, 1949–1963* (Cambridge, Mass.: Harvard University Press, 1968) and Jerome A. Cohen, ed., *Contemporary Chinese Law* (Cambridge, Mass.: Harvard University Press, 1970). On the subject of law and foreign relations, the following specialized books are quite useful: Jerome A. Cohen, ed., *China's Practice of International Law: Some Case Studies* (Cambridge, Mass.: Harvard University Press, 1972), Jerome A. Cohen and Hungdah Chiu, eds., *People's China and International Law: A Documentary Study,* 2 vols. (Princeton, N.J.: Princeton University Press, 1974), James C. Hsiung, *Law and Policy in China's Foreign Relations, A Study of Attitudes and Practice* (New York: Columbia University Press, 1972), and Shao-chuan Leng and Hungdah Chiu, *Law In Chinese Foreign Policy: Communist China and Selected Problems of International Law* (Dobbs Ferry, N.Y.: Oceana Publications, 1972). Victor Li, *Derecognizing Taiwan: The Legal Problems* (New York: Carnegie Endowment for International Peace, 1977) is a thorough treatment of the subject.

INDEX